Soviet Urban Housing

Alfred John DiMaio, Jr.

The Praeger Special Studies program—
utilizing the most modern and efficient book
production techniques and a selective
worldwide distribution network—makes
available to the academic, government, and
business communities significant, timely
research in U.S. and international economic, social, and political development.

Soviet Urban Housing
Problems and Policies

Praeger Publishers   New York   Washington   London

PRAEGER SPECIAL STUDIES IN INTERNATIONAL ECONOMICS AND DEVELOPMENT

Library of Congress Cataloging in Publication Data

DiMaio, Alfred John.
    Soviet urban housing: problems and policies.

    (Praeger special studies in international economics
and development)
    Bibliography.
    1. Housing—Russia.   2. Cities and towns—
Planning—Russia.   I. Title.
HD7345.A3D53   301.5'4   73-15183

PRAEGER PUBLISHERS
111 Fourth Avenue, New York, N.Y. 10003, U.S.A.
5, Cromwell Place, London SW7 2JL, England

Published in the United States of America in 1974
by Praeger Publishers, Inc.

Printed in the United States of America

I should like to express my deep appreciation to the late Professor Merle Fainsod for his encouragement and criticism.

A special note of thanks to Susan Jo Gardos, Librarian of Harvard's Russian Research Center Library. In addition to offering the use of its library, the Russian Research Center generously gave me financial support while researching and writing this study.

I wish to express particular gratitude to my parents for their constant support. To my sister, Dolores, I owe a great debt for her excellent work in typing the manuscript.

Finally, my deepest expression of thanks to my wife, Betty, to whom this book is dedicated.

CONTENTS

Soviet Urban Housing

1

INTRODUCTION

Housing, like all essential needs, has always had to compete against other officially more favored interests in the Soviet Union. Particularly during the Stalin years of leadership, though some advances were recorded in the fight to provide shelter for all Soviet citizens, the problem of housing grew more acute. For years, top priorities given to industrialization with the consequent rapid increase in the urban population combined to turn the housing problem into an epidemic "housing crisis." The disruptions and destructions of World War II only heightened an already extreme crisis. The postwar period saw fresh initiatives in the development of new techniques in solving the housing shortages. The fifth Five Year Plan (1951-55) increased state investments in housing by 100 percent over the fourth Five Year Plan. Industrialization of the housing construction industry and prefabrication were seen as the long awaited answer to the quest for decent dwellings. By the mid-1950s the Communist Party of the Soviet Union and the Soviet government embarked on sweeping programs to solve the housing problem once and for all. The Seven Year National Economic Plan (launched in 1959) placed a new emphasis on the housing problem and unveiled plans to build more urban and rural dwellings in seven years than in the previous forty. The 1957 Decree of Housing committed the Party and government to the final solution of the housing problem "during the next ten to twelve years." Those years have come and gone, but the problem stubbornly remains. As Leonid Brezhnev pointed out at the Twenty-Third Party Congress in 1966, "We are building a great deal of housing, but the question still remains acute in the extreme."[1] Premier Kosygin emphasized during the Twenty-Fourth Party Congress in 1971, that "as international statistics show, no other country in the world built so many apartments during the past few years. But we cannot say that all our country's population has been provided with normal housing conditions. This question remains a serious problem for the years ahead."[2]

Soviet planners have claimed that within their centrally planned economic system they will be able to achieve successful and well-coordinated city planning and to solve basic urban problems, specifically that of housing all the people. "Socialism has, for the first time in the history of man," a Soviet urbanist proclaims, "created the social conditions for the solution of the housing problem: the abolition of the conditions of private ownership of the means of production, nationalization of the land, and the constitution by the state of a general housing fund."[3] This study will investigate this claim with a sharp focus on Soviet urban housing policies and the current state of Soviet public and cooperative housing in the cities. Today the Soviet government finds itself in the unique and unprecedented position of being responsible for the housing of 250,000,000 people spread over a vast and extremely diverse land. How has the central planning of housing taken local needs and peculiarities into account? Indeed, one must first ask, is there a Soviet housing system and is housing itself centrally planned in the Soviet Union? Is there a local coordinating center for planning, constructing, and administering the housing fund?

Though increasingly burdened since 1957 with great responsibilities in the field of housing and public services, do the local Soviets really possess adequate authority and funds to carry out these heavy duties? One chairman of a City Soviet Executive Committee echoes an often heard dilemma facing most local Soviets:

> The financial and material resources allotted to us by our principal guardian, the Ministry of the Communal Economy, cannot satisfy all people's needs. These resources scarcely suffice to maintain the elementary system of the city's economy. The participation of the ministries in housing construction and the organization of public services and amenities is essential.[4]

Is this "essential participation of the ministries" in fact taking place? If so, is the local Soviet "Master of the City" in developing a well-coordinated and well-built housing and municipal service system? Must the Soviets still do battle with the strong departmental interests of the ministries and their enterprises to achieve effective control over all phases and operations of housing?

Consciously subordinated for many years to the goals of industrialization, housing was treated as an incentive—part of the society's reward system for outstanding labor, service, and conduct. It has been used for attracting and keeping good workers, and ultimately for increasing labor productivity, rather than for providing a public

2

service to which all citizens had a right. Yet, during all the years
of the Soviet Union's political, social, and economic development,
housing as a public service and decent housing as the right of every
citizen were never fully lost from official view. Party and government
leaders have never tired of reminding us that the "fundamental economic law of socialism is the satisfying of the material and cultural
needs of the workers," and that:

> among those needs, housing occupies a particular place
> of importance. Besides being an element of popular
> consumption, housing also constitutes one of the deter-
> mining factors of the development of production. That
> is why it is so important that all workers have at their
> disposal comfortable housing where they can work,
> rest, and raise the younger generation in the best condi-
> tions possible.[5]

Consequently, the history of Soviet housing to the present day is the
story of the at times troubled coexistence of two concepts—incentive
and public service. These two concepts must be kept in mind while
examining Soviet housing plans and programs. Expressing the strong
desire to achieve the goal of a separate, well-constructed and appointed
apartment for each family, Soviet authorities and planners continually
point out that the realization of this goal is crucial for the society's
further advancement into the full phase of communism, for an improvement in labor productivity, and for convincing the world of the superi-
ority of the centrally planned socialist economic system. In the realm
of housing, Soviet spokesmen are not alone in proclaiming that soon
the citizens of the Soviet Union will be the best housed of any in the
world. Reporting to the Subcommittee on Urban Affairs of the Joint
Economic Committee of the U.S. Congress in 1969, A. Allan Bates
of the Department of Commerce, who has watched carefully the Soviet
progress in housing over the years declared:

> The Soviet Union is the first, and thus far, the only nation
> which has solved the problem of providing acceptable low-
> cost housing for its masses of citizens.
>   Within a few years—perhaps a decade—it will prob-
> ably be generally acknowledged internationally that the
> best housed inhabitants of any large country in the world
> are those of the USSR. The political impact of this situ-
> ation will be profound. The United States will suffer
> devastating comparisons.[6]

However, Bates was pleading his own cause before the U.S. Congress—
that is, he was attempting to convince Congress of the need for the
United States to develop industrialized low-cost methods of housing
construction—and his advocacy role may have caused him to use
hyperbole in evaluating the state of Soviet housing.

In addition to a consideration of the immense problems of planning, designing, constructing, and coordinating housing, the question
of the role of the local Soviets and of the public in organizing and
managing the operations of housing and life within the apartment
buildings is a vital one. Public participation in matters concerned
with the daily living of the majority of the inhabitants takes on added
significance in the Khrushchevian concept of the State of the Whole
People with its accent on the increased involvement of mass public
and voluntary organizations in carrying out control and checking
activities and in administering everyday needs. During the years of
the development of the concept of the State of the Whole People, that
is, with the announcement in the late 1950s of the period of Soviet
society's transition to full communism, the domkom (domovyi komitet),
or house committee of tenants, was taken out of the dustbin of history
where it had more or less been languishing since the late 1930s, in-
jected with new life, and encouraged to take an active role in the
operation and maintenance of the apartment building. The domkoms
were specifically mandated to instruct and organize residents in
their obligations to maintain the housing fund in good condition, "to
wage a tireless struggle to preserve the housing fund," to mobilize
the talents of the inhabitants for whatever jobs had to be done, and
to increase the efficient use of existing housing. Post-Khrushchev
policies and practices have attempted to define more fully the house
committee's role and to impose greater organizational discipline in
the use of such public organizations. The 1968 Decrees on House
Committees, for example, seem to be part of the larger process of
"rationalizing" and institutionalizing the increased political participation of the Khrushchev years, in the course of this rationalization
reimposing clearer controls on the activist participants. The same
germinal period of the State of the Whole People also saw renewed
emphasis on the local Soviet deputies and the participation of public
and mass organizations in deciding questions of allocating housing,
in channeling housing complaints, and in inspecting the tempo and
progress of construction. We must ask, however, whether the frenzied
activities of a myriad of quasi-voluntary public, party, and governmental control organizations have in fact resulted in a vast system
of noncontrols, where actual responsibility is almost impossible to
discover. Instead of making life more manageable by decreasing
the bureaucratic involvement in the housing field, has the opposite
occurred and have these public administrative committees resulted

in yet another twist of the bureaucratic labyrinth, further dispersing an already too diffuse administrative authority? These are some of the basic questions posed by the Soviet housing situation.

NOTES

1. Leonid I. Brezhnev, "Report of the CPSU's Central Committee to the Twenty-Third Congress of the CPSU," Pravda, March 30, 1966 (Current Digest of the Soviet Press [hereafter cited as CDSP] XVIII, no. 12: 21).

2. A. N. Kosygin, "The Directives of the Twenty-Fourth CPSU Congress for the Five-Year Plan for the Development of the USSR National Economy in 1971-1975," Pravda, April 7, 1971.

3. A. Tomsen, "Zhilishchnyi vopros: -vazhnaia sotsial'naia problema sovremennosti" ("An Important Social Problem of Our Time: Housing"), Voprosy filosofii, no. 12 (1959), pp. 22-34 ("Un grand probleme social de notre époque: le logement," Recherches internationales à la lumière du Marxisme VII-X, cahiers 20-21 [1960]: 10).

4. Ye. Kachalovsky, Chairman of Dnepropetrovsk City Soviet Executive Committee, "Harmonious Development for the City," Izvestia, August 27, 1969, p. 3.

5. A. Tomsen, op. cit., p. 11.

6. A. Allan Bates, "Low Cost Housing in the Soviet Union," in Industrialized Housing, Subcommittee on Urban Affairs of the Joint Economic Committee, U.S. Congress (Washington: Government Printing Office, 1969), p. 1.

2

SOVIET HOUSING PROBLEMS AND POLICIES IN PERSPECTIVE

The Soviet housing problem is a complex one, difficult to define and even more difficult for leaders of the USSR to overcome. Several major reasons emerge as underlying causes of the persistent housing shortage in the Soviet Union. It should be noted that regime spokesmen themselves have recognized the fundamental political decisions that led to the perennial housing lag. First in our evaluation of Soviet housing policies and problems we must briefly examine the materials inherited by the Bolsheviks in 1917—the tsarist legacy. The early Soviet housing policies and official attitudes toward private builders and the place of housing during the Stalinist era provide the necessary background for a thorough appreciation of present housing troubles.

THE TSARIST LEGACY AND THE POST-REVOLUTIONARY SITUATION

The urban housing situation in pre-Revolutionary Russia was one of the worst in the modern world. In addition to the overcrowding, most of the workers' housing was without any semblance of modern conveniences and lacked basic sanitary necessities. Often dark and damp, with next to no ventilation at all, these miserable hovels served as breeding grounds for plaguing disease, and even worse, despair and eventually revolution. According to the 1912 census, a single Moscow or St. Petersburg apartment held an average of more than eight occupants.[1] By way of contrast, the average number of occupants of a 1900 Parisian apartment was 2.7 persons, and of a Berlin apartment four.[2] In pre-Revolutionary Russia (1912-1914), the amount of living space available to the combined urban population has been estimated at seven square meters per person, or two square meters less than the universally recognized minimum sanitary standard of nine square meters.[3] Though the average living space standard was low, it was almost intolerable for workers, to whom housing meant a dark corner or bunk in a shack-dormitory attached to the factory. In the first decade of the twentieth century a fictitious young Englishman, Russell, visits Moscow. Russell's observations dramatize the worker's life "at home." Through his eyes the reader discovers that all the large Moscow factories had sad looking buildings which were "simply warehouses of labour"—"civilian barracks."

> Inside, a dark and narrow corridor was flanked by thin
> plank doors, which opened into dormitories for twenty
> or thirty workers or into minute rooms (Kamorki)
> each sheltering several families. Each family strove
> to mark off its modest domain in the Kamorka with
> hangings made of old pieces of cloth and plaited mats.
> But these flimsy partitions were not enough to ensure
> the privacy of couples. The beds (simple plank beds)
> touched one another. One chair and one table served
> ten persons. Men, women and children mingled their
> voices, odours, illnesses, quarrels and reconciliations.
> Yet the tenants of a Kamorka were envied by those who
> lived in the dormitories.[4]

The same visitor points out that in certain workers' houses only two square yards of space and three or four cubic yards of air per person were all the tenants could expect. Since all big factories worked on a continuous twenty-four-hour schedule, quite often the same beds were occupied on a rotation basis by two workers, one on the day shift and the other on the night shift. The startling fact is that conditions were even worse in workers' housing connected with smaller factories.[5]

In most pre-Revolutionary Russian cities, sewage systems were unknown, water systems, where they existed, were serving at most 10 percent of the homes, and central heating was a luxury for the very few.[6]

Indeed, this overall picture of housing in the closing years of tsarist Russia is very bleak. Accomplishing the Revolution in the name of the Russian proletariat, the Bolshevik leaders would be faced with the heavy burden of the past and the workers' needs of the present—decent housing being one of the most outstanding needs of all. As John Hazard wrote in 1939:

> One of the most spectacular demonstrations to the working
> men of what the Revolution really could mean to them was

the moving of people, who had been living in the cellars and hovels and little shacks out in the poverty-stricken suburbs, to the palaces and mansions of the former rich. A worker had only to open his eyes in the morning and see the golden and crystal chandelier instead of the old kerosene lamp to realize that something tremendous had happened and to draw the conclusion that as the chief beneficiary he owed allegiance to the cause.[7]

With the uproar of war and Revolution and the swirling waves of anarchy, the new Russian government could do little else but recognize and approve the precipitous actions of the toiling people. On the road to Revolution, Lenin had called for "peace, bread and land," and in November 1917 he proposed the requisition of apartments of the rich to alleviate the needs of the workers. One of the first acts of the Second All-Russian Congress of Soviets was to adopt the Decree on Land (November 9, 1917), which would, along with subsequent decrees, lead to the nationalization of all lands and the "municipalization" of many urban dwellings. Finally on August 20, 1918, the cornerstone of Soviet housing policy was laid with the ratification of the Decree on the Abolition of the Private Ownership of Urban Real Estate. This fundamental decree resulted in summary expropriations and confiscations of the living quarters and personal property of individuals who were in "nonworking" categories. Persons so labeled found not only that they were evicted from their dwellings, but that in many cases their clothing, furniture, household utensils, and food provisions were confiscated. Those fortunate enough not to be classified as "bourgeois parasitic elements" were forced to give up part of their living space to other citizens. Approximately 500,000 persons in Moscow and 550,000 in Leningrad improved their living conditions by this general redistribution of dwelling space.[8] Under the August 1918 act, the local Soviets were given sweeping powers. All land within the town limits was placed under control of the Soviet. At the same time, in cities with a population of more than 10,000 inhabitants, the housing policy pattern was being set by municipalizing all dwellings whose value and size exceeded a minimum defined by each local Soviet. In Moscow and Leningrad, buildings with more than five apartments were municipalized regardless of the number of rooms in each apartment. In urban settlements of more than 10,000 residents, the right to build (and not only to control building activity) was declared to be the sole right of local authorities. Urban types of settlement with fewer than 10,000 residents were authorized to issue ordinances with the consent of the central government, making the decree applicable to their territories.

As John Hazard and others have concluded, the act of August
20, 1918 meant that only large capitalist owners were to be expropri-
ated. It did not aim at those property interests considered too small
to amount to possible sources of unearned income or political power.[9]
Overzealous local Soviets and citizens, however, did not pay careful
attention to the law's restrictions or defined intention. Consequently,
many dwellings not intended to be included in the decree's scope were
nevertheless either taken over completely or vastly altered. The
conclusion seems justified that the 1918 law seemed to sanction, at
least to some extent, the spontaneous movement of workers from their
miserable dwellings in the outskirts of the city and from their stifling
cellars into the central districts with better housing, expelling the
old inhabitants in the process without bothering to ask permission of
the local Soviet.[10]

With this momentous law, abolition of the private ownership of
land and nationalization of many privately owned and operated houses
became fact, creating for the state a nearly complete monopoly over
the construction of new housing, the complete control over all land,
and the job of managing its newly acquired housing fund.

Confusion was compounded by the evictions, quarterings, "concentration," "compressings," and countless shiftings of urban residents, plus the acute inexperience of the departments of the weak
municipal government, working through hastily constituted and often
vindictive "house management committees of tenants" and "house
committees of the poor" who were settling questions of housing assignments on the basis of class consciousness or class label. In the midst
of the turmoil of War Communism, the urban resident could never
be sure just what his housing rights were. As a result, tenants became increasingly indifferent to the maintenance of their dwellings.
Daily concern for minor repairs evaporated. This led to the need
for capital housing repairs, which also were neglected. Those private
homeowners who still retained ownership of their dwellings, growing
steadily unsure of their situation, either lacked the means or were
becoming more and more reluctant to make necessary repairs for
the upkeep of their property. Between the years 1917 and 1923, the
important private housing sector (more than three-fourths of the
entire housing fund) remained virtually unmanaged.[11] In turn, this
state of affairs led to the rapid deterioration of many residential
buildings, and in some cases, to the actual disappearance of entire
buildings. As a result of Civil War and War Communism, 17 percent
of Petrograd's residential dwellings and 10 percent of Moscow's fell
into ruin. Stories have been recounted of the tearing up of flooring,
door frames, window sashes, and rafters to get fuel for the stove.
With little or no heating, pipes burst, resulting in sunken floors and
caved-in ceilings.

In some cases the workers who had been moved into the
great houses made holes in the partitions and walls for
chimney pipes, cut wood on the kitchen floors, broke
the tiles, or ruined the plumbing and water closets whose
use they did not understand.[12]

According to Alexander Block, who was a census enumerator in Petrograd in March 1923, Petrograd, which was never bombed or
shelled during World War I or the Civil War, experienced major setbacks in housing. In 1910 the city had 37,523 buildings with residential dwellings. By 1920 the figure had fallen to 29,350 buildings. The
total number of dwellings in 1910 was put at 282,946, and in 1920 at
246,874. Of the total number of dwellings, those inhabited in Petrograd in 1910 were 225,987, and by 1920 only 192,146. During the first
five years after the Revolution, about one-fourth of all the housing fund
of Moscow was lost.[13] Block further recalls that it looked "as if not
only building materials and tools had vanished, but that the very art of
building and maintaining houses of relatively high standards reached
before the Revolution had been unlearned and lost."[14] By 1923 municipalized houses (that is, the public sector) were housing eight million
persons, 38 percent of the total urban population, while the private
sector was attempting to handle some thirteen million, about 62 percent of the urban population. Though the municipalization policy had
resulted in near disaster, and in spite of a partial demunicipalization
beginning in 1921, the number of municipalized properties grew at an
annual rate of almost 10 percent until 1923.[15]

By the end of 1920 Russia was in the throes of a serious housing
crisis. Yet, to the present day, Soviet writers, politicians, and planners are reluctant to concede that the housing problem inherited from
the pre-Revolutionary period was aggravated to the disaster level
through their early policies and as a result of the revolutionary upheaval and the subsequent breakdown of all social discipline. Tenants
who had moved up from the festering cellars and dilapidated outskirts
of the city into better quarters "behaved not like responsible owners,
but like a licentious army of conquerors."[16]

As the housing fund continued to deteriorate, officials tried to
solve the deepening crisis by issuing decree after decree. At the
same time the People's Commissariat of Labor (NKT) went so far
as to promise every worker's family "a separate apartment with
total floor space of at least 50 square meters [550 square feet] consisting of two habitable rooms, a vestibule, kitchen, bath, and a separate storage room or cellar."[17]

While the entire economic fabric was being torn apart under
the policies of War Communism, economic production was drastically
falling, and the economic life of the country was becoming increasingly
chaotic. On February 7, 1921, Pravda wrote:

The economy of our cities is steadily deteriorating. Due
to the increased number of fires, tardy repair of buildings
and insufficient sanitary inspection, the shortage of dwelling space in the cities is becoming more and more acute.
The municipal water system is increasingly unable to
cope with its tasks; in some cases entire sectors are cut
off from the water supply; in others, water is provided
only at certain very limited hours and in numerous instances half of the water collected in reservoirs is lost
in transit, seeping into the earth as the result of damaged
conduits. Power stations, sanitary and fire brigades and
other segments of the urban economy are likewise in a
most deplorable state. In a few years, nothing will be
left of many cities except ruins.

A significant part of early housing policies and woes was the
official position on rent. In 1919 the law of July 10 froze rents at
the July 1, 1919 level. Even before this 1919 law, decrees were
passed declaring a moratorium on rent for certain categories. The
government seemed to be bringing the goal of free housing closer to
reality. In another step, subsidies were provided for those who could
not meet their rent payments. The new regime was trying to provide
all loyal citizens with shelter, regardless of their economic means.
By 1920, John Hazard points out, citizens were beginning to receive
wages not in money but in kind, and wages in kind included provision
of living quarters by state enterprises.[18]
Finally, on January 1, 1921, all rents were abolished. During
the years of the Civil War and Intervention, the large Russian cities
lost a considerable number of inhabitants who fled to the countryside.
Once peace seemed to be assured, these same citizens, joined by
thousands of newcomers, flocked back to the urban centers. This
sudden influx of residents, many seeking jobs in state factories, placed
an intolerable burden on the already inadequate housing fund. Deterioration, lack of repairs, poor or no management at all, and no system
of control led to a state of supreme chaos. Something had to be done.
But what could be done? The government's earliest policies seemed
to sanction the citizenry's notion that it had a "right to living space"
and that the government had a duty to supply that space. As we have
seen, the official rent policy appeared to signal the arrival of the
"New Way of Life" by declaring an end to all rents. Modification or
abandonment of this policy carried political dangers. Imposing unified
control of the shrunken housing fund might mean countless evictions.
Yet if there were to be anything left of the existing housing, urgent
repairs would have to be made and funds would have to be found to
make them. The inhabitants of the dwellings were the only conceivable

sources of money for repairs. With the Law of July 18, 1921, "On Inducing Inhabitants of Municipalized Houses to Repair Installations for Supply of Water, Central Heating and Sewage," the groundwork for a reintroduction of rent payment was laid. This law stipulated that repairs could be charged to the occupants of a building requiring repairs. Furthermore, persons who carried out such repairs and kept their living quarters in good repair were promised exemption from eviction for three years. This "guarantee" was an appeal to those still able to effect such repairs—namely the "bourgeoisie."[19]

Under the New Economic Policy (NEP), rent was reestablished as part of the housing policy and on June 4, 1926, an all-Union rent law was adopted.[20] The rent rates, however, were set so low that rent revenue could not possibly cover all or most of the cost of building repairs and maintenance. Significant government subsidies would still be required to uphold the housing fund in livable condition. In the long run, tenants would actually be the primary source of funds, but only through wage-labor policies, not through direct rent payments.

During the NEP, denationalization, demunicipalization, and emphasis on private capital building in housing became the corner-stones of Soviet urban housing policies. An August 8, 1921, decree "On Reviewing Lists of Municipalized Houses by Communal Sections" was a call to the entire population, especially to former house owners, to help repair and save existing residential buildings. The Executive Committees of the local Soviets were given the task of reviewing within two months their lists of municipalized buildings and of producing lists to be approved by the People's Commissariat of Internal Affairs (NKVD) of those houses that because of their small size or "unsuitability to public needs" could be returned to former owners. Always cautious to avoid the charge of encouraging the growth of capitalist activity and of conditions for engaging in extensive exploitation, the Soviet lawmakers made it clear that in provincial towns a building consisting of more than two units with a total floor space of about 1,250 or more square feet, and in Moscow or Leningrad a building of more than five units could not be considered for demunici-palization. The small, demunicipalized houses were to be turned over to their previous owners on a concession basis. In return for receipt of his property, the property owner was required to make complete repairs within one year and to set aside 10 percent of the living space in the building for disposal by the local Soviets. This "leasing-management" type arrangement was to be in operation for a specific period of years, after which the dwelling was to be turned over to the city government.[21] A number of articles of the same decree (August 8, 1921, SU RSFSR, 1921, No. 60, arts. 408, 410, 411) were also designed to reassure small property owners and to encourage private builders of housing. Though these policies, especially demunicipalization, did help stabilize the chaotic housing picture, since only 17 percent of the housing had been nationalized in the first place, the overall effects were small and disappointing. Few former owners wished to lease back municipalized houses.[22] Within a few years privately held housing leases were being unilaterally liquidated on government initiative.

In spite of all official exhortations for entrance of more private capital and initiative in house construction, the nepmen, private investors, and builders remained reluctant to invest in the housing field. Uncertainty as to future policies and the thinly veiled anti-private property attitude of the regime were enough to dam the flow of big private capital in housing construction. But as late as January 1928, the government was searching for ways to attract capital. The January 4, 1928, decree "On Housing Policy" admitted that "the housing question throughout the territory of the USSR continues to remain in a distressing state." "In order to accelerate housing construction and expand dwelling space, it is necessary . . . to attract big private capital." As the decree clearly stated, this would require "preferential treatment."[23] The "preferential treatment" to attract big capital was spelled out in a following law with the advantageous terms including (1) organization of stock companies for building and operating large apartment houses, without the participation of state and cooperative capital; (2) organization of private construction companies without restrictions on the number of hired employees; (3) extension of the terms of the construction lease to eighty years for stone, reinforced concrete or mixed structures, and sixty years for wooden structures; (4) use of the dwelling space as the builder saw fit, with the possibility of using up to 20 percent of the dwelling space for commercial storage or other nonresidential purposes; (5) as long as the construction lease was valid, the owners would have complete freedom to fix rental conditions, that is, mode of rent payment and length of lease; (6) immunity from administrative interference in renting residential and commercial space; and finally, (7) (intended to be a big incentive) preferential tax treatment. Revenues deriving from residential property were exempt from income and local property taxes. Land involved in the construction lease "was rent-free for a three-year period starting from the date of the building's completion, and thereafter was assessed at half the normal rate until expiration of the construction lease."[24] These 1928 actions had little real effect, as NEP was soon to give way to the ambitious Five Year Economic Plans.

Individuals did construct private houses during the 1920s, but these houses were usually small one-story affairs, designed to secure "for the builder's family minimum shelter away from state control." As the All-Union Population Census of December 17, 1926, indicated:

Private housebuilding during the past few years has been
decidedly of a purely residential character, for the
builder's personal use. The average size of dwelling
space in a private builder's house equals no more than
twenty-eight square meters; this scarcely meets the
minimum requirements of an urban family.[25]

Sosnovy's estimates of dwelling space constructed in the private
sector in comparison to total housing construction during the years
from 1923 to 1928 put the private sector at 17.4 million square meters
(including 7.4 to 9.2 million square meters of restored dwelling space),
in contrast to the public sector of 6.7 million square meters, thereby
indicating the important role private housing played in easing the
early Soviet housing crisis.
    Even though the housing crisis seemed to be growing worse as
urban populations swelled faster and faster, Soviet governmental
and Party leaders maintained the view that the housing shortage was
only a short-range, temporary phenomenon. They believed that if
they could put the general economy on a sound basis and develop a
strong industrial base, the housing shortage would be liquidated in
the process. At the same time, Party leaders emphasized the connection between the housing crisis and the need to raise labor productivity. "The Party and the State must in the immediate future,"
warned an April 1926 Party resolution, "attach great significance to
housing construction, in view of the fact that the further growth of
industry, increases in labor productivity and better living conditions
are hampered by the housing crisis."[26] A later Party resolution
(July 23, 1926), describing the housing situation as "catastrophic,"
went on to explain the causes of the catastrophe. Besides the tsarist
legacy and the state of pre-Revolutionary Russian capital, the decree
mentioned inadequate rents as promoting the progressive deterioration
of existing buildings; failure to put housing affairs into some kind of
order and to create a steady source of revenue for new housing construction; failure to develop production of building materials; absence
of well-organized and managed construction organizations; lack of
sensibly designed models; and finally, dispersal of available resources
among tiny projects.[27]
    With the launching of the first Five Year Plan and the emphasis
on the rapid development of heavy industry in subsequent plans, the
story of Soviet housing policy is dramatically directed by the speed
of urbanization and the decline in urban dwelling space per capita.
The ratio of expenditures for housing construction to total capital
investments during the first, second, or third Five Year Plan was
only one-half that of the period from 1923 to 1928.[28]

From 1923 to 1940 urban living space per person dropped 40 percent, from 6.45 square meters to 4.09 square meters, just large enough for a double bed, bedstand, and chair.[29] But in the 1930s the "housing crisis" suddenly disappeared, at least in official Party-government pronouncements and leadership utterances. As the housing situation deteriorated, the "housing crisis" gave way to what Molotov called "housing closeness" (zhilishchnaia tesnota) (Pravda, March 16, 1939). By 1950 the per capita average of dwelling space dipped to its all-time low of 3.98 square meters, or 44.2 percent of the generally recognized sanitary norm of 9 square meters per person[30]—closeness indeed.

The stubborn housing crisis in the Soviet Union up to World War II resulted from the deliberate ordering of economic priorities that placed housing far down on the list. Housing was consciously sacrificed to the desire of maintaining a high tempo of industrial development. As Khrushchev put it in 1957, "in the prewar years we were forced to economize in everything, even including the construction of dwellings, saving every little kopeck for the creation of heavy industry."[31] Other political and economic reasons contributed to the prolonged scarcity of housing during those years. In the course of Soviet industrialization, housing itself had become more closely linked to the rewards system. Since most consumer items were hard to come by, the enterprise could "pay" skilled workers or needed technical people with better, highly sought-after housing. This practice not only attracted important workers but greatly increased the stability of the labor force of the particular industries. The overcrowding and strict rules and regulations connected with housing were also part of the regime's desire to have additional control over the population's mobility and over the population's sense of personal security, for, indeed, "housing closeness" became a significant element in the drive against all private life. The conscious desire to bring uncertainty into the home and to close the doors of the haven that the home traditionally represents were the logical extensions of the atomization and isolation of neighbor from neighbor that characterized the period of the Stalinist personality cult. The enormous destruction of World War II brought a new element into the Soviet housing picture—premature "urban renewal." Some six million buildings were reported as damaged,[32] robbing twenty-five million persons of shelter. Government action instituted a crash program to build housing as rapidly as possible, to develop new construction techniques, and to help the individual builder in as many ways as possible (1943, 1944). This policy did not mean that ideological suspicions about private builders ceased to exist. First of all, several of the decrees were adopted at a time when ideological discipline had not yet fully recovered from wartime slackness. Moreover, the aid to individual builders could be carefully

15

controlled by the state's monopoly over designs and its power to determine the availability of building materials. As Stalin was tightening his ideological and economic grip over the nation, private buildings were put under the further restriction of not being allowed to exceed two stories and a total of five rooms (law of August 26, 1948).

But even with all the postwar efforts in housing—which between 1946 and 1956 produced some 300 million square meters of housing, more than 50 percent of all urban housing in pre-Revolutionary Russia[33]—the final judgment on the Stalin years must be in Leonid Brezhnev's words that "it is no secret to anyone that in the years of Stalin's personality cult housing construction was much neglected and the housing problem quite acute."[34]

This Soviet housing problem, which grew out of the early years of revolutionary chaos and zeal, out of the trials of high-speed industrialization, the destruction of World War II, and postwar reconstruction, has left a deep mark on present policies and problems. The continuing shortage of architects is one example of long-term policy. As a result of keeping housing very near the bottom of the Party's and government's list of priorities for such a long period of time, an entire sector of the USSR's economy, which was needed to maintain the housing fund and to service residential buildings, was also sadly neglected, underdeveloped, and very poorly organized. This condition in turn led to the rapid deterioration of existing dwellings and situations in which capital repairs were often required soon after occupancy and where repairs could actually run higher in costs than the construction of new quarters. Low priority likewise meant a piecemeal approach to the planning and construction of housing, many times leaving it to the ministries and overburdened enterprises, which treated the whole business as a secondary concern. Increasingly, industrial enterprises ignored legal restrictions and general urban plans and expanded their own facilities, bringing more workers to the city and thus upsetting any long-range, city-wide housing plans. Unable to attract highly skilled workers, the poorly organized and low-status house construction industry became noted for its waste of time and limited materials, dispersal of resources, reluctance to implement new techniques, habit of turning over unfinished buildings for occupancy, and most of all, exceedingly low-grade building. The 1969 resolutions of the Central Committee of the Communist Party of the Soviet Union (CC CPSU) and the USSR Council of Ministers on reform in the construction industry testify to the fact that "there are still serious shortcomings in housing construction and city planning. In the majority of the country's cities, the architecture of areas of mass housing construction is monotonous and unattractive. The quality of construction, installation and finishing work in housing construction is still low."[35]

NEW DAY IN SOVIET HOUSING

It is this legacy of low priority and neglect, affecting all organizations and agencies involved with housing, that adds to the Soviet Union's difficulties in overcoming its housing shortage. The year 1957 marks more than the great reforms and reorganizations in the Soviet economic system—it marks the dawn of the new day in Soviet housing. The Twentieth Party Congress in 1956 spoke of the urgent need to improve the country's housing situation, but it was only after Khrushchev's dramatic struggle with the so-called anti-Party group in June 1957 that the Party adopted an extensive program for expanding housing construction "with the view of eliminating the country's housing shortage within the next ten to twelve years." That the fate of that housing program was caught in the political struggle is illustrated by K. Ye. Voroshilov's speech on February 4, 1957, celebrating the award of the Order of Lenin and the Red Banner of Labor to the Moscow Housing Construction Finishing Trusts. In addition to Voroshilov, Bulganin, Kaganovich, Malenkov, Mikoyan, Furtseva, and Khrushchev appeared on the platform in the Sports Palace of Lenin Stadium. Only Voroshilov's speech was reported in Pravda. Admitting that there is still not enough housing to go around, and that "it is an open secret, therefore, that the first demands upon government agencies are for housing," Voroshilov reassures the audience of construction workers, architects, and personnel of the building materials enterprises that "the Soviet state understands the need and is taking steps to accelerate housing construction further." Then he goes on to remind his comrades:

> that the imperialists are preparing another war and are brandishing weapons of mass destruction. In these conditions, the Soviet government is doing all in its power to frustrate the vile schemes for unleashing war and is fighting without pause for a lasting, enduring peace. At the same time, it is necessary to spend money on defense if our country is to be reliably protected against any hostile encroachment.

What was Voroshilov trying to tell the builders and the Soviet public? What practical conclusions should the builders draw? Voroshilov seemed to be saying to his audience that though there would be increased state allocations for housing, the housing problem would be solved not by more money, but only by building "more rationally and more economically."[36] Yet, several months later the July 31, 1957, Decree on Developing Housing Construction in the USSR committed the Party and government to the "major nationwide task of eliminating the housing shortage in the country in the next few years." The decree called for an increase of 100 percent in the volume of planned new housing during the 1956-1960 Five Year Plan, as compared to the preceding Five Year Plan, upped the volume of state housing to be opened to tenancy in 1956-1960 from the 205 million square meters envisaged by the directives of the Twentieth Party Congress to 215 million square meters of total floor space, and increased the volume of housing construction with private funds and state credit from an earlier planned 84 million square meters to 113 million square meters.[37] In his struggle to power, Khrushchev seemed to be advancing the position of the popular cause of improving Soviet housing.

The 1957 Decree on Developing Housing Construction is also important for its further clarifying the causes of the housing shortage. In addition to the usual causes cited of Russian backwardness at the time of the Revolution, the need to build up the Soviet industrial base, the devastation of the Great Patriotic War, and the tripling of the total urban population between 1927 and 1957, "grave shortcomings that still exist in the construction of housing" are put forward as basic reasons for the inadequate amount of housing. State funds allocated for building new housing have not been fully used in many parts of the country. Men and materials were found scattered among numerous projects. The planning of housing seems to come in for particular criticism. "Instead of large, residential sections," asserts the Decree, "we often build housing in a scattered fashion, on isolated lots in various parts of a city." In fact this practice of "scattering" and fragmentation turns out to be at the heart of the Soviet planning process for urban dwelling, that is, the problem of a unified, well-coordinated, city-wide planning program and authority in the field of housing. For example, the author of an important Novyi mir article entitled "Cities That We Are Building," while discussing the problems of new Soviet cities, emphasized this point, writing that "there are specific agencies that are responsible for the general plans of new cities, but none whose functions is to make sure that these plans are carried out."[38]

This condition seems to be especially true in the field of housing construction. Then, too, a phenomenon much criticized in Soviet construction practice is that the construction of new housing in cities is often accompanied by unjustified large-scale demolition of old housing, which results in a loss of housing and needless dislocations. Another contributing factor to the housing lag is the state of private building. As the decree makes clear, in many cases local Soviets and directors of industrial enterprises and institutions hinder private housing construction and offer little or no assistance in organizing private builders or in supplying materials and parts. Though the Decree chides Party and trade union organizations for their neglect in guiding individual builders, it does display the Party's and government's preference for the cooperative forms of housing construction over the individual.

Cited as further causes of the lingering housing shortage were shortage of building materials, neglect of local materials, the slow introduction of up-to-date prefabricated parts and the lagging development of pre-fabricated standard housing, and the inferior quality of construction and finishing work, which is called "particularly poor." According to the decree, these shortcomings were "largely due to the fact that many Party, government, economic and trade union agencies . . . do not always pay the proper attention to these matters."[39]

In summary, the 1957 Decree and Program on Housing, while never refuting the primary needs for first developing the nation's heavy industry, nevertheless offered a realistic and honest analysis of the major reasons for the overburdened and underdeveloped housing sector. However, overcoming the built-in interests of ministries and enterprises, the resistance of construction organizations to new construction techniques and organizations, the jealousies between local Soviet and industrial organs, as well as the nascent rivalries between the newly formed regional economic councils (Sovnarkhozy) and local authorities was to remain a crucial problem involving risky questions of power and control. The 1957 decree could only point in the general direction of needed reform without producing the great change in organization and decision-making necessary for the creation of an efficient and adequate housing system.

Throughout the history of the Soviet Union the housing question has managed to occupy a considerable amount of space in the Soviet press, either in official pronouncements on the "housing crisis" or "housing closeness" or in citizens' personal letters of complaint. Occasionally the tensions of close quarters and poor housing have led to a questioning of the system's ability to provide for fundamental human necessities. Such was the case with a certain frustrated Leningrad mechanic, Vladimir Vasil'ev, who sent a registered letter to his Raion Party Committee and to the newspaper Leningradskaia Pravda threatening to renounce his motherland, to refuse, along with his relatives, to participate in any election campaign, and to write to the International Red Cross and foreign correspondents if his demands for a transfer to his wife's place of residence were not met.[40] An isolated and very extreme example, the case of the Leningrad mechanic does, however, point out the regime's awareness of the close connection between its ability to satisfy its citizenry's needs and the retention of its citizenry's loyalty and active cooperation. Consequently, since 1957 the government has become more and more committed to finding the "final" solution for Soviet housing troubles and for developing a comprehensive housing program.

RECORD OF ACHIEVEMENT AND ACTUAL
HOUSING PROGRAMS

According to the 1961 Program of the Communist Party of the Soviet Union:

> The CPSU sets the task of solving the most acute problem in the improvement of the Soviet people—the housing problem.
>
> In the first decade, the national shortage of housing will be eliminated. Families that still live in crowded and inadequate dwellings will receive new apartments. At the end of the second decade, every family, including newlyweds, will have a comfortable flat conforming to the requirements of hygiene and cultural living. Peasant houses of the old type will, in the main, give place to new modern dwellings, or—wherever possible—they will be rebuilt and appropriately improved. In the course of the second decade housing will gradually become rent-free for all citizens.[41]

The figures of the following tables and other supplementary reports in the Soviet and western press testify to the USSR's growing success and increasing concern in solving its housing shortage. The five-year period from 1956 to 1960 alone saw the building of more housing than in the entire period from 1918 to 1946, and the period from 1956 to 1969 produced over 150 percent more housing than all the housing built in the Soviet Union from the time of the Revolution to the end of 1955 (see Table 1). For the first time in its history of central economic planning, the state began during the 1950s to fulfill its proposed plans for housing.[42] What these statistics do not show, however, is the quality of housing construction and the "pernicious" practice of seriously underfulfilling the national economic plan and "idling" during the first half of the year and "storming" in the second. The 1958 Belorussian plan, for example, stipulated the completion of only 4.6 percent of the total housing construction in the first quarter, 17.1 percent in the second quarter, 31.9 percent in the third quarter, and 46.4 percent in the final quarter! Neither do these figures clearly reflect the other "pernicious" practice of falsely reporting unfinished housing as completed and misusing allocated funds for nonhousing projects such as clubs and sports facilities.[43] (These problems of planning and housing construction will be discussed in another section.) But the overall situation of Soviet housing does convey a picture of great achievement.

20

TABLE 1

Housing Constructed by State and Cooperative Enterprises
and Organizations, by Kolkhozes and by Individuals
(in millions of square meters of aggregate floor space)

Period	Total Built	Built by State and Enterprises Housing Coops/ Sovkhozy	Built by Individuals' Means and with State Credits	Built in Kolkhozy
1918-71	2544.2	1311.2	470.3	762.7
1918-28	203.0	23.7	27.5	151.8
1929-32	56.9	32.6	7.6	16.7
1933-37	67.3	37.2	7.1	23.0
1938-June 1941	81.6	34.4	10.8	36.4
July 1941-Jan. 1946[a]	102.5	41.3	13.6	47.6
1946-50[a]	200.9	72.4	44.7	83.8
1951-55	240.5	113.0	65.1	62.4
1956-60	474.1	224.0	113.8	136.3
1961-65	490.6	300.4	94.0	96.2
1961	102.7	56.6	23.6	22.5
1962	100.0	59.8	20.7	19.5
1963	97.6	61.9	17.4	18.3
1964	92.7	58.9	16.2	17.6
1955	97.6	63.2	16.1	18.3
1966-70	518.5	352.5	72.8	93.2
1966	102.1	65.9	15.9	20.3
1967	104.5	68.7	15.6	20.2
1968	102.1	69.3	14.2	18.6
1969	103.8	72.0	14.1	17.7
1970	100.0	70.0	13.0	16.4
1971b	108.3	79.7	13.3	15.4
1972c	106+ (preliminary figure)			
1973d	117.6 (planned figure)			

[a]Includes restored or reconstructed housing.

[b]The 1971 planned figure was 117.8 million square meters; the total built was considerably less (Ekonomicheskaia gazeta, no. 5 [January 1971]: 3).

[c]"Report of the USSR Central Statistical Administration on Results of the Fulfillment of the State Plan for the Development of the USSR National Economy in 1972," Pravda and Izvestia, January 30, 1973, (CDSP XXV, no. 5: 14). The 1972 planned figure was 115 million square meters (Pravda, November 25, 1971).

[d]N. K. Baibakov, Chairman of the USSR State Planning Committee, "On the State Plan for the Development of the USSR National Economy in 1973," Pravda and Izvestia, December 19, 1972, (CDSP XXIV, no. 52: 9).

Source: SSSR v tsifrakh v 1971 godu (Moscow: Statistika, 1972), pp. 208-209.

TABLE 2

Capital Investments in all Types of
Housing Construction
(in millions of rubles)

	1959	1960	1965	1969	1970
USSR	2,300	9,456	9,638	12,419	13,439
RSFSR	1,452	6,041	5,989	7,557	8,148

Source: Narodnoe khoziaistvo SSSR v 1970, p. 541.

We have seen that a significant portion of that achievement and
success must be credited to the policies initiated in 1957 and later
in the Seven Year Plan (1959-1965). In addition to dedicating the
nation's energies to eliminating the housing shortage in ten to twelve
years, the 1957 Decree on Developing Housing Construction placed
heavy emphasis on the development of prefabricated large-panel housing and industrialized housing techniques. Enterprise directors, with
the agreement of trade union organizations, were given the right to
use up to 70 percent of an enterprise's fund, the director's fund, and
the consumer goods funds, as well as any prizes received, for the

TABLE 3

Housing Fund in Cities and Urban Types of Settlement
at the end of the year
(in millions of square meters of floor space)

	1913	1940	1960	1965	1966	1967	1968	1969	1970	1971
Total urban housing fund	180	421	958	1238	1290	1350	1410	1469	1529	1590
Public	—	267	583	806	854	906	959	1014	1072	1133
Private	180	154	375	432	436	444	451	455	457	457

Source: Narodnoe knoziaistvo SSSR v 1968 g., p. 580; Narodnoe
khoziaistvo SSSR v 1970 g., p. 546; SSSR v tsifrakh v 1971 godu, p.
211.

construction of housing. As an added boost to housing construction
and at the same time to the economy, industrial enterprises and economic organizations were authorized (with the permission of their
ministries, agencies, and economic councils) to build housing with
additional funds over and above those paid into an enterprise's fund
and director's fund in the amount up to 30 percent of the total above-
plan profits obtained by the given enterprise. Much excitement was
generated over the so-called Gorkii method of voluntary labor in housing construction. The Decree pointed to the example of the Gorkii
automobile workers, who beginning in 1955 were constructing houses
on their own initiative and in their spare time, often with industrial
waste and cheap materials. Hailed as a model of high socialist consciousness, the "method of voluntary labor," it was hoped, would become the beginning of a nationwide movement and would "assume
vast importance everywhere."[44] The "Gorkii Method" produced a
scattering of poorly constructed houses and eventually faded out of
fashion in the 1960s.

The important 1957 Decree on Developing Housing Construction
also spoke of "organizing individual builders into housing cooperatives." It is interesting to note that while calling on Party, government,
and trade unions to help individual builders, the decree seems to be
searching for new "socialist ways" to solving the housing problem.
This attitude was to come to fruition in 1961-1962 with a wave of
confiscations of privately owned houses and with a turning to cooperative forms of housing construction and ownership. Even before the
1957 program for expanding housing construction, there had been a
call to revive the housing construction cooperative, which had some
importance in the 1920s and 1930s but which had been given the coup
de grâce by the October 17, 1937 decree prohibiting the granting of
loans to housing cooperatives for construction.[45] Other sections of
the 1937 decree laid the cooperative housing form to rest and resulted
in the confiscation of most of the then existing cooperative buildings.
(For a fuller treatment of cooperative housing and its legislative history, see Chapter 7.) Always in search of new means to increase
the pace of socialist house construction, N. S. Khrushchev on March
14, 1958, in a pre-election speech asked the nation for fresh thoughts
about attracting into the housing construction program "the means of
those strata of the population who have savings and who at the same
time are in need of better living conditions." Khrushchev himself
then put forth the "fresh idea" of organizing housing construction
cooperatives.[46] One analyst of the role of private housing feels that
Khrushchev's main point was not to seek new ways of tapping private
savings, since nonsocialist investments had always been significant
in housing, but rather to attract that potential source to the idea of
socialist housing.[47] Less than a week after Khrushchev's suggestion,

the USSR Council of Ministers issued a Decree on the Cooperative
Construction of Dwellings and Summer Cottages, March 20, 1958,
which put official approval on the dormant cooperative construction
form, which would assume an increasing role in Soviet housing during
the 1960s.

It was around this time (late 1957 to early 1958) that the earlier
expressed desire to provide each family with a separate apartment
began to assume the status of national policy. N. S. Khrushchev repeated the goal, saying that "we want to insure every family an apartment, not a room, but an apartment,"[48] and the New Party Program
in 1961 incorporated this goal as one of the main tasks of the next
two decades. Finally in 1963 the RSFSR Council of Ministers set
down model rules on housing, establishing the impermissibility of
placing two or more unrelated families in apartments built for one
family.[49]

THE GRAND DESIGN—THE SEVEN YEAR PLAN
(1959-1965)

In the years preceding the Twenty-First Party Congress many
of the ideas for the development of housing were proposed individually,
but it was only in 1959 that these ideas came together in the Seven
Year Plan. At the Twenty-First Congress of the CPSU, Khrushchev
revealed government plans to invest a total of from 375 billion to 380
billion rubles in housing and communal construction, an 80 to 83 percent increase over the previous seven-year period, and at the same
time he reported that capital investments in the amount of 110 billion
to 112 billion rubles were being allocated to develop the building and
building materials industries, 78 to 82 percent more than was allocated
in the previous seven-year period.[50] The ambitious Seven Year Plan
called for the construction of 650 million to 660 million square meters
of total space of housing in towns and urban-type settlements (around
15 million apartments). As the July 1959 CC CPSU Plenum pointed
out, in 1956 the entire urban housing fund consisted of 673 million
square meters. In effect, the program Khrushchev was presenting
was seeking a doubling of urban housing within seven years.

How was this sweeping plan to increase the amount of Soviet
housing to be realized? Industrialization of construction and enormous
emphasis on prefabrication were to provide the answer. From his
years of leadership in the Ukraine, Khrushchev had been experimenting
with and advocating the development of industrial techniques and prefabrication for the solution of the housing shortage. In the field of
housing, "prefabrication" and "large prefabricated panels" became
linked to Khrushchev's name as "corn" and "plastics" did in other

branches of the economy. The more costly and slower traditional methods of brick construction were to give way to the progressive methods of large prefabricated structurals and panels—where units of from two to six rooms are made up of only four or five panels—precast reinforced concrete, and assembly-line techniques of building erection. The decisive changeover to the new procedures, requiring a near total refashioning of the construction industry, was to take place between 1959 and 1965. Not only housing, but all capital construction work must be turned, in Khrushchev's own words, "into a mechanized, continuous-flow process of assembling and erecting buildings and structures from large precast blocks and prefabricated units."[51] In anticipating resistance and footdragging in the adoption of reform methods, the ebullient Soviet leader warned that "perhaps it will be necessary to adopt a special decision, setting dates for carrying out this measure, with the aim of compelling conservatives at long last to take to the new methods of work."[52]

To meet the lofty goals of the Seven Year Plan, it was necessary to solve three basic problems: (1) to erect more than twice as much housing as in the preceding seven years, (2) to provide each family with separate apartments, and (3) to reduce construction costs sharply.[53] In responding to this challenge, Soviet urban planners and architectural institutes created thousands of experimental housing designs and low-cost buildings to be applied on a mass industrial scale. American housing experts have even calculated that for the last several years the USSR has been producing nearly twice the number of dwelling units produced in the USA.[54] By 1960, disregarding quality and availability of municipal services and size, the Soviet city planners proudly claimed that the Soviet Union occupied first place in the world in the number of apartments built per 1,000 population. In 1959 Britain built 5.4 apartments per 1,000 population, France 7.2, and the USA 7.9, while the Soviet Union reported a record 14.5 units per 1,000.[55] By the beginning of 1967, the number of apartments built per 1,000 of the population stood at 7.3 in Britain, 8.4 in France, 6.4 in the United States, and 9.8 in the USSR. By then, however, the Soviet Union had slipped from first place to a tie with the Netherlands for third place, after Sweden and West Germany (see Table 4 for comparisons).[56] And, indeed, the record of achievements stemming from the mid-1950s is impressive (see Table 1). Clouding the record, however, are the regular reports of "nonfulfillment" or underfulfillment of the housing plans. On August 11, 1963, for example, Pravda exclaimed that plans for housing construction on the whole throughout the country during recent years have systematically not been fulfilled, "although the necessary means and material resources for doing this have been expended." In 1963 only Belorussia, Lithuania, Armenia, and Estonia fulfilled or somewhat overfulfilled their plans for opening up new

TABLE 4

Number of Apartments Built per 1,000 Population
in Socialist and Capitalist Countries

Country	1950	1960	1965	1969	1970
USSR	6.0	12.1	9.7	9.3	9.4
Bulgaria	—	6.3	5.5	5.6	4.5
Hungary	3.8	5.8	5.4	6.0	7.7
East Germany	1.7	4.7	4.0	4.1	4.5
Poland	2.8	4.9	5.6	6.3	6.1
Rumania	3.0	7.3	6.4	7.2	8.0
Czechoslovakia	—	6.0	5.9	6.5	8.7
Yugoslavia	2.1	4.1	6.2	5.9	—
Austria	6.7	6.0	6.8	6.6	—
England	4.2	5.9	7.4	6.9	—
Denmark	4.8	6.1	8.5	10.2	—
Spain	1.9	4.2	9.0	8.2	—
Italy	1.6	5.8	7.3	5.5	—
Canada	6.5	6.9	7.8	9.3	8.2
Netherlands	5.4	7.3	9.4	9.6	9.0
Norway	6.9	7.9	7.4	8.6	9.5
USA	13.7	7.2	7.8	7.3	6.9
West Germany	7.5	10.3	10.1	9.3	—
France	1.7	6.9	8.4	8.7	—
Switzerland	6.3	9.4	10.1	9.5	—
Sweden	6.4	9.1	12.5	13.7	13.7
Japan	—	4.6	8.6	13.2	—

Source: Narodnoe khoziaistvo SSSR v 1970 g., p. 118.

housing. In 1964 plans of the RSFSR, Kirgiz, Tadzhik, and Kazakh
republics were unfulfilled and the country as a whole fell short of
the 1964 plan by almost 2 million square meters of housing space or
65 thousand apartments.[57] The resistance to the development and
application of new construction techniques that Khrushchev had fore-
seen in 1959 was cited in an authoritative 1965 article in Kommunist
as the main reason for the still high costs of apartment construction
and for the lack of plan fulfillment. The same article pointed out that
by the beginning of 1963 factories capable of producing 20 million
square meters of large prefabricated paneling were supposed to be
in full production. In fact, capacity had reached only 12 million square

meters. The Tadzhik Republic had fulfilled its 1963 target for large
panels by only 25 percent, the Uzbek, Armenian, and Moldavian republics by 33 percent, and Kazhakhstan by 40 percent. As a result,
only some 9 million square meters of housing had been built in the
entire country by the large-panel method in 1963, instead of the planned
21 million square meters![58]

We saw that at the time of the unveiling of the Seven Year Plan
in 1959, Krushchev was searching for new socialist ways to solve
the housing problem. It was also at this time that the Party First
Secretary displayed a growing concern for communist morality and
uprooting the survivals of capitalism in the minds of the people as
the nation moved into the era of the full development of Communism.
One of the most stubborn survivals seemed to be that of a private
property psychology, most evidently manifested by the private home-
owner. The campaign against so-called "parasites" that began in
the second half of the 1950s and took concrete form in the anti-parasite
laws of the major republics in 1961 became part of the broader crusade
against bourgeois survivals. In addition to a series of confiscations
of privately built houses during 1961 and 1962 and restrictions on
individual home construction in large cities, the official attitude aided
many republics to adopt measures aimed at reducing individual house
construction and boosted the widespread practice of making it more
difficult for individual builders to obtain building materials and decent
municipal services. All these measures led to a sharp reduction in
individual construction, which fell off from 27 million square meters
of total area in 1960 to approximately 16 million square meters in
1964.

An important post-Khrushchev article in Kommunist strongly
criticized the policy, and condemned "artificial restrictions on individual construction where it does not interfere with anything else
(primarily in small towns and settlements)" for hindering the elimination of the housing shortage. The author, B. Svetlichny, a prominent
architect and prolific writer on housing problems and city planning,
also criticized the view that individual construction must gradually
be curtailed in favor of expanded cooperative housing construction.
But cooperative housing construction cannot take the place of individual
construction, argues Svetlichny, or individual construction of the
cooperative form. Since those who join the cooperatives are "mostly
well-to-do city dwellers, specialists, and highly skilled workers,"
their housing requirements and desires are different from those of
the individual builder. On the one hand the cooperative member,
according to Svetlichny, usually wishes to improve his living conditions, lives separately from grown children, and moves from an overcrowded communal apartment into a separate, comfortable apartment
in a modern building. On the other hand, the individual builder is

27

most often a man recently come from the country to the factory who is not yet highly skilled and is therefore interested not only in a dwelling but also in a personal subsidiary plot so he can feed his family better. Finally, "most cooperative members are by no means attracted to the idea of an individual house in a suburban settlement, without plumbing, bath or gas."[59] The post-Khrushchev leadership has indicated a less restrictive attitude toward private house building, and in his Report to the Twenty-Third CPSU Congress, Premier Kosygin stressed development of all types of housing construction, "assistance should be given to factory and office workers and collective farmers in building homes with their own money or with the aid of credits."[60]

Still, with all the setbacks, the Seven Year Plan (1959-1965) did represent a major effort to overcome the housing crisis. According to Soviet reports at the Twenty-Third Congress, between 1956 and 1966 about one-half of the country's population moved into new apartments or improved its housing. New houses with an aggregate floor space of 556 million square meters were built in the seven years, which is 90 percent more than was built in between 1952 and 1958.[61] However, the Seven Year Plan fell short of its 650 to 660 million square meter target and fulfilled only 85 percent of the housing construction plan. Despite the achievements of the Seven Year Plan, it was still too little. "The housing question remains acute in the extreme," Brezhnev told the Twenty-Third Party Congress in 1966.

THE TWENTY-THIRD PARTY CONGRESS
AND THE 1966-1970 FIVE YEAR PLAN

At the Twenty-Third Party Congress Brezhnev launched a new drive to put an end to the shortage. The volume of housing construction from 1965 to 1970 was to expand by 30 percent over the previous five-year period. Brezhnev announced plans to build in the new five-year period 480 million square meters of living space in cities, worker's settlements, and on state farms, 100 million square meters more than in the last five-year period. On a yearly average this would mean about 90 million square meters of new housing compared to 65 million between 1961 and 1965. Capital investments in housing and communal construction were to be in excess of 45 billion rubles as against the 35 billion rubles spent in the past five years.[62]

The figure presented to the U.S. Congress by the Library of Congress' Senior Specialist in Soviet Economics, Leon Herman, does not give a true picture of amounts to be invested in Soviet housing. Herman reported to the Joint Economic Committee of Congress that during the 1966-1970 plan the Soviet government promised annual outlays for housing to run at the rate of 15 billion rubles, the annual

share of housing in total new capital investments to reach 25 percent.
The Economic Directives spoke of about 75 billion rubles to be invested for housing, municipal, and public buildings during the plan
years. This 75 billion rubles would be a little less than 25 percent
of the total new capital investments of 310 billion rubles, but represents
more than investment in housing alone. Statistics for three plan
years, 1966-1968 (see Table 2) and 1969, and 1970 estimates would
indicate capital investments in housing to be between 45 and 53 billion
rubles for the period from 1966 to 1970, or approximately between
14.5 and 17.1 percent of the original planned total capital investments
of 310 billion rubles or 14.9 and 17.5 percent respectively of the re-
vised total capital investments of 303 billion rubles.[63]

Kosygin reiterated that "housing is one of the cardinal social
problems." He outlined plans for greater centralized investments
in construction and urged enterprises to make wider use of their fund
for social and cultural measures and housing construction. "Every
encouragement must be given to cooperative house building," Kosygin
stressed, "the volume of which is to increase by 200-300 percent."
In brief, the house construction program envisaged for 1966-1970
was to move some 65 million people into new houses as compared
with 54 million during the preceding five years. Though the program
was seen as a sweeping one, the Chairman of the USSR Council of
Ministers had to admit "but even this will not fully solve the housing
problem."[64]

The Twenty-Third Party Congress Directives continued and
increased the previous emphasis on industrializing construction and
called for an increase in productivity of labor in building by 35-40
percent.[65] It was clear from Congress reports and post-Congress
articles that in the area of industrialization of construction the factor
of increasing prefabrication and factory preparation of structural
elements was most important. By 1969 the output of prefabricated
parts used for large-panel construction, the major method of residential construction, was to amount to 50 percent of the total, and in
1970 to 80 percent.[66] In accord with the directions of the overall
economic plan, economic incentives in building work were to be increased. The Party Directives declared that:

> building organizations shall be given considerable eco-
> nomic independence and profit shall play a greater role
> in construction, in making building workers materially
> interested in reducing time limits, improving quality
> and reducing costs.[67]

By the end of 1966, the results of the first year of the new Five
Year Plan began to be tallied, and in the field of housing these results

were not encouraging to those still on the waiting lists for new apartments. Only 80 million square meters of new urban housing out of the first-year target of 90 million square meters were constructed (Izvestia, January 29, 1967), though later reports upped the amount constructed to 81.8 million square meters.[68] Before the end of the next plan year, 1967, the goal was lowered from 480 to 466 million square meters (Izvestia, October 10, 1967). As Donald Barry has pointed out, when the achievements of the 1967 plan were disclosed, the official announcement failed, for the first time in recent years, to reveal the exact amount of urban housing erected.[69] Instead, the Pravda report only gave the total of 103.1 million square meters, the figure for urban and rural housing (Pravda, January 28, 1968). This practice has continued through the reporting of the 1970 plan fulfillment. Previous to the report on the 1967 plan, separate figures had been given for urban construction, presented in square meters, and rural construction, expressed in dwelling units. The combined 1968 total of 102.1 million square meters was less than the 1967 final total of 104.5 million square meters.[70] And even though the amount of total housing opened for occupancy in 1969 expressed in terms of the percentage of that opened in 1968 was 100.4 percent, the figure of 102.5 million square meters was still below the 1967 achievements and seems to indicate that the urban housing target was once again underfulfilled.[71] The 1969 plan had called for a combined urban-rural goal of more than 121 million square meters, or 14.4 percent more than in 1968.[72] As we have seen, the actual 1969 increase over 1968 was only .4 percent. And though in 1969 some 11 million people (55 million from 1966 through 1970) (Pravda, February 8, 1971, p. 2) moved into new or improved housing, "the plan for housing, cultural, and service construction for the national economy as a whole, and for a number of republics, ministries, and departments was underfulfilled."[73]

This sagging record may help explain why in 1968 the ministries and departments of the USSR and the Councils of Ministers of the Union Republics had been authorized to put up to 5 percent of the total volume of centralized construction operations with respect to construction sites for production purposes into residential and communal construction in addition to the established plan.[74] Despite this provision for diversion of funds from plant construction, during 1968-1969 the rate of growth of investment in housing grew more slowly than in 1966-1967, the increasing decline in private house construction contributing to this slowdown.[75] In 1968 a series of resolutions was passed implementing major reforms in the construction industry and the decision was made to increase the wages and economic incentives of a large category of builders.[76] These reforms may now be yielding positive results, since the figures for the fulfillment of the 1970 economic plan indicate that the total housing space built was 106 million

square meters, even higher than that recorded in the banner year of
1967 (see Table 1). Subsequent years have also shown an increase
over the previous five years.

Further complicating the evaluation of factors holding back the
actual achievement figures in housing is the growing rate of demolition
of existing housing, often as a result of poor or uncoordinated planning.
M. Vershinin, sector head of the CC CPSU's Construction Department
highlighted this problem by stating that "for the country as a whole,
unfortunately, demolition of usable housing in connection with reconstruction is increasing." From 1966 to 1968 the total housing space
demolished came to approximately 10 million square meters, or an
amount equal to 5 percent of new housing built during those three
years![77] Turkmenia was singled out for its demolition of housing.
In Armenia demolition reached 10 percent of new housing space.[78]
Between 1960 and 1963 in the RSFSR, house demolition brought on
by urban reconstruction increased by 50 percent.[79] Throughout the
nation, general city plans, where they exist, are often violated by the
city agencies themselves or by industrial enterprises with the help
of impatient bulldozers and wrecking crews. These often unwarranted
actions simply prolong the housing shortage and cause major disruptions in the lives of many communities and individuals.

THE TWENTY-FOURTH PARTY CONGRESS
AND THE 1971-1975 PLAN

While there was again the recognition that the housing shortage,
particularly in the cities, had not yet been solved, Leonid Brezhnev
underlined the fact that almost 60 billion rubles had been spent to
combat the problem and more than 500 million square meters of
housing had been built during the past five years. "This means the
equivalent of more than fifty large cities with a population of a million
each was built from scratch in this country." The General Secretary
went on to assure the Twenty-Fourth Congress that "housing construction will assume a still greater scope" in the new Five Year
Plan (Pravda, March 31, 1971). The Party Congress Directives
(Pravda, Izvestia, April 11, 1971) and the Draft of the 1971-1975 Five
Year Economic Plan (Pravda, Izvestia, February 14, 1971) both called
for the building of housing with a total space of 565 million to 575
million square meters from all sources of finance during the plan
period. At the same time, there was note of the need to improve the
architecture and exterior finishing of the buildings. Housing construction cooperatives, which were considered "very important in
improving the population's housing," and individual housing construction were to be encouraged. Later in the year (1971), Premier Kosygin

announced an increase of the planned housing target to 580 million square meters, a 12 percent increase over housing constructed during 1966-1970 (according to Radio Moscow, November 23, 1971). This increase may reflect the leadership's concern over the unsettling events in Poland in December 1970, a concern which seems to have delayed the unveiling of the ninth Five Year Plan (1971-1975). With a view toward satisfying growing pressures for an improved way of life, the plan set a goal of bringing the level of gas service for housing in cities and urban settlements to 65-75 percent, and of increasing the volume of everyday services by at least 100 percent for the country as a whole, and by 180 percent in rural localities (Pravda, Izvestia, February 14, 1971). The ninth Five Year Plan appropriated 78.5 billion rubles (from all sources) or 21.6 percent more than during the previous five-year period. Despite this plan for an accelerated pace, actual performance has fallen below yearly targets. Whereas 117.8 million square meters of total dwelling space had been planned for 1971 (Izvestia, December 10, 1970, p. 2), only 108.3 million had been opened; the 1972 plan envisaged 115 million square meters (Pravda, November 25, 1971), but according to preliminary figures, realized only a little more than 106 million square meters (see Table 1).

What have these recent Soviet housing programs actually meant to the Soviet citizen? From the point of view of the "sanitary standard" or amount of living space per person, real progress has been slow. The ten-year period from 1957 to 1967 recorded an average annual gain of only about 3 percent, from 5.29 square meters to 7.18 square meters of living space. Living space does not include bathrooms, kitchens if communal, and hallways. According to Soviet economist David Broner, the living space may be determined by taking the total space of housing per person and multiplying by a correction coefficient of 0.7, since in buildings of new construction the so-called auxiliary (kitchen, bath, hallways) space of the apartment on the average comprises 30 percent of the total space, and living floor space is about 70 percent of the total space.[80] In 1922 the universally recognized sanitary standard of nine square meters per person of living space was established in Russia ("Sanitarnye pravila po postroike zhilykh zdanii," approved by Narkomzdrav RSFSR August 20, 1922). Broner calculated that at the end of 1964 the urban living space in the Soviet Union per person amounted to 6.8 square meters, still below the health norm of nine square meters. Timothy Sosnovy, western expert on Soviet housing conditions, arrived at the lower figure of 6.42 square meters living space per urban resident in 1965.[81]

Applying the Broner procedure to more recent statistics, we find that at the end of 1971 the living space per urban dweller in the USSR was 7.84 square meters (based on an urban population of 142.5 million and an urban housing fund of 1,590 million square meters).

By contrast, in 1950 the figures stood at 3.98 square meters, and at
the end of 1960 at 6.17 square meters of living space per urban dweller.
Table 5 indicates a slow but steady growth of urban housing space
per resident since the mid-1950s. In contrast to rural housing, urban
housing is more costly because of "amenities," central heating, sewerage, gas, and running water. Another indicator of housing conditions
is the density of occupancy per room in urban communities. Table 6
indicates the density of urban occupancy and also shows a very gradual
decline in crowded housing conditions.

The continued rapid urbanization of the country must explain
in part the slow pace of providing and increasing the amount of housing
space available to the urban resident (see Table 5). In the eleven-year
period from 1959 to 1970, the urban population increased by 36 million
persons. Of these, 14.6 million represents the natural increase in
the cities, 5 million the transfer of formerly rural communities to
urban status, and the largest part, over 16 million persons, the movement from rural to urban population.[82] The slow increase in urban
housing space also reflects a failure of Soviet officials to enforce
their own restrictions limiting migration to the large cities and urban
centers, and a miscalculation of Soviet planners in estimating population growth. Preliminary 1970 census figures for Moscow, for example, reportedly "astonished" the Moscow City Council. The Moscow
population in January 1970 was actually 7,061,000, instead of the estimated 6.7 million upon which the Moscow government had based its
projections of housing and transportation. In fact, V. Promyslov,
Chairman of the Moscow Soviet Executive Committee (a position
somewhat analogous to that of mayor), revealed in 1966 that the Moscow
general plan envisaged a population of from 6.6 million to 6.8 million
during the plan period, that is, up until 1980! (Izvestia, October 5,
1966). The Leningrad General Plan drawn up in 1962 anticipated a
population of 3.2 million in 1980. By 1971, however, the Leningrad
population had surpassed 4 million. Kiev's plans had been based on
an estimated 1.5 million population after 1980. But by 1971 the
Ukrainian capital held 1,632,000 persons (Izvestia, March 7, 1971).
Despite existing curbs, the 1970 census gave further evidence of the
fact that big cities experienced steady increases in population, reflecting the attractiveness of existing urban complexes for industrial
expansion, the desire of people for the better material and cultural
life offered in urban areas,[83] and a greater pressure on the urban
housing fund (see Table 7).

Although most union republics have set nine square meters of
living space per person as the sanitary housing norm, some republics
are exceptions and reflect the national policy of looking to greater
housing allowances. The Belorussian, Lithuanian, and Moldavian
civil codes, for example, stipulate that for certain cities or towns

33

TABLE 5

Growth of Urban Housing Space per Resident

Year (at end of year)	Urban Housing Fund		Urban Population		Average Floor Space per Person (square meters)	Living Space per Urban Resident (square meters)	
	Aggregate Housing Space (millions of square meters)	As Percent of 1950	Millions	As Percent of 1950			As Percent of 1950
1950	513	100	73	100	7.0	3.98	100
1957	723	140.9	95.6	130.9	7.6	5.29	135.4
1958	832	162.2	100.0	137.0	8.3	5.82	146.7
1959	896	174.7	103.8	142.2	8.6	6.04	151.8
1960	958	186.7	108.3	148.4	8.8	6.17	155.0
1965	1238	241.3	124.7	170.8	9.9	6.95	174.6
1966	1290	251.5	128.0	175.3	10.1	7.06	177.4
1967	1350	263.2	130.9	179.3	10.3	7.18	180.4
1968	1410	274.9	134.2	183.8	10.5	7.35	184.7
1969[a]	1469[a]	286.4	136.0	186.3	10.8	7.56	189.9
1970[b]	1529[b]	298.5	139.0[c]	190.4	11.0	7.70	193.5
1971[b]	1590[b]	311.9	142.5[c]	195.2	11.2	7.84	197.0
1973[d] (Planned Figure)					11.6[d]	8.12[d]	204.0

[a]Narodnoe khoziaistvo SSSR v 1970 g., p. 546.
[b]SSSR v tsifrakh v 1971 godu, p. 211.
[c]Narodnoe khoziaistvo v 1922-1972, p. 9.
[d]N. K. Baibakov, "On the State Plan for the Development of the USSR National Economy in 1973," Pravda, December 19, 1972.

Source: D. L. Broner, "Zhilishchnaia problema v trudykh i gosudartsvennoi deiatelnosti, V. I. Lenina," Vestnik Statistiki, no. 3 (1970): 10.

TABLE 6

Density of Occupancy per Room in Urban Communities
of the USSR in 1923, 1960-63, and 1965

Year	Persons per Room
1923	2.60
1960	2.78
1961	2.72
1962	2.59
1963	2.55
1965	2.33

Note: Under standards in effect in most West European countries and in the U.S., occupancy by more than 1.5 persons per room
is regarded as excessive.

Source: Timothy Sosnovy, New Directions, 1966, p. 545.

the sanitary housing norm may be raised. Consequently, in Vil'nius
the norm is twelve square meters per person; in the Ukraine 13.65
square meters per person has been established as the norm; Georgia
and Azerbaidzhan have set twelve square meters as their norm.[84]
The Moscow General Plan envisages twelve to fifteen square meters
per resident as the optimal norm of living space by 1980.[85] The
latest population statistics may prove a major setback to achievement
of this goal. In the continuing battle of square meters versus apartments, there have been serious suggestions that the placement norm
or norm of living space per person be enlarged by approximately
two square meters per person. Such an increase, argue the proponents,
would decrease by 20 percent the number of families receiving new
living quarters annually. Greater population stability, longer tenancy,
and presumably more careful treatment and upkeep of apartments on
the part of the tenants are the desired results of the proposal. Furthermore, instead of planning housing construction "according to the gross"
on the basis of total quantity of space, housing construction should
be planned on an apartment basis.[86] Since the goal of a well-built
and appointed apartment for each family was elevated to the position
of national policy in the late 1950s and in the 1961 Party Program,
an increasing number of planners have been talking in terms of the
number of rooms as well as the amount of square meters. In simple

TABLE 7

Population of USSR Cities
(in thousands)

City	1970 (on January 15)	1972 (on January 1)
Moscow	7,061	7,300
Leningrad	3,950	4,066
Gorky	1,170	1,213
Novosibirsk	1,161	1,199
Tashkent	1,385	1,461
Odessa	892	941
Tbilisi	889	927
Cheliabinsk	875	910
Dnepropetrovsk	862	903
Omsk	821	876
Volgograd	818	852
Erevan	767	818
Saratov	757	790
Riga	732	755
Voronezh	660	693
Krasnoiarsk	648	688
Alma-Ata	730	776
Perm	850	881
Kazan	869	904
Donetsk	879	905
Frunze	431	453
Dushanbe	374	400
Vil'nius	372	400
Zaporozh'e	658	697

Source: SSSR v tsifrakh v 1971 godu, (Moscow: Statistika, 1972), pp. 13-15.

formulas, "from K = n - 1 to K = n + 1," Broner illustrates Soviet housing policy. At the stage of the living space norm of nine square meters per person, Soviet planners and architects must employ the formula K = n - 1, where K equals the number of rooms in an apartment and n equals the number of persons in the family. At the second stage in solving the housing problem, when the average living space will grow to twelve square meters per person, K = n will express the planner's guiding formula—that the number of rooms in an apartment should be equal to the number of persons in the family. When the size of living space per person will be fourteen to fifteen square meters, the third stage formula $K = n + 1$ will represent the task of providing every person with a separate room plus one room for common use.[87] The advance of the housing front is to march in cadenced step with the advance of the nation into communism.

What consequences will the achievement of this appealing goal have on the organization of collective life? On the individual's energies directed to his private and collective life? Up to the present, the Soviet urban dweller has not looked to his home as his "castle," the place for the enjoyment of a protected private life. In fact, in many cases the home turned out to be the least private place of all, a living example of the ever present collective. Would the policy of separate apartments for all families lead to a new, somewhat unique condition for both the Soviet public and Soviet public organizers alike? With more room, less interference by nonfamily tenants, greater comforts, would Soviet man continue to become the new Soviet man, motivated by concern for the collective life, or would he become more able to resist participation in voluntary communal activities? Certainly the picture of Soviet housing, though changing slowly, still presents new challenges to the mass-movement regime. Soviet decision-makers may not be totally unaware of the social aspects of their housing policies, and such awareness may partially explain the slowness in eliminating the housing shortage once and for all. Could the revival of the house committees of tenants, active in the late 1950s and during the 1960s, be one answer to the dilemma of private versus collective life? The domkoms (further examined in Chapter 6) do represent the official aim of getting the inhabitants involved in the problems of administration and of organizing all aspects of life within the apartment house with strong guidance by party organizations and local Soviets.

Soviet urban housing policies since the mid-1950s have been consistently directed to liquidating the housing shortage and to improving the housing conditions of the Soviet citizens. Programs initiated in 1957 and 1959 and continued by the post-Khrushchev leadership have made substantial advances in the housing sector over the much neglected and inadequate housing fund of the Stalin years. Placing their faith in industrialization and prefabrication of the construction industry, Soviet leaders have significantly heightened the tempo and lowered the cost of housing construction and made it a year-round possibility. Balancing the scales of progress in providing housing is the heavy weight of an unplanned and seemingly uncontrolled urban population (largely the result of migration to urban areas). At the same time, the inability to match the pace of house building with that of urban migration and growth may be providing Soviet sociologists and politicians with the necessary time in which to develop the institutions needed to meet new social aspects of separate, comfortable apartments, creating conditions for life centered around the hearth instead of the collective or common room.

NOTES

1. Entsiklopediia mestnovo upravleniia i khoziaistva (Moscow, 1927), p. 609. Cited in Timothy Sosnovy, The Housing Problem in the Soviet Union (New York: Research Program on the USSR, 1954), pp. 3-4.

2. Sosnovy, op. cit., p. 3.

3. Bol'shaia Sovetskaia Entsiklopediia, (Moscow, 1930), XVIII, 146.

4. Henri Troyat, Daily Life in Russia under the Last Tsar (London: Allen and Unwin, 1961), pp. 90-91.

5. Ibid., pp. 92-94.

6. Only 215 of 1,063 cities of pre-Revolutionary Russia, that is, 20.2 percent, had a water system; 23 cities, or 2.1 percent, had sewage systems. Only 5 percent of all houses had electricity. See A. N. Marzeev, Kommunal'naia gigiena (Moscow, 1951), p. 2, and B. B. Veselovski, Kurs ekonomiki i organizatsii gorodskogo khoziaistva (Moscow, 1951), pp. 83, 92. Cited in Sosnovy, op. cit., p. 5.

7. John N. Hazard, Soviet Housing Law (New Haven: Yale University Press, 1939), p. 3.

8. Problemy ekonomiki (Moscow, 1937), nos. 5-6, p. 177, in Sosnovy, op. cit., pp. 14-15.

9. Hazard, op. cit., p. 4.

10. See Alexander Block, "Soviet Housing—The Historical Aspect: Some Notes on Problems of Policy—I," Soviet Studies III, no. 1 (July 1951): 12-13.

11. Alexander S. Balinsky, "Non-Housing Objectives of Soviet Housing Policy," Problems of Communism X, no. 4 (July-August 1961): 17.

12. See: Kommunal'noe khoziaistvo (March-April 1922) printed in English translation in "European Housing Problems Since the War," no. 15 (Geneva: International Labour Office, 1924), p. 476. Cited in Hazard, op. cit., p. 7.

13. Alexander Block, "Soviet Housing—The Historical Aspect: Some Notes on Problems of Policy—I," Soviet Studies VIII, no. 1 (July 1951): 15; also Karass, Ocherednoi vopros zhilishchnogo stroitel' stva, 2, Ezhenedel'nik sovetskoi iustitsii, no. 989, p. 192; Sosnovy, op. cit., pp. 37-41.

14. Alexander Block, "Soviet Housing—The Historical Aspect: Some Notes on Problems of Policy—II," Soviet Studies III, no. 3 (January 1952): 230.

15. B. B. Veselovskii and D. I. Sheinis, eds., Gorsovety i kommunal'noe khoziaistvo (Moscow: 1927), pp. 194, 199, 202.

16. Zigurds L. Zile, Private Rights in a Collectivist Society: A Study of the Non-Socialist Effort in Soviet Urban Housing Construction, Thesis for Doctor of Juridical Science, Harvard Law School, 1967, p. 15.

17. Marzeev, Kommunal'naia gigiena (Moscow: 1951), quoted in Sosnovy, "Housing in Workers' State," Problems of Communism V, no. 6 (November-December 1956): 31.

18. Hazard, op. cit., p. 6.

19. Sobranie uzakonenii i rasporiazhenii rabochego-krest'ianskogo pravitel'stva RSFSR [(SU RSFSR) (Collection of Legislation), 1921], No. 56, Art. 355.

20. Decree April 20, 1922, SU RSFSR, 1922, No. 30, Art. 349.

21. August 8, 1921, SU RSFSR, 1921, No. 60 Art. 409. See also Zile, op. cit., pp. 23-25; Hazard, op. cit., p. 9.

22. Balinsky, op. cit., p. 18.

23. Sobranie zakonov i rasporiazhenii raboche-krest'ianskogo pravitel'stva SSSR (SZ SSSR, 1928) (Collection of Laws of the USSR) (Moscow, 1928), No. 6, par. 49. Also cited in Sosnovy, op. cit., p. 49.

24. SSSR God raboty ravitel'stva (1927-1928) (Moscow, 1929), pp. 430-431. Cited in Sosnovy, op. cit., p. 50.

25. Vsesoiuznaia perepis' naseleniia 17 dekabria 1926 goda, Part I, p. 9, in Sosnovy, op. cit., p. 46.

26. Direktivy KPSS i sovetskogo pravitel'stva po khoziaistnym voprosam 1917-1957 (Moscow: Gospolitizdat, 1957-1958), I, 570.

27. Ibid., p. 588; Zile, op. cit., p. 81.

28. Sosnovy, op. cit., pp. 55 and 57. Investment in housing construction as a percentage of the total state capital investments was 17.4 percent between 1923 and 1928, 9.2 percent during the first Five Year Plan (1929-1932), 11 percent during the second Five Year Plan (1933-1937), 8.1 percent during the third Five Year Plan (1938-1942), and 16.9 percent during the fifth Five Year Plan (1946-1950).

29. Ibid., pp. 105-106.

30. Ibid., p. 106.

31. N. S. Khrushchev, Sorok let Velikoi oktiabr'skoi sotsialist-icheskoi revoliutsii (Moscow: Pravda, 1957), p. 47.

32. Chossudovsky, "The Development of Housing in the USSR," U.N. Housing and Town and Country Planning Bulletin, no. 5 (1951), pp. 81, 82-83. N. S. Khrushchev, Sorok let, p. 47; and A. Shneerson, Chto takoe zhilishchnyi vopros, (Moscow: VPSiAON, 1959), p. 63.

39

33. "Decree of the CC of the CPSU and USSR Council of Ministers: On Developing Housing Construction in the USSR," Pravda and Izvestia, August 2, 1957, p. 1 (CDSP IX, no. 31: 3).

34. Pravda, May 12, 1964.

35. CC CPSU and USSR Council of Ministers, "On Measures for Improving the Quality of Housing and Civil Construction," Izvestia, June 20, 1969, p. 4; Pravda, June 21, 1969, pp. 1-2, (CDSP XXI, no. 25: 11).

36. Speech by Comrade K. Ye. Voroshilov, in "Celebration by Moscow Builders," Pravda, February 5, 1957, p. 1 (CDSP IX, no. 5: 27-28).

37. Decree of the CC of the CPSU and USSR Council of Ministers, "On Developing Housing Construction in the USSR," Pravda and Izvestia, August 2, 1957, pp. 1-3 (CDSP IX, no. 31: 4).

38. A. Nezhny, "Goroda, kotorye my stroim" ("Cities That We Are Building"), Novyi mir, no. 10 (October 1969) (Current Abstracts of the Soviet Press [hereafter cited as CASP] II, no. 3 [March 1970]: 26).

39. Decree "On Developing Housing Construction in the USSR, July 31, 1957," Pravda and Izvestia, August 2, 1957, (CDSP, IX, no. 31: 3-4).

40. Leningradskaia Pravda, November 15, 1963.

41. In Jan F. Triska, ed., Soviet Communism: Programs and Rules (San Francisco: Chandler, 1962), pp. 92-93.

42. Timothy Sosnovy, "The Soviet Housing Situation Today," Soviet Studies XI, no. 1 (July 1959): 13-14.

43. See Kommunist, lead article, March 24, 1961, and Izvestia, September 2, 1970, p. 2.

44. "Decree on Developing Housing Construction in the USSR, July 31, 1957" (CDSP IX, no. 31: 3-6, 32).

45. Pravda, December 17, 1956.

46. Izvestia, March 15, 1958.

47. Zile, op. cit., p. 165.

48. Pravda, November 19, 1957.

49. A. I. Mal'ginova, D. P. Vatman, "Spornye voprosy obmena zhilymi pomeshcheniiami" (Controversial problems in the exchange of apartments and rooms), Sovetskoe gosudarstvo i pravo, no. 6 (June 1968): 112.

50. N. S. Khrushchev, "Control Figures for the Development of USSR National Economy in 1959-1965—Report to the Twenty-First Party Congress," Pravda and Izvestia, November 14, 1959 (CDSP X, no. 48: 6).

51. N. S. Khrushchev, "On Control Figures for the Development of USSR National Economy in 1959-1965," Pravda, January 28, 1959 (CDSP XI, no. 3: 4).

52. Ibid., p. 5.

53. Kucherenko, "On the State of Urban Development in the USSR and Measures for Improving It," report delivered at the June 1960 Conference on City Planning and Construction, Pravda, June 8, 1960 (CDSP XII, no. 23: 14).

54. See Bates, op. cit., p. 10.

55. Kucherenko, op. cit., p. 13.

56. Central Statistical Board (Administration) of the USSR Council of Ministers, Soviet Union 50 Years: Statistical Returns (Moscow: Progress Publishers, 1969), p. 251.

57. B. Svetlichny, "Improved Housing for Soviet People," Kommunist, no. 6 (April 1965) (CDSP XVII, no. 22: 10).

58. Ibid.

59. Svetlichny, op. cit., pp. 12-13.

60. "Report on the Directives for the Five Year Economic Development Plan of the USSR for 1966-1970," delivered by A. Kosygin on April 5, 1966, in Twenty-Third Congress of the Communist Party of the Soviet Union (Moscow: Novosti, 1966), p. 245.

61. Twenty-Third Congress of CPSU, pp. 318-319.

62. L. I. Brezhnev, "Report of CC CPSU to Twenty-Third Congress CPSU, March 29, 1966," Pravda, March 30, 1966.

63. See Leon M. Herman, "Urbanization and New Housing Construction in the USSR," in Industrialized Housing, p. 29; Directives, Twenty-Third Congress CPSU, 1966 p. 368; Pravda, December 17, 1969, January 25, 1970.

64. Twenty-Third Congress of the CPSU, p. 245.

65. Ibid., p. 370.

66. A. K. Gaiduk, "Increasing Labor Productivity in Construction," Bulleten stroitel'noi tekhniki, no. 12 (1968): 28-30.

67. Twenty-Third Congress CPSU, p. 370.

68. Narodnoe Khoziaistvo SSSR v 1968 g., 1969, p. 573.

69. Donald Barry, "Cities and Towns," Problems of Communism XVIII, no. 3 (May-June 1969): 4. The statistical annuals, however, Narodnoe Khoziaistvo SSSR, do present figures for achievements in urban and rural sectors.

70. Narodnoe Khoziaistvo SSSR v 1968 g., p. 573.

71. Pravda, January 25, 1970.

72. Izvestia, December 11, 1968.

73. Pravda, January 25, 1970.

74. A. Repenko, Ekonomika stroitel'stva, no. 2 (1969): 3-8.

75. Scot Butler, "The Soviet Capital Investment Program," in Economic Performance and the Military Burden in the Soviet Union Joint Economic Committee, U.S. Congress (Washington: 1970), p. 47.

76. "On Improving the Planning of Capital Construction and Increasing Economic Incentives in Construction Work," Pravda, June

20, 1969, pp. 1-2. "On Measures for Improving the Quality of Housing and Civil Construction," Pravda, June 21, 1969, pp. 1-2. "On Improving Design and Estimate Work," Pravda, June 22, 1969, pp. 1-2. V. Isayev, "Make Good Preparations for the Economic Reform in Construction and Carry It Out Successfully," Ekonomicheskaia gazeta, no. 26, June 1969, p. 34 (CDSP XXI, no. 25: 8-16, 21).

77. M. Vershinin, "The Soviets and the City Economy: The Fate of a Residential Building," Izvestia, April 11, 1970, (CDSP XXII, no. 13: 18).

78. Ibid.

79. Ekonomicheskaia gazeta, June 23, 1964, p. 38.

80. David L. Broner, Zhilishchnyi vopros i statistika (Moscow: Statistika, 1966), p. 7.

81. Timothy Sosnovy, "Housing Conditions and Urban Development in the USSR," in New Directions in Soviet Economy, 1966, Joint Economic Committee, U.S. Congress (Washington: 1966), p. 544.

82. S. I. Bruk, "Ethnodemograficheskii protsessy v SSSR (po materialam perepisi 1970 goda)," Sovetskaia etnografiia, no. 4 (1971): 11.

83. The New York Times, April 19, 1970; Izvestia, April 19, 1970.

84. Iurii K. Tolstoi, Sovetskoe zhilishchnoe pravo (Soviet Housing Law) (Leningrad University, 1967), p. 78.

85. V. F. Promyslov, "Principles of the General Plan for the Capital," Izvestia, October 5, 1966.

86. N. Kordo and M. Fradin, "Housing: Comfort of an Apartment and Placement," Izvestia, July 15, 1966 (CDSP XVIII, no. 28: 22-23).

87. Broner, op. cit., p. 60.

3

URBAN PLANNING
CONCEPTS AND PROCESS

Since housing policies and problems of construction are intimately linked with Soviet city planning principles and planning processes, the present chapter will attempt to describe Soviet theories
and practices in urban planning and to analyze the major problem of
coordinating central economic planning, local urban planning, and
house construction. Is centralism of urban planning a reality and a
success? Has central economic planning resulted in a unified housing
program and system at the local level, in a rational use of urban land,
and in a well-balanced development of public services in livable urban
areas? Have post-Stalin developments enhanced the standing of local
city governments to the position of "Master of the City" in designing
and enforcing solutions to city problems? In brief, what power does
the local Soviet have in the urban planning process, particularly when
it is concerned with housing? Or is the local Soviet only an instrument
of the central planning authorities and a victim of the powerful industrial ministries? Finally, what have the Soviet concept of "dwelling"
and recent Soviet housing policies meant for the designing of urban
housing, and to what extent has central planning improved or hindered
practical housing design at a local level? Have the economic and
planning systems helped to hasten the elimination of the housing problem in the Soviet Union? Questions of housing construction will necessarily have to be discussed in this section, but a more concentrated
treatment will be presented in Chapter 4.

SOVIET VIEW OF THE CAPITALIST CITY

Stemming from the Marxist ideological tradition with its emphasis on the "idiocy of rural life," Bolshevik theory has always demonstrated an urban bias. Soviet policy consequently has often been

expressed in terms of eliminating the distinction between town and country in favor of the town. The entire thrust of post-Revolutionary programs has been in the direction of city building and urbanization, direct results of industrializing the nation. No Jeffersonian suspicions of the city and its evil ways existed in Marxist thought to hamper the Soviet leadership's and even Soviet public's drive to the cities. The life of the future, the life of Communism, is to be centered in the modern, highly organized city. "The city is the most accomplished form of human establishment," a prominent Soviet architect and city planner writes. Throughout Soviet history, in fact, there has been no dearth of praise for the potential of man's highest achievements and fullest development in the harmoniously organized rhythms of cities, in which have been amassed "immense material treasures, to which entire generations, one after the other, have brought their contribution."[1] Neither has there been a dearth of criticism of the capitalist city and capitalist city planning. In analyzing the condition of the city in capitalist countries, Soviet planners have at the same time defined and underscored claims to their own system's superior planning abilities and successes. Time and again one hears that a fundamental characteristic of the present capitalist city is individual or corporate selfishness— "each one wants only to consider his own interests." The absence of an economic plan, retention of private ownership of the means of production, private ownership of land, and competition all lead to the disordered, uncontrolled development of great capitalist urban areas. This self-centered, selfish attitude is seen in the capitalist who wants to install his enterprises in the already crowded cities to insure the greatest number of clients and the cheapest manpower. In search of work, thousands flow into the large cities. Nothing opposes this process, which eventually leads to the city's growing beyond all rational limits.[2] Many of the serious problems facing our western cities have been very sharply spotlighted by Socialist critics: "Plants and factories cover the (capitalist) city with clouds of smoke and dust which empoison the health of the inhabitants, and in particular that of the working population." The more the city is seen extending itself, the greater becomes the distance to work. "Nature becomes, for the majority of the urban population, something far off and inaccessible." Slums with no decent health services for their population spread out to the city limits. "To these characteristic traits of capitalist cities must be added social wounds such as criminality, prostitution, alcoholism, and various diseases caused by a lack of hygiene."[3] Do these Soviet observers see any hope for the nonsocialist city? They take their cue from Engels' writing in The Housing Question, when he said:

> In reality the bourgeoisie has only one method of settling
> the housing question after its fashion—that is to say, of

settling it in such a way that the solution continually poses
the question anew. . . .
    . . . the most scandalous alleys and lanes disappear
to the accompaniment of lavish self-glorification by the
bourgeoisie on account of this tremendous success, but
they appear again at once somewhere else, and often in
the immediate neighborhood. . . .
    The breeding places of disease, the infamous holes
and cellars in which the capitalist mode of production con-
fines our workers night after night, are not abolished; they
are merely shifted elsewhere.[4]

Their conclusion then is that in the existing social structure, all
envisioned attempts to correct the faults of a capitalist city are bound
to failure.[5] Can master plans be implemented with private ownership
of land? Can construction and city service costs be lowered and developed in a balanced way in the face of land speculation? Can the
swallowing up of the land into an unmanageable megalopolis be halted
and reversed without a central economic planning authority? The
questions alone seem to ring with an emphatic negative answer.
    The major problems of most cities are usually discussed in
terms of the "size" of the city and of urban agglomerations. In conditions of capitalism, with an extraordinarily high concentration of
population in several of the largest cities, the small and middle-sized
population areas are continually shrinking. As the city giants develop,
the contradictions between city and country, between industrialized
centers and agrarian regions become stronger. When these city giants
come together and merge into urban agglomerations, they spontaneously
push together many economically diverse centers, fusing them into
a chaotically built territory extending hundreds of miles and deprived
of necessary green plantings. This fusion process actually results
in separated population places displaying vast contrasts in planning
and development, depending on social and racial groups. Iu. P.
Bocharov points to Chicago as a concrete illustration of the processes
where all peculiarities and contradictions characteristic of the development of large North American cities are manifested. Chicago is the
first American city to have established a general plan. In its time
the Chicago General Plan of 1909 served as a model for American
town planning and also exerted a noted influence on the development
of a number of European cities. Bocharov notes that city planning is
one of those fields of the economy where bourgeois society first attempted to adopt the principles of planning. With Chicago, however,
only part of the proposals of the General Plan was ever realized.
Bocharov concludes that the planning administration created at the
outset of the Chicago General Plan was transformed, in the final count,

into simple, powerless advertising agencies, since it did not have any real laws regulating the conditions of private ownership of land. Since there was no authority over economic forces of the area and over land ownership, the development of the city took place without control, resulting in a present metropolitan Chicago that consists of many competing towns, with more than a thousand independent local administrative organs.[6] Bocharov further concludes that class and racial segregation of population in capitalist cities to a significant degree defines the planned structure of these towns and is not its consequence, as non-Soviet researchers sometimes assert.[7] One thing is made absolutely clear in the writings of all Soviet city planners—that the growth of industrialization is the basic city-forming factor. Consequently, in contrast to western capitalist city planning (claim Soviet authorities), under the socialist economic system "it is possible to make a rational redistribution of the intensity of productive concentration between the large industrial center and its surroundings."[8] It is, therefore, only under the conditions of centralized economic planning and fully directed placing of industrial forces that the harmonious development of new social and spatial forms of settlement and the full exploration of their advantages are considered possible. "The absence of these conditions under the capitalist system of economics leads to agglomerations as the most complex and complicated forms of settlements, which most sharply manifests the crisis of bourgeois city planning."[9]

HOW LARGE SHOULD THE IDEAL CITY BE?

This brief discussion of the Soviet view of capitalist city formation and development reveals a basic concern of the Soviet Union's planners over the question of the optimal size of the city, a question that has been at the eye of a raging and sometimes bitter controversy. The optimal size debate also points to some of the basic principles of city planning in the USSR. In Soviet theory, the law of the development of cities states that the growth of industrialization is the basic city-forming factor. To build and encourage the vigorous life of well-serviced and healthy cities, the population must be limited, and the way to limit urban population growth is to plan carefully by directing the location and expansion of industries. Closely tied to this placement of industry is the principle of proportional, relatively even distribution of industry and population over the entire country, with the goal of abolishing the essential differences between town and country. In its drive to realize the ideal, well-ordered, attractive city as the dominant place of activity, Soviet theorists and leaders have stressed that the city must be a unified "living organism," whose basic cells must be

46

a rich communal life raised to a heretofore unknown level of human experience and intensity. To control its urbanization process, the Communist Party as early as 1931 approved a resolution forbidding the construction of new industrial enterprises in Moscow and Leningrad as of 1932. It declared "inexpedient the agglomeration of a huge number of enterprises in big urban centers."[10] Later this resolution was extended to other major cities and became all-union policy. At the Twenty-Second Party Congress in 1961, Khrushchev again underlined an updated version of this policy in saying that "while preserving large cities as industrial and cultural centers but at the same time preventing their excessive growth, we must develop and build small and medium-sized towns having all facilities."[11] A similar decision was re-enforced at the Twenty-Third Party Congress in March 1966 when the Party Directives specified that new industrial enterprises shall be built mainly in small and medium-sized towns.[12] The Twenty-Fourth Party Congress (1971) once again stressed the policy of curbing the growth of large cities, halting the siting of new industrial enterprises in these cities, and improving the distribution of productive forces. A great part of the concern for the development of middle and small-size towns is not just the possibility of stemming the tide to the large cities. It is seen as a way to make better use of labor manpower, which is now underutilized. Implications of the policy are that these middle and smaller urban areas are to grow through a program of industrial location and development that may well take them out of their classification as small and middle-size towns. Yet the results of all these attempts to limit the population growth of cities have been far from successful. Long-term planned population ceilings for a significant number of Soviet cities have often been greatly surpassed within the first few years of the plan period. In 1960, for example, the planned population for 1975 of several important cities was reported. Population plans, however, were soon made obsolete, as may be seen from the following: [13]

City	Population Planned for 1975	Actual Population January 1, 1969	Actual Population January 1, 1972
Gorky	840,000	1,159,000	1,213,000
Tashkent	800,000	1,354,000	1,461,000
Novosibirsk	850,000	1,098,000	1,199,000

Earlier we noted that by January 1970 Moscow's population had unexpectedly exceeded its maximum population projection for 1981. Such demographic miscalculations—often the result of unchecked enterprise expansion and building—have caused and are causing costly plan revisions, severe labor shortages in most urban areas, and prolonged housing shortages, as well as casting more fuel on the debate over the optimal size of the city.

Population growth through migration to large cities has been a significant factor in the failure to realize a planned living space per urban dweller of 8.12 square meters by 1965. As Soviet economists and planners admit, it is not the lack of meeting planned housing targets, but rather "the growth of the urban population in excess of the planning projections" that has led to this negative phenomenon.

> Moreover, Leningrad and a number of other large cities
> have long ago exceeded their optimal size, and their
> further growth will lead to progressive increases in
> irrational budgetary outlays, to environmental pollution,
> and to other negative consequences. . . . The Party de-
> mands a halt to the construction of new enterprises in
> large cities regardless of the form in which it is done—
> directly or indirectly (under the guise of reconstruction).[14]

At the same time, population restrictions have probably resulted in a somewhat more planned urban growth than would otherwise be the case. Without population controls of any kind, Moscow might well have turned into another Tokyo or New York. Perhaps more than any other factor, these demographic phenomena illustrate the weakness of the Soviet urban planner in relation to the dominating economic and industrial ministries. Considerations of industrial development still outweigh all urbanists' arguments and well-calculated projects.

Soviet city planners and economists have calculated that cities with a population of one million are less economical than those with 200,000 to 250,000 inhabitants; the city of 100,000 is more economical than one with 20,000 from the point of view of the smallest per capita material expenditures for construction and the exploitation of the whole complex of urban economy.[15]

The optimal size of the Soviet city may vary between 20,000 to 250,000 residents (in the RSFSR, a population of 12,000 is needed to be classified as a city). Once the city limits go beyond certain boundaries, as a result of excessive population, great expenditures are called for in organizing the network of urban transportation, constructing a highly complex system of municipal services, and in achieving effective sanitation, not to mention increased time and energy wasted in traveling to and from work. Though this has been the prevailing view in the past, it has not been the only one advanced. Within the last few years some Soviet economists, sociologists, and demographers have argued that the "optimal size theory" is unrealistic and that so-called towns of "optimal size" display no special advantages.[16] At the All-Union Conference on the Prospects of Soviet City Planning,

held in Moscow in February 1970, the concept of the "optimal size"
of a city came under general attack and may have been mortally
wounded. What could be more "unoptimal," it was argued, than medium-
sized towns with limited cultural opportunities isolated from other
urban centers? The various shortcomings of these "optimal towns"
can only be eliminated by converting them into large ones! Perhaps
the strongest point in this "anti-optimal" position is the contention
that labor productivity is much higher in large urban areas, far out-
weighing increased outlays for municipal services, and that lowest
housing costs and fastest rates of construction are attained precisely
in the very largest cities.

One well-known Soviet urban economist, V. Perevedentsev
points out the results of a study made by the USSR Gosplan
that showed 1961 labor productivity in various sized industrial cities as a percentage of the average for all cities:

Size of City (number of residents)	Gross Output per Worker	Return on Assets
Under 50,000	90%	82%
50,000 to 100,000	97	90
100,000 to 250,000	100	101
250,000 to 500,000	100	94
500,000 to 1,000,000	108	111
Over 1,000,000	138	211

The conclusion Perevedentsev draws from the data is clear,
namely, that:

Superlarge cities have enormous advantages in comparison
with small, medium-sized and even large cities in the field
of industrial production. Hence, the concentration of population and production in superlarge industrial cities is economically advantageous. Therefore, . . . the optimal city
from an economic standpoint is one in which the disparity
between what the urban resident consumes and what he
produces is the greatest, not the city in which outlays per
urban resident are the smallest. . . .
However, the restrictive regulation of the growth of
cities agrees poorly with the necessity of increasing the
efficiency of the national economy. Moreover, a large
city, with its possibilities for choice in all respects, offers people far more than medium-sized and small cities
do. These economic and social advantages are the main
reasons for the ineffectiveness of restrictions on large

cities, which have been unable to prevent the further concentration of the urban population.[17]

Since 1958 urban policy has been moving in the direction of emphasis
on the development of the small and medium-sized towns and reflects
less concern over artificial population restrictions. Antagonist of the
"optimal-size" theory, Perevedentsev, seems to favor the experiment
of "opening up" cities to a free influx of population. He stresses recognition of the fact that "conurbations" (urban agglomerations) constitute
the most characteristic feature of twentieth-century urban growth
patterns, with currently more rapid growth of outer sections of conurbations than their centers. Instead of continuing to exert an effort
in artificial administrative regulation of migration—which Perevedentsev
concludes has proved ineffective in the extreme, compelling people to
live tens of kilometers from their place of work—urban planners should
pay greater attention to better organization of large cities. Besides,
where administrative population regulation has enjoyed some success,
it has led to a shortage of manpower. Perevedentsev is convinced
that with the increased importance of the "geographic situation" of
an enterprise as a result of the economic reform, the increased effectiveness of enterprises situated in large cities will inevitably promote
the tendency toward the priority development of them.[18]

WHERE SHOULD THE ENTERPRISE BE LOCATED?

This question of the location of industrial enterprises has been
central to the optimal-size debate and to the success or failure of
urban plans, particularly those concerning the construction of housing.
Practically all participants in the debate agree that the construction
of a new enterprise is almost always easier and faster in a large city
with highly developed transportation, electrical, and water systems—
and that is why it is so often built there. But, for every 1,000 new
workers in an industry, the population of the city increases by around
4,000 persons.[19] Naturally, the economic ministries desire to take
the most economical and easiest route from their own point of view.
The consequences of this fact usually spell disaster for neatly re-
searched general plans of city development. In the Ukraine, for
instance, for several years the seven largest cities, including Odessa,
have been prohibited from constructing new enterprises and expanding
existing ones. Yet, in 1969 the Chairman of the Planning Commission
for the Southern Economic Region of the USSR complained that nevertheless such construction continues "by way of exceptions," resulting
in population increases that are outstripping all plan estimates. By
1967 Odessa's population forecast for the end of the Five Year Plan

(1970) was already reached. What is more, a number of ministries, "guided purely by departmental considerations," were planning further development of Odessa's industries and construction of new productive units, exacerbating serious problems with housing, communal, social, and cultural services.[20] This persistence on the part of the economic ministries has created an "excessively rapid expansion" of Odessa's territory, which in 1969 was already stretched out forty or fifty kilometers along the Black Sea coast and within the next few years will extend fifty-five to sixty kilometers. As to proposals for major enterprises to be established in small and medium-sized cities, ministries of the Odessa area have given flat disapproval. These problems are viewed as characteristic of other important industrial centers in the USSR.[21] Thus the actual lines along which cities develop are often drawn out in the offices of branch ministries. City and territorial planning agencies are simply ignored or circumvented. The conclusion, "it turned out that the city's general plan of development was in need of serious corrections," is one sadly repeated by countless chairmen of City Soviet Executive Committees. Dnepropetrovsk, for example, is faced with the cold fact that its population figure for 1985 will be reached in 1973. Why? "The growth rates of industrial construction, it turned out, were three times as great as those in housing and social and cultural construction." In the case of Dnepropetrovsk there had been general agreement a few years ago on the advisability of reducing industrial construction. It seems the city already had many plants, not enough workers, and considerable housing difficulties. Evidently, the ministries' general agreement meant very little. Enterprises were and are being built on an even grander scale,[22] leading to even more aggravated labor shortages, mainly because so little housing was erected to shelter new workers. Not all the blame, however, can be placed on the ministries. Local city governments themselves encourage the location of new or expanded industries within their town limits. More industries mean more of the "basic city-forming factors," greater financial resources to city budgets from industry taxes, and hopefully a larger slice of the centrally divided economic pie. The USSR State Planning Commission (Gosplan) and planning commissions of union republics do not sincerely participate in determining the economic prospects of towns. "All too often," one urban planner comments, "planning agencies are content to formally endorse economic prognoses submitted by town planners." "This endorsement," however, "does not commit them to abiding by town plans in distributing and locating new industry."[23]

A major incentive for the industrial enterprises' often flagrant disregard of general city plans has been the widespread view of the low "value" of land, expressed in extremely low land rents. Land cost has just not been an important concern when calculating the economics of industrial expansion. It has been relatively easy for industrial enterprises to be allocated excessively large amounts of city land. And because of the very low ground rents, plant directors can hold on to vacant lots "just in case."[24] In 1960 it was reported that in most Soviet cities, areas occupied by industrial enterprises per head of population were nearly double those in U.S. cities,[25] and there does not seem to have been any significant reversal of this situation. If the danger of land shortage exists in the Soviet Union, it is not from overpopulation, but rather from present-day "appetites" of industry.[26] The idea that urban land in the Soviet state is not a material value has been declared "an unforgivable error" by the Chairman of the USSR Gosstroi.[27] Yet this "unforgivable error" still continues to affect the conduct of factory managers, as well as some housing planners, who up until the last few years had little thought of building upward. To be fair to the housing builders, official policy, with an eye to short-run economic advantages, has more often than not encouraged the development of "vacant" lands before the "renewal" of older sections of the city. Khrushchev's preference for the five-story walkup also seemed to influence the "upward development of apartment building." Since Khrushchev's ouster, his successors and many urban planners have criticized the excessive construction of such buildings as uneconomical and unwise.

SUBURBAN ZONE AND SATELLITE CITIES

For the last fifteen years or so the Rules of Soviet City Planning (1958) have made clear the importance of surrounding cities with specially protected suburban zones intended to serve as the city's "oxygen tanks" and areas for mass recreation. Agriculture is to be the major activity within the suburban zone, and industrial activity producing things not required by the city is to be severely restricted. The suburban zone's inner ring closest to the city, of a width anywhere from three to ten kilometers, is to be the so-called "green belt" or forest-park belt (Lesopark), where all construction not connected to mass recreation, agriculture, forestry, or transportation is prohibited. Although some success has been achieved in carrying out this plan, because only the largest cities, such as Moscow and Leningrad, have a single master plan for the city and its suburban zone. City Executive Committees are not always able to regulate the type of construction in the suburban zone. The high-priority economic interests have consequently also violated this progressive spatial arrangement.

In their attempts to slow down and decentralize large city population growth, with the aim of improving the quality of urban life, Soviet decision-makers embarked upon a policy of building a network of satellite towns (Goroda-Sputniki) in the suburban zones around the largest cities but beyond the forest-park belt. Once again the question of industrial location became an essential one in defining the role of these satellite cities. As early as 1954, at the Second All-Union Conference of Builders, N. S. Khrushchev strongly suggested satellite towns as a realistic means of limiting the growth of large cities. Soviet planners had been keeping a curious eye on the "satellite city" programs of European cities, giving special attention to London's experience. Planners and politicians both seemed to agree (though not absolutely) that the creation of satellite towns dissociated from industry does not bring any positive results in attempts to disperse the population of large cities.[28] The satellite towns are planned to hold anywhere from 30,000 to 80,000 inhabitants each and their distance from the big city center should, in the opinion of some economists, be not less than 80 to 100 kilometers.[29] Other urbanists suggest a distance of 60 to 80 kilometers.[30] By 1958 Moscow was in the process of constructing its own satellite near Kryukovo Station. This satellite town was to have a population of 65,000. To avoid turning the satellite into a mere "bedroom" town, some of the capital's enterprises—primarily precision machinery and instruments plants—were to move to the satellite.[31] The timing of the satellite town program seemed to indicate an organic link with the economic reorganization and decentralization launched in 1957. The biggest obstacle to the successful decongestion of population through the satellite-cities program is the continued high priority on economic development, which has led to the ministries' encouraging, even pressuring for industrial plant expansion regardless of regional restrictions. Without the town and regional builders' effective control over the behavior of the economic administrator and industrial enterprise, the satellite may actually prove to be the vehicle for transporting even greater numbers into merging urban conglomerations. This danger was clearly recognized by those persons involved in working out satellite cities. In the case of Moscow, for example, there was the expressed fear that the growth of satellite cities in the Moscow suburban zone would lead to a reduction of the forest areas and open spaces and to excessive concentration of populated places.[32]

In view of the Soviet policy, re-emphasized in the late 1950s, to limit the growth of large cities and especially to promote the location of industry in small and medium-size cities, there was a major effort to define the concept of "satellite town" and to create a typology of satellite places. Of course, populated settlements around large cities may be termed satellite towns; a satellite town does not have to be an "artificial," newly created satellite. V. G. Davidovich has been a primary contributor to the discussion of the satellite town concept. Satellites, in Davidovich's opinion,

are those cities, towns and villages that develop around a
large central city and are related to it by common features
in the life of the population—commuting to places of employment and for cultural and other service purposes, or
only for cultural and other service purposes (on a sufficiently intensive scale). Satellites that are most closely
related to the central city both in employment and cultural-
service commuting may be termed "first-order satellites"
(situated within the inner part of the suburban zone) and
those that are related chiefly or only by cultural-service
commuting "second-order satellites" (in the outer part of
the suburban zone).[33]

Davidovich's suggested definition and subsequent elaborations strongly disagree with the widespread view that satellite cities constitute a
single functional type of city.[34] In Davidovich's interpretation, satellites include places that differ in function. Functions that may qual-
ify the city for the satellite label are heavy and light manufacturing
and mining, transportation, administrative-cultural institutions of a
raion seat, higher educational and research institutions, residential
or even "dormitory," as well as resort functions—health resorts,
sanatoria, summer resorts, or agriculture. Actual study of satellite
places showed that most satellites do tend to contain industries serving the needs of the central city and relatively rarely contain concen-
trations of large heavy industrial enterprises. The primary function
of the first-order satellite town is providing the place of residence for
a large number of persons employed in the central city—the so-called
"dormitory-town" function. Second-order satellites are usually not
places of permanent residency of those employed in the central city;
rather they are classified by their cultural-service gravitation toward
the central city, in other words they serve as places of seasonal residence, resorts, outings, camping.[35] The evident tendency seems to
be for the growth of large urban centers to be limited while the surrounding satellites expand very rapidly, though this conclusion is now
in the process of being modified by the latest census figures. What
this situation may now be requiring is limiting the growth of the resulting excessively large urban agglomerations as well as the big
cities alone. However, what this regional limitation implies is extensive decentralization of productive forces of the USSR with all the
political difficulties and changes involved. As Davidovich proposes,
"enterprises and institutions moved out of the central city need not
necessarily be located in its satellite cities. In many cases they
should be moved outside the agglomeration even to other regions."[36]
A less radical alternative discussed would be the replacing of
single large enterprises by a whole complex of small ones in close

cooperation, in this way taking advantage of an urban agglomeration
defined as a "system consisting of interconnected [though not fused]
populated points of different size that are 'drawn' into a single complex
by the large industrial center."[37] Specialization is put forward as
increasing the feasibility of this proposal. Leaders of the Soviet Union
may be assumed to be sincere in their desire to create the beautiful,
well-planned city of Soviet man and to house him in well-built dwellings
with convenient services. The satellite-town program may yet prove
to be an aid in finding the livable city. But at the same time the stronger
leadership goal of continued economic growth and concern over the
rate of economic production clashes with and often supersedes the
actual carrying out of social theories and urban plans. By no means
is this a phenomenon unique to the USSR. Indeed, most industrialized
and industrializing nations have had the tendency to make "production"
reigning monarch and the Gross National Product the predominant
index of national health. In recent years there seems to be less of
an attempt to carry through a satellite-town program as a major
means of limiting population growth. In its place, a policy of greater
development of small and medium-size towns has been emerging.
That no one policy has become rigid is an indication of the relatively
high degree of flexibility in Soviet urban planning, in which pragmatism
has occupied a prominent place.

MICRORAION

The idea that perhaps best translates into concrete form the
Soviet concept of dwelling is the microraion, an evolution from the
"superblock" concept of the 1930s. The superblocks were to be basic
planning units consisting of large blocks of residential apartment
dwellings and some public services, with groups of superblocks forming residential districts. The microraions (also called microboroughs
or microdistricts) are to be small communities of several thousand
inhabitants within a larger urban setting. Schools, nurseries, stores
catering to daily needs, sports and recreational facilities, cinemas,
clubhouses, cafeterias—in short all elements of cultural and public
service are to be fully integrated into the microraion plan. And the
satisfaction of man's many and growing everyday and cultural needs
will more and more assume a communalized character and will cross
the boundaries of the individual apartment. As a basic city planning
rule, all new housing should be located in these large complexes.
The accent here is not on the individual apartment as the basic unit
of city building, but rather on the community and the collective life.
In this connection Soviet writers are fond of quoting N. K. Krupskaia's
definition of the home. "A home," she said, "should not simply be

55

the sum of the rooms, but rather it should be a (living) organism."38
Since the home is not simply the place where one lives, but is in es-
sence a vital part of the community—in fact in Soviet urban theory
people do not live in houses but in communities—urban planners in
the USSR have begun in earnest to put the microraion program into
large-scale practice during the last few years, especially since the
late 1950s, though the idea itself has had a long theoretical history.
One American observer recently commented that in America the
house and not the community is erroneously regarded as the "housing
problem."39 By contrast, in the Soviet Union the "housing problem"
is almost always viewed as the problem of developing a more intense
and hence satisfying communal life for all citizens. And the microraion is the place for the daily acting out of this communist way of
life and the development of the collectivist spirit of its inhabitants.
Whether the more intense communal life is actually more satisfying
has never really been questioned. The expanded social content of the
notion of dwelling, with its focus on the unified ensemble and network
of services, is also seen as the way to furnish the means for the progressive liberation of women from the burdens of housework and for
the speedier passage to the collective education and upbringing of
children.40 Freed from oppressive household chores, women would
then have more energy to devote to productive labor. Advancing at
a time when the Soviet Union was officially declared in transition to
communism, the new forms of daily living embodied in the residential
complex of the microraion may be seen as a major step forward in
rearing the collective in the spirit of building communism and in creating real possibilities for bringing about the "state of the whole
people" by transferring into the hands of the public a number of the
state's functions in the field of organizing housing, daily life, and
culture.41

    Previously this new approach to city planning that the microraion
represents was hampered by the limited volume of construction and
especially by the departmental system of economic management where
each ministry was primarily concerned with promoting its own interests. The 1957 economic reorganizations, by aiming at the entrenched
ministerial system, may have initially provided the necessary climate
for the microraion idea to take root in actual planning practice. Even
in the 1960s and early 1970s, however, the practice often continues
by which different organizations and departments go right on building
houses, children's institutions, shops, cultural establishments, laundries, and other public buildings without a single plan for providing
the number of housing units with an adequate number of cultural and
public services. The November 1962 CC Plenum noted the great importance of an integrated development of residential sections so that
schools, kindergartens, nurseries, cultural and service institutions

would be built at the same time as apartment houses. Nevertheless, even in many cases where an integrated plan does exist, completion of cultural service and communal facilities lags woefully behind completion of apartments.[42] Such facts cause serious setbacks to the complete success of the microraion idea and tend to raise the volume of complaints of the Soviet urban resident.

The chief hindrance to the integrated development required for the microraion's success seems to be that planning and financing spring primarily from different sources. The City Soviet receives its capital investment plans for social, cultural, and communal construction from individual republic ministries and agencies; for the construction of schools and children's institutions, plans come from the Ministry of Education; for public health institutions, from the Ministry of Public Health; and for communal construction, from the Ministry of the Communal Economy. "For these institutions, integrated plans for development are a dead letter." The results—apartment houses are built in the microdistrict, people move in, but cultural and service enterprises either do not get built at all or go up much later. Between the planning and construction of the microraion, the plans must go through a great number of approval stages. A plan envisaging the building of a housing complex costing more than 2,500,000 rubles, for example, had to be reviewed and approved by the enterprises involved, at the time of the sovnarkhozy, by the economic councils, the city or province Soviet Executive Committee, the Union-republic State Construction Committee, and the Union-republic Council of Ministers. What this leads to in practice are skillful attempts on the part of many organizations to avoid such a complicated and protracted procedure by breaking up the integrated microraion into several sections. Plan approvals are inevitably speeded up by employing such methods of getting around the law, but the goal of integrated planning and construction is flagrantly violated.[43]

Most city dwellers have lived in houses on conventional city blocks encircled by streets on all sides—streets that are costly to build and maintain, hazardous to cross, and that can take up to a third of the surface of a residential district. In addition, the layout of city streets usually forces the mechanical alignment of buildings, depriving many of sunlight or the free flow of fresh air. The microraion innovation is pointed to as the way out of these rigid, traditional urban forms. Vast islands of land ranging from twenty to forty hectares in size, bounded by local traffic arteries, the microraions exclude through traffic and most roads from their interior. Complete separation of pedestrian routes from transportation roadways is a main principle in this new town planning. As a result of this new design, buildings may be arranged facing many different directions, presumably in directions most advantageous for light and air. A green zone is to form the center of the microraion.

In 1958 the Soviet government made the decision to undertake
the construction of an experimental section in the Southwestern Borough
of Moscow, with the aim of producing a national prototype for modern
residential ensembles, that is, the microraion. At the same time a
contest was announced for the plan favoring

> the best possible organization of personal and collective
> life of the population; the participation of adults in public
> life and social production; reduction of work and time
> spent in housework, and the perfecting of forms and
> methods of education of children and development of the
> physical and intellectual culture of the inhabitants

with stress on economy and industrial methods of construction.[44]
Soon many new and old Soviet towns were being built or rebuilt on the
basis of the microraion. Usually the microdistrict covers 25 to 30
hectares and has a population of eight to ten thousand living in groups
of about two thousand persons each.[45] In microraions for a population
of six thousand people, expenditures for construction of public buildings
have been shown to amount to 17 percent of the cost of housing construction; in one for nine thousand, they drop to 15 percent; and for
twelve thousand, to as little as 13 percent. In microraions built for
eighteen to twenty thousand these expenditures are estimated not to
exceed 11 percent of the cost of housing construction.[46] Houses within
the complex are to be of several different types. The hotel type, composed of one room from ten to fourteen square meters, is designed
for single people and families of two. Such houses are to be closely
integrated with a public service block, enabling their residents to
have laundry service, club-dancing, and public catering facilities.
Four- to five-story apartment houses (now upped to nine or more
stories in large cities) for medium-size families were the type most
frequently built during the Khrushchev years. Finally, houses for
large families included two-story cottages.[47] Schools were to be no
more than 500 meters from the farthest dwelling; nursery and kindergartens no more than 200 meters. The food shops and a department
store were to be located in the heart of the district, no more than 500
meters from the outermost apartment house.[48]

At the time of the microraion launching, the Soviet press hailed
the concept as a significant program to introduce greater variety and
style in urban housing construction. Within a very few years the
results were being strongly criticized. The problem of monotony and
uninteresting architecture seemed to have invaded the microdistrict.
Even the much heralded Southwestern Borough of Moscow was singled
out for its deadly "sameness," where "five-story buildings had been
put up everywhere for the sake of economy."[49] One Soviet architect

sadly concluded, "It is obvious that the esthetic formalism that impeded the formation of Soviet architectural style for many years has not yet been overcome completely. There is still some evidence of it even in the construction of the Southwestern Borough" of Moscow. The buildings are almost identical in form and height. Color has not been used adequately.[50] A good deal of what was said about the Southwestern Borough applies to other areas. A visitor to a new borough of Kharkhov or Rostov or Dnepropetrovsk or Donetsk would be hard put to tell where he was, or to recognize distinctive features of the particular city.[51]

PUBLIC SERVICES SYSTEM

The system of public services, with an emphasis on communal activities, is to be the major achievement of the microraion form of urban settlement. A five-stage system of services has been worked out and is now in the process of being brought into life. It is a system paralleling the movement from the microraion or microdistrict, made up of groups of dwellings, to the residential districts, composed of several microdistricts, to city districts, encompassing the residential districts, and finally to the city itself, containing all the city districts. The first service level or primary service (pervichnoe obsluzhivanie naseleniia) includes enterprises and establishments directly connected with the dwelling and serving a group of houses for 2,000 to 3,000 persons within a 100 to 150 meter radius. Each cluster of 2,000 or so persons will have its primary servicing post providing delivery service, automatic vending machines for foodstuffs, ready-cooked meals and semiprepared food, dining room, recreation hall, nursery, self-service laundry, house workshops, and studios. There are also premises for storing children's carriages, sleighs, bikes, skiis, etc. At the second level of services, enterprises and establishments will be concerned with everyday needs of the entire microraion. Here one will find a grocery store, a restaurant or dining room, the Housing Office, receiving places for laundry and repairs, and an everyday service center (kombinat bytovogo obsluzhivaniia or KBO) operating within a 400-meter radius, or a ten- to fifteen-minute walk. There will also usually be a building easily transformed from a dining room, cafe, or club to an auditorium for spectacles, physical culture, cele-brations, meetings, or even a sports area. Soviet architects and planners stress the fact that the network of services defines the size of the microraion and not the opposite. The third service level, designed for the dwelling or residential district and catering to from 25,000 to 70,000 inhabitants within a radius of from 900 to 1,300 meters, will include gastronomes (grocery stores), department stores, spe-cialized stores—such as a photo studio, barber, savings bank, and pharmacy—restaurants, cafés, an everyday service center (KBO), and other enterprises. This then is the commercial or shopping center of the residential district, fulfilling periodic needs of the population for various goods and dining, communal, and living services. At the next level, the city districts, more public administrative functions are incorporated. This level seems less defined than either the preceding residential district shopping centers or the final all-city shopping and commercial center. The latter is, as a rule, the social center of the city. Planners emphasize the need of taking into account the possibility of growth of the city itself when constructing or reconstructing the all-city shopping area. At the lower residential district shopping center this is absolutely unnecessary, since the growth of the city theoretically does not change the size or population density of the existing districts. For the residential districts, therefore, it is possible to work out and apply standard models for shopping centers. By contrast, at the stage of the all-city center individual projects relying heavily on standard elements of building are encouraged. This new system of services has been put fully in action for the first time, from the drawing board to actual operation, in the construction of the scientific town of the Siberian Branch of the USSR Academy of Sciences—a town, known as Akademgorodok, of 50,000 in microraions of 7,000 persons each, twenty kilometers from the industrial center of Novosibirsk.[52]

By the end of 1966 certain critical observations were reported on the experience of using the microraion. It was noted that food shops in the microraions were half empty, while those near bus and subway stops were heavily patronized. It appeared more convenient to shop on the way home from work than to shop in the microraions. This complaint may point to the fact that the service system was never really fully developed, for it was often linked with the call for the establishment of "consumer goods and food store complexes," that is, shopping centers.[53] Such criticism may indicate that the microraion idea might have to be changed to fit inhabitants' daily practices and that planners have not fixed on one microraion form. Furthermore, in the apartment houses themselves, designs did not sufficiently allow for variations in family size. The shortage of either housing or money was forcing the majority of large families to keep together, resulting in enforced sharing of apartments by "families within families."[54] More recently many letter writers have complained that public services and amenities, particularly in areas of new apartment houses, have not been organized, "so that with the onset of spring and autumn there is no reaching them 'either on foot or by vehicle.'"[55] "Why is the New Tenant Unhappy?" asked Pravda in September 1969. The paper went on to answer the question by describing the difficulties of those who had just moved into a new residential area in Chelyabinsk. "There wasn't a single kindergarten to be found in the entire district," and so the children had to be taken to the other end of town. New residents found no movie theater, no everyday-services establishment, no public dining room, no drugstore, or any stores selling manufactured goods in the community. When the muckraking newspaper delved into the causes of this sorry situation, it found from the City Mayor that "from the very beginning [local governmental planners and officials] were required to violate the most elementary norms of urban construction. Important municipal, cultural, and everyday structures were not included in the construction plans. The city budget simply didn't have funds for them." It seemed that when the idea for developing the sector was conceived, it was assumed that funds for an integrated plan of construction, "which were still lacking," would be provided by interested departments and ministries whose workers would be living in the project area. Convincing the factory managers and ministry bosses to provide the money proved to be an altogether dismal fiasco.[56] Despite consistent pleas that the city Soviet ought to be authorized to handle all questions of the integrated construction of new microraions— and that for this purpose strict procedure be instituted for the allocation of resources by the appropriate ministries and departments and for transferring the requisite funds to the city in some centralized fashion—the coordinating procedures remain extremely weak, and consequently the new occupant remains unhappy. At the end of 1972 Pravda once again asked "Why Is the New Tenant Unhappy?" In addition to the usual complaints about the lack of services, the newspaper claimed that the chief reason for the deplorable situation is that construction organizations consider trade and public catering enterprises secondary installations "and are unwilling to take on their construction: if they do take it on, they drag out the work for years." Pravda explains:

> Builders greatly dislike these trade "points," especially
> cafeterias: these are a lot of bother, and the desired
> profit in rubles is lacking. The same rubles could be
> expended more easily and more quickly in constructing
> square meters of housing space. . . . [A] housing con-
> struction combine's plan fulfillment, for example, is
> determined chiefly in terms of the number of residential
> buildings put into operation. If they have been put into
> operation—especially ahead of schedule—it means the
> plan is achieved and there will be a bonus. While the
> "Incompletes" (frequently including unfinished trade and
> consumer service enterprises) can be put off for "some
> other time." This "some other time" is then delayed for
> an indeterminate time.[57]

And finally, the 1972 Plan Fulfillment announced that the annual plan for provision of cultural and everyday services to the population was underfulfilled.[58] Earlier, soon after the November 1962 CC Plenum decision to bifurcate the middle-level Party and Soviet organizations along industrial and agricultural lines, the number of bureaucratic personnel and the amount of space they required rapidly expanded. Izvestia noted in January 1963 that under the pretext of reorganizing Party and Soviet agencies, schools, hospitals, and service enterprises were being taken over by administrative institutions in several cities and that the excessive expansion of administrative buildings was being misrepresented as the construction of dining rooms, barbershops, and other services. Almost a decade later, Premier Kosygin reiterated that funds are still being diverted to the construction of unnecessary administrative buildings and that "the spending of money in this function is impermissible."[59]

Still, when all is said and done, the microraion is a major new concept of urban living, designed to bring to life Soviet theories of unified communities. It is true that decades of neglect and the low priority of public services present formidable obstacles to the complete realization of the microraion experiment. Administrators, construction organizations, and a long line of bureaucrats, trained for and taught by the requirements of the old priorities, find it all too easy to divert monies allocated for public services and housing to other "pet" projects. But there are signs that at least some headway has been made in overcoming this barrier. The search for community is now being conducted on a world-wide scale. In the United States, recognition of the urgent need for a sense of community grows clearer with every daily news report of urban blight, social upheaval, and violence. During the last few years, American architects, urban designers, sociologists, and politicians have been bombarding the American public with endless studies on the American city. Some have gone so far as to predict the demise of the city form of life in the not too distant future. Others have put forth what is called "a most immodest, outrageous, but serious" proposal for the largest of American cities—New York. This "most radical proposal" calls for complexes of residential dwellings of varying height and design, built with huge prefabricated wall panels, closely integrated with daily services and the metropolitan transportation system. No traffic is to pass through these residential complexes, where the pedestrian is to be king. Playgrounds, gardens, cinemas, day-care and nursery centers, and sports fields are to be a few of the main attractions of this idea. Bringing persons of different economic and social backgrounds together in the same living area is one of the primary concerns of the proposal's authors. A major part of the project is low-cost, prefabricated, flexible housing.[60] Perhaps the most startling aspect of this "radical" proposal is its extraordinary similarity to the Soviet microraion, which was being planned and built more than a decade

ago. What this American plan seems to indicate is that in our own
country some urban planners, and presumably social scientists and
economists, are finally realizing that the American housing problem
is the problem of the American community and not just the American
house.

PLANNING PROCESS: COORDINATING URBAN PLANS

We have seen that many of the difficulties involved in the full
implementation of the microraion idea are a direct result of priorities,
the poorly coordinated planning process, and the practice of channeling
funds for public services and a considerable amount of housing through
various economic ministries and departments. The call for the creation
of one organ to conduct the financing of city planning and development
has been heard for many years and appears to be getting louder.[61]
The separation of the planning of capital investment for housing construction and communal economy from that for the development of
production is a central problem of the Soviet city planning process.
Because of the involvement of so many organizations and of the necessity of gaining approval at so many levels, plans for housing and urban
development are often changed many times, causing delays and a lack
of unified development. For a particular housing project to go from
the drawing board to finished construction, it must be included in a
number of separate economic plans. The picture one gets of the
planning and directing of the communal and housing economy is indeed
complex and somewhat confused. The Executive Committee of the
local Soviet is given the job of confirming plans for capital construction, but even before this stage, the State Committee for Civil Construction and Architecture, under Gosstroi (State Committee for
Construction of the USSR Council of Ministers) is responsible for
design of the houses for city Soviet consideration and for encouraging
standardization. The ministry of the industry of building materials
is responsible for technology. The central authorities have been particularly vigorous in insisting on the use of standard designs and in
some cases have turned down local initiative in this field (see the
example of Vilnius later in this chapter). In the case of the RSFSR,
the RSFSR Ministry of the Communal Economy must confirm limits
on labor. The Ministry of Finance plays a major role in confirming
financial indicators, in composing the economic plan that includes
the particular housing project, and in insuring that the city's plans
are in accord with the national budget. Though the Department of
Finance is often a part of the Executive Committee of the local city
Soviet, it almost always has direct lines with the republic Ministry
of Finance and seems to exert a major influence on the financial end

63

of house planning. The republic Gosplan sets the limits on capital
investments, which have been determined at an even higher level,
that of the USSR Gosplan. Funds for materials and equipment are
mainly confirmed by Glavsnabsbyt (glavnoe upravlenie material'no-
technicheskogo snabzheniia i sbyta) and the republic Ministry of the
Communal Economy. In addition, plans for the actual allocation of
materials and for credits and financing involve (Gosbank) the State
Bank and (Stroibank) the Construction Bank. Project planners must
get their plans incorporated into the city budget, and the city in turn
must lobby for inclusion of the city budget in the state budget of the
republic. As one frank deputy minister puts it, "Is it necessary to
prove that even with the optimum good will in regard to the needs of
the local Soviets, to reach the complexity of planning, reciprocal coordination of deliveries on time, in the right quantity and right assortment, becomes highly difficult, and in a number of cases almost
impossible."[62] Just to make planning a little more harrowing, location
of the housing project itself may have been determined or changed by
a powerful local industry over which the city Soviet has virtually no
control. This lack of coordination at the local level is usually a reflection of the situation higher up. An example of the lack of coordination at a relatively high level is the fact that in 1969 the RSFSR
Gosplan established the volume of capital repairs of dwellings of local
Soviets at 370 million rubles, but the Ministry of Finance of the RSFSR
established the plan for financing those repairs at 298 million rubles![63]
    In an attempt to consolidate the Moscow city planning process,
it was announced in June 1968 that state capital investments in housing,
municipal, and public-service construction would be transferred from
the ministries and departments to the Moscow City Soviet.[64] The
process of allocating all centralized capital investments to the Moscow
Soviet was actually begun the year before. Before this change occurred,
however, Moscow had more than 500 different clients for housing,
municipal services, and cultural construction. After the change, which
aimed at carrying out the financing of almost all city planning and
building through the Moscow Soviet, the Moscow Soviet and its Main
Board of Capital Construction took upon themselves the responsibility
of a single central client for such construction. It does appear that
the larger cities have been more successful than smaller ones in their
battle to control and coordinate city plans. When compared with the
average Soviet city, the larger cities have also been able to attract
better trained city officials and planners. (Because of its relatively
weak power position and low status, the average local city Soviet is
usually staffed by personnel with less education and skill in handling
city tasks than the personnel directing industrial enterprises.) David
Cattell's study of Leningrad, based on close-up observation, provides
a more detailed picture of the planning process and of Leningrad's

desire to have deciding control over its urban construction, especially housing. First of all we learn that those concerned in erecting housing—the raions, housing cooperatives, or enterprises—must submit an annual building request by September 1 to the City Architect-Planning Department. Cattell points out that unlike many other Soviet cities, in Leningrad new housing requested by particular enterprises is not turned over to the enterprises for control, but instead is managed by the Leningrad Soviet, insuring a more unified system of housing operations. Once the Architect-Planning Department has all requests for construction of housing, it coordinates these requests with its own building plans and then draws up a tentative city plan as a "title list." Although the Architect-Planning Department is the focal point for preliminary planning, many other organizations must be brought into the process and consulted. In the field of housing construction, the head of the Leningrad Architect-Planning Department has extensive control, with the approval of the Executive Committee (Ispolkom) of the city Soviet. Within the Architect-Planning Department itself, the projects must pass through the Expert-Technical Section, which in turn must get clearance from the Sanitation, Fire, Parks and Gardens, Communal Services, Enlightenment, and Welfare Departments. The Chairman of the State Committee for Civil Construction and Architecture under the USSR Gosstroi, M. Posokhin, has suggested that in order to reduce the time for this long process of reviewing plans, it would be desirable to abolish the requirement of obtaining the agreement of the sanitation, state fire inspection, and other agencies before plans are approved, but leave these organizations the right to check adherence to safety and health standards during plan realization.[65] Earlier we mentioned involvement of the Ministry of Finance, Gosstroi, and Stroibank, which influence the type, the timing, and costs of the housing. Cattell also found that the cost-level of the particular housing or urban project determines the various levels of government through which the project must pass for approval or change. The city's Executive Committee has the right to approve projects of less than 200,000 rubles; for plans calling for 200,000 to 500,000 rubles, republic Gosplan verification is also necessary; 500,000 to 1 million rubles projects require the approval of the republic Gosplan; and between 1 million and 2.5 million rubles the republic Gosplan gives approval but only with verification by the USSR Gosplan. All projects seeking more than 2.5 million rubles must gain an affirmative decision of the USSR Gosplan.

The final "title list" for all new building is drawn up by the city's Executive Committee and is approved by the republic Council of Ministers only after all negotiations of the city agencies and important city leaders with Gosplan, the ministries of Construction, and USSR Gosstroi in Moscow are completed.[66] Leningrad represents the case of

an unusually strong and well-organized city Soviet. But even in regard
to Leningrad, the center in Moscow has absolute veto power over the
city budget and hence strong say over city plans. If local needs change
or conflict with officially titled and approved needs, success in carrying
through a change usually requires the reopening of protracted negotiations. In many instances the unplanned for need is simply neglected
because of the low status of the local government. Particularly in
the area of housing and communal services, where the Ministry of the
Communal Economy views itself as chief benefactor and defender of
the rights and interests of the local Soviet, the local city planning
agencies under the local Soviet are often subject to interference and
added confusion from its great protector—the Ministry of the Communal
Economy. If the Executive Committee (Ispolkom) of the city Soviet
makes changes in lists already confirmed by the Ministry of the Communal Economy, planning delays and discrepancies become inevitable.
A city may be in need of a public bath, but the Ministry may approve
a new hotel instead. "Does the Ministry, which is in Kiev, really know
better which streets in Kharkov need gas?" queries one staunch home-
rule advocate.

> At present, the Ministry of the Communal Economy con-
> firms plans for passenger traffic and the runs of cars on
> city electric transit system, the water supply through the
> water mains, flow of sewage through the sewers, the at-
> tendance of public baths, amount of linen subject to wash-
> ing in the laundries. . . , etc. Who needs this centraliza-
> tion?[67]

Most troubles of Soviet urban planning are a result of the sometimes fierce conflicts between the much overburdened but weak local
Soviets and the nearsighted but powerful ministries and departments
and their enterprises. Time and time again top government and party
spokesmen emphasize that there can be only one "master of the city"—
the local Soviet. At the Twenty-Third Party Congress in 1966, the
declaration of V. Promyslov, the Mayor of Moscow, that "the question
of the expansion of rights of local Soviets in construction planning and
the building of cities must be finally resolved," met with great ap-
plause.[68] In 1971, on the eve of the Twenty-Fourth Party Congress,
the Central Committee of the CPSU issued a resolution on district
and city Soviets designed to strengthen the hand of the local Soviets.
The Party resolution charged that

> the Soviets are still inadequately coordinating the work of
> the enterprises and organizations of different departmen-
> tal subordination in the field of housing and communal

construction, the construction of social, cultural and
everyday facilities and the production of consumer goods.

Because many enterprises and organizations are directly subordinate
to the territory and province agencies, or to republic ministries and
departments, explains the resolution, the responsibility of the local
Soviets for the state of affairs on their territory is reduced and their
initiative in solving city problems is curtailed. Admitting that plans
for housing and city developments carried out by the ministries and
departments are frequently unfulfilled, the central Committee goes
on to blame the local Soviets for tolerating this situation and for not
stopping "manifestations of departmental narrow-mindedness." In
other words, the Party is criticizing the weakness of the local Soviets
in city planning, a weakness the Party itself has insured by its past
policies of strong central control. With an eye to correcting past
weaknesses, the Party is now calling for an increase of local government in deciding "all questions of local importance on their territory"
and in coordinating and controlling "within the bounds of their com-
petence [author's emphasis], the work of all enterprises and organizations regardless of their departmental subordination." Even more
important is the fact that the Party and state have moved to remedy
a fundamental weakness of local governmental authority, namely, the
lack of a solid financial base. Part of the profits of non-Union enterprises and economic organizations are to be transferred to the budgets
of districts and cities. The local Soviets are also being instructed
to step up their activity in pooling of resources of the economic institutions allocated for housing and communal development. In addition,
the district and city soviets have been empowered to examine draft
plans of enterprises, institutions, and organizations situated within
their areas but subordinate to a higher jurisdiction with respect to
the development of housing and public utilities, roadbuilding, socio-
cultural and consumer service facilities, the production of local
building materials, consumer goods, amenities, trade, public catering,
education, health, and other matters of public services. The decrees
clearly lay down the right of the district and city Soviets to confirm
plans for all the aforementioned questions. As one Soviet specialist
on local Soviets states, "Until recently the practice in this area has
been in different directions. Some heads of enterprises and organizations not subordinate to the local Soviets have generally disputed this
right of the local Soviets" (see footnote 69). Furthermore, both district and city Soviets have been empowered to suspend the carrying
out of illegal orders and instructions of heads of and enterprises and
organizations under higher jurisdiction on matters of land use, construction of populated points, housing, public utilities, and cultural
and consumer facilities. In the event that local Soviet decisions on

these matters are ignored by heads of various organizations under
higher jurisdiction, the district and city Soviets may appeal to the
appropriate higher-echelon organs to ask for disciplinary action
against these leaders, including their dismissal from the posts they
occupy.[69] Actual practices, however, indicate that the local Soviets
have little muscle in instructing enterprises to allocate any sums for
urgent or projected needs, and in turn many enterprises are skillful
in ignoring directives of the local Soviets. Usually the enterprise
director is aware of city needs, particularly those involving his workers. But being further removed from local problems, the central
ministries are often not very cooperative, appreciative, or even concerned with worries of the city in which their enterprise is located.
Housing plans and solutions to shortages of housing and communal
service are further hampered because regulations requiring that the
City Soviet Executive Committee approve any planned assignment for
the construction of new enterprises or the reconstruction and development of existing ones are frequently disregarded. It is clear that the
state funds allocated to the local Soviets are not nearly enough for
these local governments to handle all city needs in housing and communal services. Consequently, the local Soviet must turn to the
industries and enterprises within the city's limits. Response from
these industries is more often than not noncommittal or out-and-out
negative. Sometimes individual enterprises have to be "beaten down"
to insure their agreement to construction of facilities vital for services to people working at these very enterprises. When it is a question
of all-city facilities, arguments break out not only among agencies of
the local Soviets, but also among managers of the enterprises involved.
"We have to provide the settlement with public services and amenities,
but why should we exert ourselves not only for our workers but also
for yours." "We would be glad to do it," another says, "but after all,
strangers will use them too."[70] What usually happens is that the
enterprises work on their own and the Soviet works on its own, or the
two work against each other. The heart of the problem seems to lie
in shortcomings in planning of capital investments. Guided by their
departmental interests and major concern for plan fulfillment, the
ministries' planning agencies naturally give preference to industrial
facilities, relegating housing and communal construction to secondary
concern. "Thus, disproportions in the development of the city are
willy-nilly built into the planning process itself."[71] Evidently the
ministry planning agencies assume that the city will be able to obtain
the funds it lacks from the interest on state capital investments on
the development of industry or through noncentralized sources of
financing. The ministry executives, however, act differently, aided
by the fact that interest deductions for the development of the communal
economy are concentrated in the hands of the ministries themselves.

The latter distribute this money as they see fit. A Gorky city official, for example, complained that not a kopeck of these rather large sums was spent in Gorky during 1967, but instead all the money was absorbed by the central ministries. The same official proposed that this interest money should be deducted automatically, taken into account by the ministries' planning agencies—regardless of their departmental subordination—sent to the cities where the enterprises are located, and then disposed of by the city Soviet Executive Committee.[72] Even in large cities such as Dnepropetrovsk, not only are the Executive Committee's financial resources scattered and dependent on many ministries, but even the city government's knowledge of what the enterprises are planning is often very little and too often merely learning of a fait accompli. If the city Executive Committee should be fortunate enough to learn in detail the plans of the ministries and departments, it is not always able to influence them.[73] How then is it able to plan for immediate or future housing needs?

After the regional economic councils were organized in 1957, the planning process became still more complicated and the local Soviet found that many of its previous powers over city development were further diminished. In addition to battling enterprises for the inclusion of new housing and communal development of plans, the city Soviet had to take on the new regional economic councils (sovnarkhozy). Decentralization of the economy into the economic regions led to decentralization of the planning and constructing of new housing. The resulting chaos spurred on the recentralization of all planning for construction in 1959. At the time of the great reforms in 1957, the local Soviets were supposed to be major beneficiaries, playing a leading role in the local economy, in unified city planning, and in control over housing. The burden of supplying the daily needs of the people was to be shifted from industry to the back of the local Soviet. "This permits plants, factories, and institutes to be free from what is not their peculiar function of authority in the housing economy."[74] In reality, the sovnarkhoz took a major role in communal services at the expense of the local Soviet, and to the misfortune of the local populace. Coordination of housing plans became increasingly more difficult to achieve. Many times the economic council would make a decision affecting the housing or communal development of a city without being fully aware of that city's needs and without knowing that the decision was in direct conflict with the city's own plans. Lack of communication between local government, ministries, and agencies increased. Planning authority seemed even more removed from the local level than before the reform.[75] The later reforms initiated in November 1962 seemed to deal another debilitating blow to local Soviet influence over economic and cultural construction. In 1962 almost all the local industrial enterprises that had been transferred to local Soviet control as a result of the 1957 reforms were taken away from the authority of the local Soviets and transferred to the sovnarkhozy. Opportunities were reduced for local initiative and activity in city functions such as transportation, everyday services, trade, and other questions of the municipal economy.[76] Naturally the sweeping away of the sovnarkhoz system in 1965 was viewed as a strengthening of local prerogative. Not all, however, have seen this as taking place. The Chairman of the Presidium of the Armenian Supreme Soviet, in arguing for an all-Union law guaranteeing and strengthening the rights of local Soviets, wrote in December 1966 that local government's difficulties in establishing "business contacts" with the administrations of Union enterprises had actually increased "since amplification of centralized leadership on the part of the Union ministries."[77] What these various reforms and subsequent changes in the planning process illustrate is the basic contradiction between the desire to run a centrally planned economic system, with an emphasis on national economic goals and on decision-making and control from the center, and the desire to encourage local initiative, with the aim of attaining more rational planning and operation of communal facilities and housing to meet local needs. There has been a great deal of talk about strengthening the role of the local Soviet. But as long as local governments must go begging for their funds from a host of sources, and as long as economic development remains the primary Party-state goal, for the majority of local Soviets, unified city planning will remain buried in a dispersed process continually escaping their control.

DESIGNING OF HOUSING

Laying the groundwork for an invigorated housing program, the Central Committee of the CPSU and the USSR Council of Ministers issued a joint decree in November 1955 "On Eliminating Waste in Design and Construction." The battle had actually been joined the year before at the December 1954 All-Union Conference of builders, in which superfluous, showy facadism and lack of economy and comforts in design and construction were criticized and condemned. At this conference Khrushchev spoke out against grave shortcomings in the work of designing offices and architects, who frequently feel that designs are much too "modest." Khruschev expounded:

We can no longer reconcile ourselves to the fact that
behind a screen of phrases about combatting constructivism and about socialist realism, many architects
spend money wastefully . . . . We are not against beauty
but we are against extravagance.[78]

70

For years Soviet architects were raised on theories reflecting Stalin's taste for neoclassical but "Russified" architectural styles. Instead of trying to speak in the language of the times, these architects addressed the Soviet nation "for almost a quarter of a century either in Old Church Slavonic (often called 'the continuation of national traditions') or in Old Italian or pseudoclassical jargon (often called 'mastering the classical heritage')."[79] During the 1930s Soviet architects departed from what is now considered the rational, economical residential complexes they were building back in the 1920s. In the process, architects in search of official favor and perhaps a lucrative Stalin prize developed an "ostentatious style of architecture, abounding in excesses," a style chiefly concerned with embellishing the facade rather than improving the interior of buildings. Not only did these now well-known "wedding cakes" abound in decorative colonnades and porticos, but they also absorbed many rubles that could have been applied to constructing more living space and hampered the widespread application of industrial prefabrication techniques. In fact, the main thrust of the 1955 Decree on Architecture and Design seemed to be directed against architects' resistance to full-scale use of standardized building designs. Of the 353 apartment houses then under construction in Leningrad, the decree sternly noted that only 14 were from standardized designs. Moscow was also reprimanded for its foot-dragging in this respect. The Party-State Decree resolved

> to consider the principal task of design organizations, architects and engineers to be the working out of economical standardized designs and standardized building parts and the use of them in construction.[80]

Soon after the decree was proclaimed a massive campaign against "formalism" and excesses in architectural design was launched. The ensuing confrontations over architectural designs took on particularly bitter shape involving Party secretaries, architects, artists, builders, and noted authors. As late as the spring of 1960 the conservative journal Oktiabr' published an article by the First Secretary of the Astrakhan Province Party Committee entitled "Esthetics and the Present Day: Against Alien Influences." The author warned against certain Soviet architects who in recent years

> have assimilated the faulty ideas of Corbusier, the leader of constructivism and his followers . . . who reduce the artistic tasks of architecture to the display of technical properties and the estheticizing of reinforced-concrete structures and supplant the ideological-graphic content of architecture with a formalist combination of concrete and glass planes.[81]

The same article attacked the "cosmopolitanism"—a word carrying ominous overtones reminding one of the worst cultural attacks during the post-World War II years under Stalin—of such architectural ideas and called for the application of the guiding principle of socialist realism.[82] At the same time, author Viktor Nekrasov, writing in Literaturnaia gazeta, was advocating a re-evaluation of constructivism and Le Corbusier. Nekrasov discusses the major theoretical tenets of constructivism as practiced by Le Corbusier and describes their rejection in the Soviet Union after 1931 "as a bourgeois trend." "But what replaced constructivism with its emphasis on logic, convenience and economy of room placement?" he asks. "Splendor and opulence and pseudoclassic pediments." Instead of architecture being subordinate to man, man became lost at the foot of grandiose structures.[83] Overcoming the legacy of the past, however, was not to be an easy or rapid achievement. The architect Danin recalled in Novyi mir that in 1954 he saw the beginning of a promising change in Soviet architectural attitudes. Soviet architects, Danin felt, would be overjoyed "at the right to write [their] own text," instead of producing architectural quotation of past centuries on "order" and "demand." By the beginning of 1961, Danin came to realize that all the architectural "sins" of the past were by no means only the result of the architects' misfortunes, but were rather a result of inner conservatism, a living part of many present-day Soviet architects.[84] Eventually the massive Party-state campaign for standardized designs would emerge triumphant, but would simultaneously give rise to a new "sin," namely, "the vicious centralism of standard design planning, [which] only strengthens the contradiction" between the use of standard design and local conditions.[85] In practical terms this means that the major urban centers of concentrated political and industrial power, particularly Moscow and Leningrad, monopolize the formulation of standard designs and dictate these designs to all parts of the Soviet Union. So we see the project planning agencies of Leningrad working out a plan on standard buildings to be applied in a Turkmen Republic city. The Chief Architect of the Turkmen city, Ashkhabad, unhappily points out that buildings being built in the city are hardly suited to the local climate—which experiences extremes from 46° C. (115° F.) of heat to -20° C. (-4° F.) of cold—or to the demographic peculiarities of the Turkmen family.[86] Still another survival from the past may be seen in the example of Tashkent. It has been written of rebuilt Tashkent that

> the housing is so standardized that one resident had to sleep at the office several times when he was unable to find his apartment among hundreds of others. This is characteristic of the entire city. . . .[87]

Vilnius' urban expansion and redevelopment represents another example of the "vicious centralism of standard design planning" and the conflict between center and region. In this case, however, how did Vilnius succeed in preserving the unique qualities of the old city, despite the fact that 80 percent of new housing consists of standard, prefabricated apartment buildings? In trying to answer the question, a Soviet observer found a history of "protracted problems, artificial contradictions and frustrating delays." In 1961 the Lithuanian Republic Urban Building Design Institute worked out a new design for apartment buildings and promptly sent it to Moscow for approval. That Moscow dominates designing—often to the detriment of improved housing in other localities—is clearly seen in what followed. Once in Moscow, the Vilnius design proposals "disappeared into the bureaucracy; a general reorganization had resulted in the assignment of all standard design work to the central institutes, and a year passed with no response from Moscow." The Soviet commentator states that "the message was clear": do it our way or don't try.[88] Vilnius planners were forced to either find a way out of the impasse or give up their development plans. They displayed unusually great initiative and managed to persuade the director of a housing construction combine to build a single model apartment building—but without authorization. Unlike the situation of less fortunate cities, the Vilnius story has a happy ending. The bold local initiative and extraordinary cohesiveness of city planners enabled Vilnius to prevail over initial central resistance.

In Uzbekistan architects from the Uzbek State Design and Planning Institute have complained about the lack of variety in standardized apartment houses and the low demand for beauty in standard designs. Once again we hear the accusation that designers ignore local conditions. Planners have the concept of "tying in" standard projects. "To tie in" a project means to adapt it to specific local conditions, taking into account the relief of the land, geology, and buildings around it. In practice, "tying in" turns out to be something quite different. "Tying in" becomes a matter only of engineering solutions and omitting everything that is beyond the building's foundation. The results are monotony, dullness, lack of color, lack of any individuality, and little attention to local climatic conditions.[89] Of the almost 800 standard designs available to architects and city planners for apartment houses, scarcely 10 percent have ever been used, "and even these have been dubbed alike as peas in a pod."[90]

Earlier we saw this same centralism phenomenon in relation to the planning of microdistricts and specifically in the development of the Southwestern borough of Moscow. It seems that the building industry's domination of architects is one of the real causes for this sameness of districts and for the lack of apartment house designs that reflect distinctive qualities of the locality. A major article in the October 1969 issue of Novyi mir stresses that "diversity among new boroughs can be achieved only when industry is put at the service of the architect, rather than making the architect dependent on what is made available by industry, as is the case almost everywhere."[91] Even when designers do come up with an outstanding design, they do not always have the means to see that construction organizations carry it through to the finish. Moscow's Chief Architect, M. Posokhin, has suggested that design organizations be given a most effective right, the right of control by the ruble; that is, to be in a position to halt or slow construction through instruction to the bank if the work is of poor quality or if there have been departures from the design.[92] There has been some limited official reaction to this proposal, which took shape in the 1969 reforms of the construction industry. A Party-state resolution dating from June 1969 stipulates that USSR Gosstroi's State Civil Construction and Architecture Committee and the Union-Republic Gosstrois have been granted the right to halt construction work on apartment buildings and cultural, service, and communal buildings, begun without approved designs, that deviates from the confirmed designs or violates technical specifications. Gosstroi was also given the right to stop the production of building materials that violate standards and technical specifications.[93] But the primary cause for the monotony and trite application of standardized housing designs was a clamorous campaign, whose theme was "anything that cost more than the minimum was bad and anything besides the bare essentials was superfluous," which swept aside the "businesslike and reasonable criticism of aesthetic overemphasis in architecture."[94] In some cases, this led to serious defects in building designs—all in the name of economizing. In September 1969, for example, the editors of Pravda received a letter from some research and technical people in construction in which the increase in calculated specific heat losses in apartment buildings was explained. The letter pointed an accusing finger at design organizations, which had decreased the thermal insulating properties of walls in their pursuit of the cheap square meter. Furthermore, explained the letter writers, permitted specific heat losses are on the average under similar climatic conditions 1.5 to 2 times greater in Soviet buildings than in those of the Scandinavian countries. The letter closed by urging that a 25 to 35 percent increase of walls' resistance to heat transmission be the minimum required in future buildings.[95] In an unusual response to these charges, the Deputy Chairman of USSR Gosstroi reported that significant losses of heat in residential and public buildings were correctly noted in the letter and for the reasons given. The USSR State Construction Committee reported that it planned corrective action to raise requirements for thermal insulating and to improve hermetic sealing of seams of

outside walls in large-panel buildings.[96] In other cases, the search
for the low-cost square meter of housing has led designers to skimp
on sound insulation and finishing plans. Designs worked out at the
center were proclaimed for their universal applicability. Thus arose
the predominance of the five-story apartment building, which became
a "symbol of faith among urban planners."[97] The Moscow building
boom of the 1950s produced hundreds of five-story residential buildings,
which are now obsolete and must be torn down to make room for taller
ones. At the Twenty-Third Party Congress, the Mayor of Moscow,
V. Promyslov, noted that instead of the uneconomical five-story buildings, more and more nine- to twelve-story panel buildings and sixteen-
and twenty-four-story buildings were being built. The five-story
buildings were explained in political terms as a "manifestation of
subjectivism" of the pre-October 1964 period (the Khrushchev years),
"which led to a number of errors in the construction and reconstruction of Moscow."[98]

The dominating sweep of centrally devised designs is also a
result of the weak condition of local government and its city agencies,
particularly of the chief city architect. The weakness of the local
Soviet often leaves the city's general plans vulnerable to pressures
for revision, damaging changes, or out-and-out violations. Some
urban areas do not have approved or up-to-date general plans. Such
large cities as Gorky, Novosibirsk, Sverdlovsk, Chelyabinsk, and
Kuibyshev remained without general plans as late as the early 1960s.
Until 1967 Dnepropetrovsk was rapidly growing without the aid of a
general plan. The 1960 Conference on City Planning and Construction
declared that every city must have a properly approved general plan
and that the practice of drawing up such plans by design organizations
in Moscow, Leningrad, and Kiev must be changed in favor of the
locality.[99] The general city plan is usually a twenty-year plan that
determines the street layout of the city, the location of residential
areas and commercial and public centers, engineering solutions for
problems of sanitation and transportation, water-supply system, the
city's greenery, and overall housing projections. The biggest difficulty
with such general plans, besides the obvious one of ministerial and
enterprisal noncompliance or disregard, is the length of time needed
to formulate them. When all the designers, economists, and politicians
are ready to present the general plan for approval, it is usually already
way out of date. Then, once the general plans are in operation, they
are violated not only by the industries but not rarely by the very city
Soviets that at one time approved them. One way considered to make
the general plans of cities the inviolable law of Soviet city planning
is to have better trained and more powerful chief city architects. In
the Soviet Union chief architects, under the city Executive Committee,
have been shifted about with great frequency. Reports at city planning

conferences have illustrated that all the positive examples of an integrated carrying out of general plans for the development of cities are related to the prolonged tenure of the chief architect and to the high level of his qualifications. This was particularly true of Leningrad, where by 1960 two architects, N. V. Baranov and V. A. Kaminsky, had filled the post of chief city architect for the previous twenty-five years. In this connection, in 1960 the head of the USSR Gosstroi, V. Kucherenko, advocated the creation of appropriate material and legal conditions for the chief architects, elevating their importance to encourage the greatest Soviet architects to seek this post. At the same time, he proposed increasing the responsibility and legal position of the State Architecture and Construction Control Service, since it is called upon to exercise day-to-day control over fulfillment of general plans and over the quality of city construction.[100]

It appears that a strong chief city architect backed by a strong executive committee does make a big difference in realizing city plans. But it also appears that the strongest chief architects are to be found in the largest, most influential Soviet cities and that their strength comes, not from a generally improved legal position, but from the favored position of the particular city.

General city plans, especially housing designs and plans, cannot be effectively formulated without relevant data on the city's present and prospective population. Urban designers and city administrators have been increasingly emphasizing the importance of demographical research and statistics for the proper planning of housing, particularly in regard to the birthrate, the structure of the family, immigration patterns, and structure of the apartments. In the two years preceding the 1970 All-Union Census, economists, urban planners, demographers, and sociologists pointed out the need for thorough studies of the contemporary family, noting that most studies up until then were unsatisfactory. Almost everyone concerned with the problem of population statistics and their application agrees that not enough information is available and that which is available is sometimes of questionable quality.[101] The Soviet urban economist David Broner has been consistently outspoken on making the timely study of the demographic composition of families the required basis for planning not only the volume of new housing construction in any specific place, but also the types of buildings and apartments. For the planning of housing it is essential to know the number of persons constituting the family and their age and sex. Two families, each having four members, for example, may have very different housing needs. One family may have two adults and two young children. The other family may be made up of parents, an adult son, and an adult daughter. Assuming both families receive the same size apartment, and taking Broner's suggested figure of thirty-six square meters as the living space, the interior design of the apartment becomes crucial in satisfying the needs of the families. The family with the young children will find two bedrooms adequate. The other family of four adults (with adult children of different sexes) will need three separate bedrooms. During the last few years planners have been encouraging sociologists to conduct in-depth studies of how the urban dweller spends his time at home. The aim of such studies is to find ways in which to make apartment designs more rational, allowing inhabitants more leisure time. Other studies conducted by the Research Institute of Housing established that in the mid-1960s only 20 to 25 percent of apartments with average living space from fifty to fifty-five square meters was occupied by individual families. What this means is that most of these larger apartments are occupied by several families on a per room basis. But 90 to 95 percent of apartments with an average living space from twenty-five to thirty square meters was occupied by individual families. These figures are not startling to Soviet statisticians and urban planners, since about 80 percent of all urban families are small families of four or less members.[102] The results of such projects have become part of the argument for better planned, smaller apartments. Leading in the field of planning standard apartment buildings, the Central Scientific Research and Experimental Planning Division of the Institute of Housing not only conducts statistical surveys, but also analyzes statistical materials and critical comments concerning the planning of apartments and attempts to have these findings incorporated into housing designs. Institute of Housing research branches also conduct such surveys as what places in the kitchen are most used or points in the kitchen most often walked between, how the kitchen and its equipment should be planned or rearranged to shorten the number of steps and make for the most rational use. Over the last decade, for example, planners have been designing apartments with direct exit from kitchen to dining room, thereby eliminating the corridor. The aim was to cut down the number of steps needed in daily household chores and to lower the cost of the apartment by cutting down auxiliary spaces. (Organizations such as the Institute of Housing have found that the average person takes 18 to 20,000 steps or walks ten to twelve kilometers per day in doing household chores. Over a forty-year span this comes to 10 kilometers x 300 days x 40 years = 120,000 kilometers!)[103] Statistical surveys, however, have shown that the apartment dwellers themselves did not approve of such design changes. According to Broner, 94 percent of all apartment dwellers surveyed (several thousand in large cities) negatively evaluated the plan of direct exit from the kitchen to another room. Why? Those questioned indicated that this results in dirty and smelly air of the living, "the best" as they called it, room. Considering that only 12 percent of the general rooms are in fact used as dining rooms, as the sample indicated, and in the remaining cases for other purposes (in that number 60 percent used as bedrooms), it becomes very clear why tenants are rejecting this new planning of apartments.[104] The survey also indicates that for most Soviet families a dining room is still a luxury. Time studies are also playing a role in the search for the ideal apartment house and apartment designs. One such time study (see Figure 1) attempted to find out how the adult Muscovite spends his time at home. This particular study revealed that out of an average twelve to thirteen hours spent at home each day, the preparation of meals and washing dishes takes the Muscovite woman two hours and thirty minutes each day. Housework, that is, cleaning the apartment, laundering linen, and putting clothes in order, consumes one hour and fifteen minutes of the woman's time at home. Caring for children takes another one hour per child. In all, seven to eight hours out of every twenty-four are spent in household work, leaving the exhausted woman with one whole hour of free or study time! The Muscovite husband finds himself in a somewhat happier situation, having two hours and forty-five minutes of free time or time to engage in studies, plus an extra forty-five minutes sleeping time each day.[105]

Looking for new forms of apartment houses to contribute to the liberation of tenants, especially women, Soviet urban designers came up with the project "House of the New Way of Life" (Dom novogo byta), which took over five years, involved fifteen research institutes, six chairs of higher educational institutions, seven branches of the boards of the Moscow City Executive Committee—in all more than 150 persons. Plans for the New Way of Life house hoped to cut the time spent by a woman in housework by two hours and fifteen minutes. The New Way of Life apartment-hotel complex of two sixteen-story buildings of large-panel construction is located on Television Street, block number ten, in the Noviye Cheryomushki district of Moscow. In 1969 the new living experiment began to receive its first inhabitants. The ground floors hold clubrooms, management offices, and children's playrooms. The two apartment house lobbies are connected by heated, glassed-in vestibules with the two-story social center, which includes a large café, swimming pool, winter garden, Finnish sauna, drycleaning establishment, and hairdressing shop. This new housing complex, whose public areas are air-conditioned, provides five to six times more in the way of social, cultural, and service facilities per person than ordinary residential blocks. In addition, the building contains a hotel for twenty guests. The New Way of Life, then, is clearly an experimental prototype for future urban living in the Soviet Union, sometime in the 1980s.

Inside the New Way of Life apartments themselves, all articles not used more or less on a continuous basis, winter clothing, for instance, are removed and stored elsewhere. Ground floor checkrooms

FIGURE 1

How Adult Muscovite Spends His Time at Home
(based on family of 3)

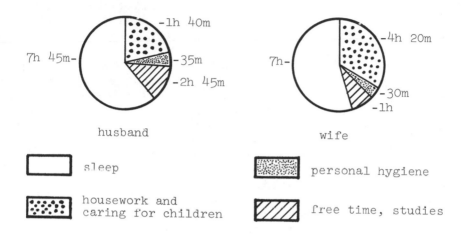

husband   wife

☐ sleep

▦ housework and caring for children

▨ personal hygiene

▨ free time, studies

Note: Data from study of 2,500 Muscovites. Adult person spends an average of 12 to 13 hours at home.

Source: Central Statistical Administration of RSFSR. Broner, op. cit., p. 66.

handle coats and boots. Thirty service rooms on the various floors contain washing machines, driers, and ironing boards, with rental of vacuum cleaners, electric floor polishers, and folding furniture. Extra chairs and tableware needed when guests drop in may be borrowed from the household service room on each floor. Perhaps the most controversial aspect of the New Way of Life apartments is the fact that they are to be kitchenless. Each apartment has a built-in kitchen compartment containing a two-burner electric stove, sink, small refrigerator, and shelves, all set into the wall and concealed when not in use. Most meals will be eaten in small dining rooms seating fifteen to twenty persons and serving only residents of the particular floor, about sixty persons. The central dining room and café in the social center provides precooked or semiprepared foods to the smaller dining rooms. The eating facilities are envisaged as the prime timesaver, eliminating the need for daily grocery shopping, preparing, cooking, and cleaning. Catering and room-service are also part of the New Way of Life. Medical services, with the accent on preventive medicine, are to be provided in the polyclinic, physiotherapy, and hydrotherapy rooms and in the hall for exercising. This is anticipated as one small step toward the ideal of the house physician. In addition to a gymnasium, swimming pool, outdoor courts, and a stadium, recreational facilities include a movie theatre with stage, a library and reading rooms, a movie-film and photo darkroom, hobby rooms, a billiard parlor, thirty lounges (one on each floor) with color television, radios, and tape recorders, a solarium, and a greenhouse. As mentioned above, providing more leisure time to each resident is a chief function of the new apartment. What is most clear from the description of the New Way of Life apartment is that this new-found free time should be used by the individual to enrich his own life by participating in and contributing to the enrichment of the collective life. The center of life is not the individual apartment, but rather the entire complex, focused in the social center. Even the management of the new complex—the cooperative form—stresses residents' involvement and collective concern. Heavy emphasis is placed on the occupants' voluntary services.106 A curious type of residential segregation is suggested in most planners' comments. These planners underline the importance of keeping these new apartments out of the hands of the ministries and departments. Department-owned or -operated housing tends to segregate people on the basis of work affiliation. The future life of communism, as represented in the New Way of Life experiment, is to be totally integrated—all types of workers, mental and physical, living together and intensely interacting. Unquestionably the New Way of Life is a bold experiment. Similar projects are also being planned and carried out in Leningrad and Kiev, though these cities have given in to critics and added full kitchens in their designs. Soviet planners hope to obtain valuable data from the experiment as to how to build future apartment houses and to intensify the socializing process. The project has been the subject of an extraordinary amount of sociological studies and experiments. All concerned repeat over and over again that the project is just an experiment, and as such must be conducted for a period of years before its practical merits can be evaluated. Unfortunately, there have been several signs that

the New Way of Life will not be given the time it needs for full operations over a long period. One of the sixteen-story towers on Television
Street has been turned over to Moscow State University. At the time
it was expected that the university would be better able to carry through
the experiment on a more scientific basis. Faced with a constant city-
wide housing shortage and growing need for university housing, Moscow
State University decided against the New Way of Life concept and instead reportedly intended to convert the building into a conventional
dormitory. In a bitter reaction to this university intention, Literaturnaia gazeta flatly stated that the shortage of dormitory space is
no reason for discarding an innovative scientific experiment. The
angry newspaper asked "if a shortage of potato storage space arose,
would the university convert its synchrophasotron into a vegetable
bin?"[107] The Soviet architectural community seems to have cham-
pioned the experiment and has pressured the university to hold to its
original agreement to carry through with the New Way of Life plan.[108]
Finally, in December 1970, the Moscow City Soviet Executive Committee decided to carry the experiment "through to the end," to the
delight of Literaturnaia gazeta and NWL planners.[109] Moscow University, however, has been very slow in carrying through with the
experiment, and is using part of the complex as a graduate student
dormitory.[110]

It goes without saying that the New Way of Life has attracted
as much unfriendly criticism as it has lavish praise. The major point
of criticism is the extent of privileges for project residents. If the
aim of the experiment is the socializing of everyday living and the
formation of the new man on the basis of the cooperative principle,
then the most vulnerable part of the New Way of Life design, according
to some detractors, is its insufficient economic rationale; in other
words, the extremely large amounts of state subsidies for a privileged
few. Public dining admittedly would save time for residents, but it
would increase living costs, being 16 percent more expensive than
homecooking. The same critics suggest that the extensive service
system restricts the category of tenants "not only to those of high
moral attributes, but also to persons of a given material status,"
and this surely cannot provide any model for the future life.[111] The
provision of all the expensive services has been defended on the grounds
that if the experiment in the new way of communal living succeeds,
it could spread and introduce a new life style, and eventually a new
form of community organization.[112] In any event, the New Way of
Life and other such projects are a consistent extension of the city-
planning ideas embodied in the microraion, with attention to increased
opportunities for socializing and socialization.

NOTES

1. B. Svetlichny, "Nashi goroda na puti v budushchii," V pomoshch politicheskomu samoobrazovaniiu, 1959, p. 10 vii-x, (Recherches internationale a la lumiere du Marxisme cahiers 20-21 (1960): 209).

2. Svetlichny, op. cit., pp. 209-229; A. Tomsen, op. cit., pp. 22-34; M. Posokhin, Pravda, July 26, July 28, August 2, August 7, 1964; Iu. P. Bocharov, "Sotsial'nye problemy zarubezhnogo gradostroitel' stva," Voprosy filosofii, no. 1 (1964): 90-101.

3. Svetlichny, op. cit., pp. 209-210.

4. Frederick Engels, "How the Bourgeoisie Solves the Housing Question," The Housing Question, Part II, in Karl Marx and Frederick Engels, Selected Works (Moscow: Foreign Languages Publishing House 1962), I, 607-608, 610.

5. See footnote.2.

6. Iu. P. Bocharov, "Sotsial'nye problemy," Voprosy filosofii, no. 1 (1964): 92.

7. Ibid., p. 97.

8. E. Ruzavina, "Economic Aspects in the Urbanization Process," Ekonomicheskie nauki, no. 2 (1969) (Problems of Economics XII, no. 4 (August 1969): 71).

9. Bocharov, op. cit., p. 101.

10. L. Perchik, The Reconstruction of Moscow (Moscow, 1936), p. 20.

11. N. S. Khrushchev, "On the Program of the CPSU," Report to the Twenty-Second Congress CPSU, October 18, 1961, Pravda and Izvestia, October 19, 1961 (CDSP XIII, no. 44: 18).

12. Directives, Twenty-Third Congress of the CPSU, 1966, pp. 387-388.

13. Ekonomika stroitel'stva, 3 (1960); p. 30.

14. P. Pavlov, "Intensifikatsiia proizvodstva i trudovye resurvy" (Labor Resources and the Intensification of Production), Voprosy ekonomiki, no. 3 (1972): 16-17.

15. D. Valentei, "On the Construction of Cities During the Transition to Communism," Voprosy ekonomiki, no. 4 (1960) (Problems of Economics III, no. 5 [September 1960]: 50).

16. See O. S. Pchelintsev, "Problems of the Development of Large Cities," Sotsiologiia v SSSR, II (Moscow, 1965), pp. 270-285; V. Perevedentsev, "Cities and Years," Literaturnaia gazeta, no. 9 (February 21, 1969): 12; Voprosy ekonomiki, no. 9 (September 1970): 34-43; and Iu. Bzhilianskii, "Methodological Prerequisites for Population Forcasting," Planovoe Khoziaistvo, no. 1 (1972): 76-80.

17. V. Perevedentsev, "Population Migration and the Utilization of Labor Resources," Voprosy ekonomiki, no. 9 (September 1970):

04-43 (CDSP XXII, no. 2, 4). See also Pchelintsev, Sotsiologiia v SSSR, pp. 270-285.

18. Perevedentsev, Literaturnaia gazeta, no. 9, February 26, 1969; Perevedentsev, "Population Migration and the Utilization of Labor Resources," op. cit., pp. 34-43.

19. Svetlichny, op. cit., p. 214.

20. B. Brig and Ye. Koppel, "Big Cities and the Ministries," Pravda, May 21, 1969 (CDSP XXI, no. 21: 27).

21. Ibid.

22. Ye. Kochalovsky, "Harmonious Development for the City," Izvestia, August 27, 1969, p. 3 (CDSP XXI, no. 35: 29).

23. B. Svetlichny, "Soviet Town Planning Today," Voprosy ekonomiki, no. 7 (1960) (Problems of Economics III, no. 8 [December 1960]: 32).

24. V. Kucherenko, "On the State of Urban Development and Measures for Improving It," speech at the 1960 Conference on City Planning and Construction, Pravda, June 8, 1960.

25. Svetlichny, "Soviet Town Planning Today," op. cit., p. 33.

26. S. Lyashchenko, "Spread of Industry, Not Cities Will Crowd Land," Literaturnaia gazeta, no. 31 (August 2, 1967): 10-11 (CDSP XIX, no. 31: 13-14).

27. M. Posokhin, Pravda, July 26, 28, August 2, 7, 1964, (CDSP XVI, no. 32: 12).

28. See V. Kucherenko, "The Future of Our Cities," Pravda, October 25, 1959 (CDSP XI, no. 42: 23).

29. See, for example, Valentei, op. cit., p. 51.

30. Kucherenko, "The Future of Our Cities," op. cit.

31. I. I. Loveiko, Chief Architect of Moscow, "Moscow Redevelopment Plan Underway," Izvestia, August 7, 1958.

32. G. Ye. Mishchenko, "Satellite Cities and Towns of Moscow," Goroda-Sputniki (Moscow: Georgraphical Publishing House, 1961) (Soviet Geography III, no. 3 [March 1962]: 42).

33. V. G. Davidovich, "Satellite Cities and Towns of the USSR," Goroda-Sputniki (Soviet Geography III, no. 3 [March 1962]: 5).

34. See A. A. Mints and B. S. Khorev, "An Attempt at an Economic-Geographic Typology of Soviet Cities," Voprosy geografii, no. 45 (1959): 79.

35. Davidovich, op. cit., pp. 5-9.

36. Ibid., p. 33. For detailed case studies of satellite town networks, see Ye. B. Lopatina, "The Formation of Leningrad's Satellite Places," Goroda-Sputniki, pp. 50-59; B. S. Khorev, "Satellite Cities and Towns of Gorky," Goroda-Sputniki, pp. 60-77; G. Ye. Mishchenko, "Satellite Cities and Towns of Moscow," Goroda-Sputniki, pp. 35-43.

37. E. Ruzanina, "Economic Aspects in the Urbanization Process," Ekonomicheskie nauki, no. 2 (1969) (Problems of Economics XII, no. 4 [August 1969]: 71).

38. Komsomol'skaia Pravda, July 15, 1929.

39. Bates, op. cit., p. 7.

40. D. Khodiaev and N. Selivanov, "Un quartier residential experimental à Moscou," Stroitel'stvo i arkhitektura Moskvy; no. 12 (1960) (Recherches internationales à la lumière du Marxisme VII-X, cahiers 20-21: 198).

41. M. Posokhin, "The City of the Future Is Being Built Today," Pravda, July 26, 1964, p. 6, July 28, p. 4, August 2, p. 6, August 7, p. 4 (CDSP XVI, no. 32: 19).

42. Ibid., pp. 21-22; V. A. Kucherenko, "The State of Urban Construction in the USSR and Measures for Its Improvement," Pravda, June 8, 1960 (Soviet Review I, no. 2 [September 1960]: 33); Svetlichny, "Soviet Town Planning Today," op. cit., p. 33; V. Danilov, "Why Is The New Tenant Unhappy?" Pravda, November 21, 1972, p. 3; V. Yegorov, "Everyday Services Center," Pravda, December 12, 1972, p. 1; V. Krugliak and R. Dal, "What Should the Microborough Be Like?" Pravda, July 23, 1972, p. 3.

43. Posokhin, op. cit., p. 22.

44. Khodiaev and Selivanov, op. cit., p. 196. This article describes fifteen entries from the USSR, satellite countries, Yugoslavia, and Communist China.

45. A. Obraztsov, "What Will Our Cities Look Like," Nedelia, December 25, 1960 (Soviet Review II, no. 4, [April 1961]: 35); E. Lenina and Ye Syrkina, "Reflections on the Microdistrict," Zvezda, no. 10 (October 1966) (CDSP XIX no. 3: 35.

46. Obraztsov, op. cit., pp. 34-35.

47. Obraztsov, op. cit., pp. 34-35.

48. Lenina and Syrkina, op. cit., p. 35.

49. D. Danin, "Material and Style," Novy mir, no. 1 (January 1961) (CDSP XIII, no. 3: 11).

50. P. Volodin, "Planned Flaws," Izvestia, June 2, 1960.

51. A. Vyatkin, "Esthetics of a City," Izvestia, April 5, 1963 (CDSP XV, no. 4: 37).

52. Much of the foregoing information on the five-stage system of services is from A. S. Obraztsov, "Novaia sistema obsluzhivaniia nashikh gorodov," Znanie, no. 10 (1968): seriia stroitel'stvo i Arkhitektura, pp. 1-46. For detailed case studies of the microraion and service system, see G. Dukelski, "Pervye microraiony pervogo goroda-sputniki," Stroitel'stvo i arkhitektura Moskvy, no. 4 (1960): 13-15; M. Biely and I. Orlov, "Naushchnigorodok pod Novosibirskom," Arkhitektura SSSR no. 6 (1960): 4-8; Michael B. Frolic, "The Soviet City," Town Planning Review (Liverpool) XXXIV, no. 4 (January 1964): 285-306.

53 Levina and Syrkina, op. oit., p. 36.

54. Ibid.

55. Letters to Izvestia, "The New Home," Izvestia, October 14, 1969, p. 4.

56. Iu. Shpakov, "Why Is the New Tenant Unhappy?" Pravda, September 8, 1969, p. 2.

57. V. Danilov, "Why Is the New Tenant Unhappy?" Pravda, November 21, 1972, p. 3.

58 . "Report of the USSR Central Statistical Administration: Stages of Growth of the Five-Year Plan—On Results of the Fulfillment of the State Plan for the Development of the USSR National Economy in 1972," Pravda and Izvestia, January 30, 1973 (CDSP XXV, no. 5: 14).

59. Izvestia, Januray 9, 1963, and Speech delivered by A. N. Kosygin at September 30, 1972, meeting of USSR State Planning Committee, Planovoe Khoziaistvo, no. 11 (November 1972): 3-8 (CDSP XXV, no. 3: 6).

60. Craig Hodgetts and Lester Walker, "Redesigning New York— An Immodest Proposal," New York II, no. 8 (February 24, 1969): 33-43.

61. For example, see Nezhny, op. cit., p. 206.

62. V. P. Semin, "Union Republic Ministry and Local Soviets," Sovetskoe gosudarstvo i pravo, no. 9 (September 1969): 92.

63. Ibid.

64. "Sovershenstvovat' organizatorskuiu rabotu sovetov" (Perfect the Organizational Work of the Soviets), lead editorial, Gorodskoe khoziaistvo Moskvy (monthly of Mosispolkom), no. 6 (June 1968): 1.

65. Posokhin, op. cit., p. 22.

66. David T. Cattell, Leningrad: A Case Study of Soviet Urban Government (New York: Praeger Publishers, 1968), pp. 124-126.

67. N. Kondratyev, "Toward One Goal," Izvestia, April 3, 1962, p. 3 (CDSP XVII, no. 27: 33-34).

68. Pravda, April 8, 1966.

69. "On Measures for the Further Improvement of the Work of the District and City Soviets," Pravda, March 14, 1971, pp. 1-2; "Decree of the Presidium of the USSR Supreme Soviet: On the Basic Rights and Duties of the City and Borough Soviets," Izvestia, March 20, 1971; p. 4; and K. Sheremet, "New Rights and New Opportunities," Sovety deputatov trudiashchikhsia, no. 5 (1971) (The Soviet Review XIII, no. 2 [Summer 1972]: 174-188).

70. M. Shestak, "Soviets and the Urban Economy: Where There Is Agreement Among Comrades," Izvestia, October 4, 1968, p. 3 (CDSP XX, no. 40: 19).

71. A. Sokolov, "Soviets and the Economy: The Autonomy of the City," Izvestia, November 3, 1968, p. 12 (CDSP XX, no. 43: 25).

72. Ibid.

73. Izvestia, August 27, 1969, p. 3. For another example, see A. Grishmanovsky, First Secretary of Novotroitsk City Party Committee, "Like Supplicants," Pravda, April 13, 1973, p. 3.

74. R. A. Safarov, Raionniye sovety deputatov trudiashchikhsia v gorodakh (Moscow, 1961), p. 43.

75. See David Cattell, "Local Government and the Sovnarkhoz in the USSR—1957-1962," Soviet Studies XV, no. 4 (April 1964): 430-442.

76. K. F. Sheremet, Kompetentsiia mestnykh sovetov (Moscow: Moscow University, 1968), pp. 34-35; lead editorial, Izvestia, December 19, 1964.

77. N. Kh. Arutiunian, "Both All-Union and Republic," Izvestia, December 29, 1966, p. 5.

78. Cited in Seymon Tutuchenko, Housing in the USSR: Notes of an Architect, (Moscow: Foreign Languages Publishing House, 1960), p. 89. Pravda, December 8, 1954, mentioned Khrushchev's address to the conference but did not print it.

79. Danin, op. cit., p. 10.

80. "Decree of Communist Party Central Committee and USSR Council of Ministers: On Eliminating Waste in Design and Construction," Pravda, November 10, 1955, p. 1 (CDSP VII, no. 43: 15-16);

81. I. Ganenko, "Esthetics and the Present Day: Against Alien Influences," Oktiabr', no. 4 (April 1960): 167-174 (CDSP XII, no. 22: 27).

82. Ibid., pp. 27-28.

83. Viktor Nekrasov, "About Past, Present and a Little Bit of the Future," Literaturnaia gazeta, February 20, 1960, (CDSP XII, no. 11: p. 4).

84. Danin, op. cit.

85. Nezhny, op. cit., p. 206.

86. Ibid., p. 205.

87. A. Nezhny, "Cities that we are Building," Novyi mir, no. 10, October 1969, (Current Abstracts of the Soviet Press [henceforth CASP] II, 3, (March 1970), p. 26).

88. Ibid., pp. 25-26.

89. V. Berezin, "Beauty and Expediency," Pravda Vostoka, April 7, 1960, p. 3.

90. Nezhny, op. cit., p. 26.

91. Ibid.

92. Posokhin, op. cit., p. 13.

93. "On Measures for Improving the Quality of Housing and Civil Construction," Izvestia, June 20, 1969, p. 4; Pravda, June 21, 1969, pp. 1-2 (CDSP XXI, no. 25: 13). Complaints continue that "the ostensible control that the architect has over the builder is nonexistent." See Komsomolskaia Pravda, September 17, 1972, p. 2.

94 Nezhny, op. cit., p. 26.

95. "But the Heat is Escaping," Pravda, September 24, 1969, p. 3.

96. "Defense Against Heat Loss," Pravda, November 24, 1969, p. 3.

97. Nezhny, op. cit., p. 26.

98. V. Promyslov, speech at the Twenty-Third Party Congress, Pravda, April 8, 1966.

99. Pravda, June 8, 1960.

100. V. Kucherenko, "Several Questions of Soviet Urban Planning," Pravda, June 1, 1960 (CDSP XII, no. 32: 24).

101. See, for example, A. V. Osipov, ed., Town, Country and People: Studies in Soviet Society, Vol. II (London: Tavistock Publication, prepared by Novosti Press Agency, 1969), especially J. K. Arkhangelskayia, "Models of Population Reproduction for Long-Term Planning of Housing Construction," pp. 100-106.

102. Broner, op. cit., p. 52.

103. David L. Broner, op. cit., p. 54.

104. Ibid., p. 55.

105. Ibid., p. 66 and Figure 1.

106. Preceding description of the New Way of Life Apartment from Posokhin, op. cit., pp. 19-20; Broner, op. cit., pp. 67-71; "The Building in Which We Shall Live," Literaturnaia gazeta, no. 45 (November 6, 1968): 10; Iuri Polukhin, "Not Dream, but Reality," Literaturnaia gazeta, no. 45 (November 6, 1968): 10 (CDSP XXI, no. 3: 16-18); Literaturnaia gazeta, no. 52 (December 25, 1968).

107. Leonid Zhukovitsky, "Will the New Way of Life Housing Complex Remain?" Literaturnaia gazeta, no. 3 (January 14, 1969).

108. "Will the New Way of Life Remain?" Literaturnaia gazeta, no. 10 (March 4, 1969): 11 (CASP II, no. 5 [May 1970]: 14-15).

109. "What's Happening to the New Way of Life Building?" Literaturnaia gazeta, no. 50 (December 9, 1970): 2.

110. "Once More About New Way of Life Housing Complexes," Literaturnaia gazeta, no. 35 (August 30, 1972): 10.

111. Yu. Zhuchok and Ye. Zuikova, "House of the New Way of Life: Building with Privileges?" Literaturnaia gazeta, no. 2 (January 8, 1969): 11 (CDSP XXI, no. 4: 15-17).

112. Literaturnaia gazeta, no. 52 (December 25, 1968).

4

ORGANIZING FOR HOUSING CONSTRUCTION: PROBLEMS OF THE HOUSE CONSTRUCTION INDUSTRY

The problems of the house construction industry are often a reflection or a direct result of the weaknesses of the complicated planning process. Just as numerous organizations, differing and sometimes conflicting departmental, ministerial, and local Soviet interests have repeatedly resulted in delayed plans and distorted urban development, so too this multi-organizational involvement in housing construction has created a housing construction industry until recently characterized by a high degree of disorganization and low degree of workers' skills.

Faced with a frightening picture of widespread destruction as a result of World War II, the postwar USSR was forced to develop new techniques and methods for rapid building of desperately needed housing. As urban planners and politicians tried to introduce these new techniques of industrialization and prefabrication into the construction industry, they gradually came to realize that their hoped for plans of increased housing construction would require a major reorganization of the industry assigned to carry out the new programs. This chapter will attempt to depict the state of the Soviet housing construction industry, its problems in getting the job done, and the quality of its work. How have the authorities coped with the question of the industry's reform in responding to the new demands of technology? Have new forms of organization evolved in the search for greater efficiency in construction work and more control over the entire construction process? Are the series of economic reforms coming out of the 1960s and continuing into the present leading to improved solutions for the enormous problems of coordinating and consolidating many agencies and levels of government? In brief, are recent developments helping to define an integrated, unified house construction system in the Soviet Union, fulfilling the claim that "the planned organization of construction in the USSR is one of the striking manifestations of the advantages of a socialist social system"? Once again, the main question revolves around the achievement of coordination of planning, financing, and constructing of housing. Inspecting is also a vital part of the house construction process. With the new emphasis— stemming from the late 1950s' notion of the State of the Whole People— on the public in control functions, we must also ask what roles have trade-union and "public" groups been assuming in inspecting and accepting newly constructed housing? Finally, what practices, if any, have some officials and individuals developed to overcome certain legalistic difficulties in housing construction?

The years of emergency reconstruction following World War II (1944-1950) saw a turning to industrialized, so-called "speed-building" methods of housing construction to relieve urgent needs and eventually, it was hoped, to solve the tight housing situation in the Soviet Union. It was during this period that prefabrication and prefabricated housing made their grand entry into the Soviet housing industry. First applications and experiments in prefabricated reinforced concrete elements and industrial techniques of house construction were made back in 1938 by the architect Andrei Burov, who taught at the Moscow Institute of Architecture. At that time Burov was designing prefabricated large-panel houses. Widespread acceptance of the idea would not, however, come until the late 1950s and early 1960s. But it was in the Ukraine that industrialized housing techniques were first developed on a wide scale in the early postwar years, and it was Nikita S. Khrushchev who stressed the Ukraine's development of such new building techniques. The Ukraine Ministry of Civil Building and its Designing Institute were commissioned to begin industrial production of new building materials and to introduce them into building practice. Ceramic sheets and tiles, gypsum blocks (ceramic tiles made of plastic), gypsum panels, prefabricated ceiling panels and sets of doors and window openings, and even built-in furniture were introduced during these years. In addition, the Ukraine was taking an active lead in the utilization of mechanization in all phases of the building industry.[1]

At the same time, the search was on for new uses of local building materials and for low-cost structurals. Plastering by the so-called "wet-method" was seen as too time-consuming and too subject to the weather, as a "relic of ancient times" that was much too costly and inefficient. Admittedly, bricks were considered excellent building materials. Yet the slow, arduous process of bricklaying meant long, drawn-out construction projects. The weight of the brick itself limited heights to seven or eight stories. Time and weight could be sharply cut down by making brick houses with thinner walls, but this in effect would "only emphasize brick's treacherous heat-conductivity."[2] Consequently, early postwar "industrialized" housing attempts turned to large-block construction, in which Soviet builders had had some prewar experience. By enlarging the size of building elements, labor costs and time were decreased. These large blocks or "slag-blocks" made from the waste of blast furnaces and boilers proved to be solid and light—as well as too excellent conductors of sound. During a Moscow Conference of Architects, a certain academician Sysin describes his "quiet life" in his new slag-block house, built with reinforced concrete floors and ceilings:

> I seldom see my neighbors, but thanks to the excellent sound-conducting properties of the partitions, ceilings and floors, I know them all by their first names. I know immediately when my right-hand neighbor's baby has a tummyache in the morning. A talented woman pianist lives on the floor above me. I have enjoyed many of her concerts at the Conservatoire, but in the evenings when I am resting or working, even Rachmaninov's wonderful preludes are annoying. . . . I was imprudent enough to get a dog. The caretaker and the neighbor above also have dogs. And the moment the caretaker's dog begins to bark, my Rex replies. They are soon joined by the neighbor's dog, and within two minutes the whole house seems to be barking.[3]

The quality of these first attempts at prefabricated housing seemed even worse than that of other, more conventional types of construction. According to a 1949 Izvestia report, the floor boards of these prefabricated houses were of varying thicknesses; window frames and doors were frequently warped. The extremely poor insulation allowed the cold to whip freely through the buildings during the winter.[4] The slag-blocks often cracked or chipped during construction and had to be patched up with plaster or cement once the building was occupied and subject to changes of temperature. The average citizen's early experience with these new prefabricated creatures made a lasting impression on his mind and helps account for his reluctance to accept for many years thereafter any housing that bore the prefabricated label. Nevertheless, the Soviet tenant would increasingly find himself sheltered in a "factory-made" world.

A series of Party-government resolutions in 1954 and 1955 sought to open up a new epoch in the life of construction. Greater industrialization of all phases of construction, lower costs, higher levels of skills, and better organization of construction enterprises were the basic aims of these decrees. It was not, however, until the late 1950s that industrial methods of construction were widely adopted

with the initiation of a drastic reorganization of the building industry.
The monumental decree of June 1957 on improving housing, the Seven
Year Plan (1959-1965), and a 1959 decree called for the positive shift
to the "progressive" methods of construction embodied in precast
large-panel components and other prefabricated construction elements.
Since then the Soviet housing and construction industries have been
involved in an ongoing revolution aimed at making construction work
a fully mechanized process of assembling and erecting buildings from
as many parts and units manufactured under complete factory conditions as possible. In his effort to find quicker solutions to the Soviet
housing problem, Khrushchev became the tireless proponent of the
further expansion of the industrialization of construction. At the
Twenty-First Party Congress in 1959, the then First Secretary of the
CPSU spoke of still newer techniques to speed the changeover of the
construction industry to industrial methods of construction. The
Congress heard Khrushchev speak of the necessity of broadly intro-
ducing vibration rolling or vertical casting to make reinforced concrete panels. These rolled panels require no welding and are joined
by bolts. In 1964 an experimental plant of the Special Rolled Elements
Design Bureau produced the first experimental apartment house in
Moscow assembled on conveyor belt. According to Pravda, building
with vibration-rolled materials allows 65 percent to 70 percent of
the work to be done by the rolling mill.[5] The major advantage of
prefabricated large-panel construction was, according to Khrushchev,
the fact that per 1,000 square meters of floor space, the required
labor is one-third needed in brick construction and labor expenditure
is one-half.[6] In 1959 erection of apartment houses assembled from
prefabricated large panels began on a mass scale. This mass-scale
prefabrication was also changing the face of the construction industry.
In 1959 there was a total of 1,851 plants producing precast concrete
elements in the Soviet Union. About two-thirds of these plants were
not large-scale operations, with an average of only 10,000 cubic meters
of finished components. By 1965 the USSR had 2,305 plants, with a
considerable number capable of large-scale production. Furthermore,
Moscow, Leningrad, and other major urban areas have seen the set-
up of some 275 specialized factories with a combined capacity of 17
million square meters of finished housing space of the large-panel
type.[7] The story of Soviet industrialization of its construction industry
is still not the history of an easy sweep forward. In an earlier chapter,
we recognized the foot-dragging on the part of many construction enterprises in applying new construction techniques. The conveyor-belt
process required considerable reform and reorganization of industry.
Even the Soviet capital, with perhaps the most favored and strongest
construction industry, was sternly criticized by its chief architect
for its building industry's obvious slowness in reorienting itself

"toward a more decisive increase in the production of advanced, large-panel houses." He charged the industry with lack of flexibility and a certain inertia—a charge echoed throughout the USSR.[8]

Yet in the ten years from 1957 to 1967, the proportion of prefabricated buildings in Moscow rose from 7.6 to 82 percent of all new construction, with the proportion of what is considered the most progressive type—large-panel structures—still rising. In 1968 the proportion of large-panel buildings reached 61 percent, or twice the state-wide average, and the planned figure for 1975 is 80 percent.[9] The 1969 reforms in the construction industry re-emphasized the further development of industrialization of housing and civil construction and the improvement of completely prefabricated housing. They also ordered USSR construction ministries to work out measures for bringing the volume of large-panel housing construction up to no less than 50 percent of the total volume of state and cooperative housing construction in the country by 1975.[10] The experiences of the Moscow Main Construction Administration were widely publicized and discussed at a 1969 Seminar on Large-Panel Building construction. The high degree of prefabrication and mechanization was described in detail. Building components delivered to construction sites of Moscow housing construction combines are almost completely finished at the plants. Large outer-wall panels are designed for two rooms, reducing the number of joints by 40 percent. These large panels are delivered from the factory with window glass and the sash ready for the final coat, inside surfaces all ready for papering, and the outer surface finished with stone or white concrete. Some plants are now even producing large panels with wallpapering or painting already completed. The inside retaining-wall panels are sent to the construction site, complete with built-in heat ducts and surfaces ready for papering. Overhead panels come furnished with electrical conduit and simply need a quick coat of paint. These new materials and methods have allowed the erection of a 143-unit nine-story apartment building in fifty-four days, with structural work and coincident jobs taking thirty days. The rapid erection of such housing has meant the necessity of vastly improved schedules of transportation and construction and the virtually total reorganization of the house construction industry.

In the early 1950s Timothy Sosnovy concluded that Soviet house building was adversely affected by the proliferation of construction organizations, each subordinated to a particular department or ministry. It was not a rare sight to see several building organizations associated with different departments or ministries "clustered together in the same general building site—or even on the same building site— using different sources of material supply and different transportation facilities."[11] Efficiency and economy of materials and men suffered in the extreme. The December 1954 All-Union Conference of builders held in the Moscow Kremlin and subsequent Soviet reports lend support to the Sosnovy conclusion of a poorly organized, highly uncoordinated construction industry. The 1954 conference pointed out that housing appropriations were often dispersed over numerous projects. Instead of concentrating on one area at a time, builders freely scattered sites, with the result that cranes and other machines installed for use on one or two houses were not uncommonly allowed to stand idle. In Novosibirsk in 1955, for example, there were more than 500 different building sites. The outcome of such practices was a drop of crane efficiency in the city to 57 percent of planned operations.[12] Small construction offices having little or no connection with city or territorial agencies seemed to dominate the building industry. Dispersal of funds, material, and cadres among numerous weak, non-specialized construction organizations only served to hamper the full-scale development of housing construction on the basis of an industrialized industry. "In the mid-1950s in every town ten, and not so rarely even 100 or so construction organizations of the different ministries and institutions were conducting the construction of housing."[13] The results were chaos and poor housing. If real headway was to be made toward a solution of the housing shortage, the many small, scattered, and low-skilled construction organizations would have to be concentrated. Specialization of skills would also be necessary in the newly amalgamated construction enterprises. For many towns and cities of the Soviet Union, the process of consolidating tiny construction facilities attached to many different enterprises is still the basic task for the future. Speaking of the nation as a whole, an important 1969 Novyi mir article summed up the situation by declaring that "above all it is necessary somehow to coordinate this [house construction] system, to concentrate its leadership in a single set of skillful hands."[14]

In response to the accelerated house construction programs and demands for industrialized house construction methods, the last decade saw a major development in the Soviet construction industry—the integrated house construction combine or trust, the "kombinat" (domostroitel' nyi kombinat or DSK). Leningrad pioneered the path of fully prefabricated house construction when, in the spring of 1959, Leningraders began the first house construction combine—the Poliustrovskii DSK. Its appearance signaled the beginning of a revolution in the organization of house building. The manufacture of parts, their putting together, and their finishing were to be united into one continuous-flow technological process. The management of the house building combine was to have total responsibility for the entire process, from obtaining unmanufactured materials to presenting the finished house. The experience of the first "kombinat" in 1959 demonstrated that labor costs could be reduced 1.7 times.[15] By the end of 1960 there were already six house building combines in Leningrad. The idea began to catch on. Volgograd tried out the new organization in 1960 and found that house construction time could be shortened by two to three months.[16] During 1961-1962 two house construction combines were formed in Moscow. Within a short period of time, the Moscow combines gained the reputation of being the strongest industrialized house construction enterprises in the country, with the Moscow House Construction Trust No. 1 leading all Moscow organizations. In three years the DSK No. 1 was credited with the erection of 500 multistoried houses. Other Soviet cities took note of the Leningrad-Moscow developments, and by 1962 large house construction combines had been formed in Kiev, Minsk, Alma-Ata, Tashkent, Dushanbe, Vilnius, Tallin, Sverdlovsk, Baku, Dnepropetrovsk, and many other areas. According to Soviet reports of the early 1960s, development of this type of housing construction facilitated the lowering of labor expenditures by 35 to 40 percent and cut the time of construction by 1.5 to 2 times. Particularly in large, specialized construction organizations, labor productivity rose 15 percent and costs were lowered 8 percent in comparison to the usual organizations.[17]

The securing of adequate materials where and when needed in the construction schedule is a major problem for efficient construction in any country. It has been a particularly severe problem in the Soviet construction industry. Thus, one of the primary purposes of the DSK is to overcome this supply difficulty, and thereby avoid idling of men and machines. Pravda relates that the Moscow House Construction Trust No. 1 of the Chief Moscow Construction Administration under the Executive Committee of the Moscow City Soviet (that is, the DSK No. 1 of Glavmosstroi under the Ispolkom of the Mossoviet) operates plants to prefabricate structures, as well as assembly departments that put up the houses. It should be noted that many of the experiences of the Moscow construction organizations are connected with very recent economic reforms that are to be implemented throughout the country during the early 1970s. In the case of the Moscow DSK No. 1, all functions related to the building's erection, except the underground communications, the foundations, and the approaches, are the combine's responsibilities. The parallel conducting of the assembly of building's elements and the inside work, combined with the precise assortment of parts in sets and container packing, accelerates the assembly work of this combine to a pace of one story in three days, nine stories in thirty days, and complete construction in less than half the time required by the norms. Materials and containerized parts arrive when needed at the construction site, thereby eliminating on-site storage and cutting down on spoilage and disappearance. In addition to the high degree of prefabrication, the Moscow House Construction Trust No. 1 was also beneficiary of the transition to new conditions for planning and economic incentive. The management of the combine had the right to approve its own staff within the limits of the centrally allocated wage fund. In practical terms, this meant that administrative personnel could be consolidated, jobs combined, and excess labor trimmed. The mixed assembly brigade, which once had sixty-five men, was now able to do the same amount of work with forty-five to forty-seven workers. According to the _Pravda_ article, this was one of the secrets of the achievement of one of the highest labor productivity marks—250 square meters of housing a year per construction worker—and of the lowest share of wages in the cost of construction-assembly work in the city.[18]

Although the house construction combine is making an important impact on the organization of the construction industry, especially in the larger cities, it is still a long way from being the predominant mode of construction operations. Small construction organizations subordinated to a multitude of different ministries and departments still characterize the Soviet construction industry. Even when a town or city has developed house construction combines, there is no guarantee that the building of dwellings will be carried out in a well-planned and city-wide coordinated fashion. The combines and pre-fabrication plants themselves are often located under the jurisdiction of various ministries and departments.[19] Attempting to find a solution to its diffuse house construction organization, the Dnepropetrovsk City Soviet, as one case in point, organized the Dnepropetrovsk Urban Construction Trust, in conjunction with the Ukraine Republic Ministry for the Construction of Heavy Industry Enterprises. But what happened? Half the construction work that the ministry assigned to the trust was on industrial enterprises, while the plans for the construction of apartment houses went unfulfilled.[20] Furthermore, let us recall that it was only at the end of the 1960s and in the early 1970s that Moscow has been attempting to centralize its house and municipal construction activities by transferring state capital investments for such purposes from the ministries and departments to the Moscow City Soviet. In relation to this move, the Moscow Board of Capital Construction has been reorganized into a Main Board (Administration) and it has assumed the function of a single client for all forms of housing, municipal, and cultural-service construction, regardless of which department or ministry owns the proposed building. At the raion level, this means there is a board of capital construction that is the single client for all housing and cultural-service construction in the raion. Hopefully this will raise the role and responsibility of the raiispolkoms in fulfilling plans for the city's capital construction.[21] In this case, however, it is not necessarily true that as Moscow goes, so goes the nation.

In the midst of calls for "more power to the local Soviets," at least in regard to matters of urban planning and construction, there are also loud dissonant voices. Some of these voices point to the local Soviets' underutilization of allocated housing and repair funds or outright misuse of such funds for showy sports palaces and questionable administrative buildings. The Soviets' defenders reply that such abuses are a result of the local Soviets' weakness in enforcing a unified city-wide construction program and that the local government is a victim of strong-willed ministries. This long-time controversy once again came to a head at the December 1969 plenary session of the Central Committee of the CPSU. In an editorial article printed several months after the important session, Pravda reported the Central Committee's findings. At the expense of housing, school, hospital, and children's institution construction, several cities and republics are still giving building priorities to the construction of "administrative and costly entertainment enterprises and sports complexes." Furthermore, "this work is sometimes carried on outside the plan and uses appropriations made for housing and industrial construction." Citing the practice in Kazakhstan, which seems to have been continually criticized for the same abuses since the late 1950s, the editorial stated that "such violations of state discipline and incorrect use of assets in urban construction are, unfortunately, not infrequent." Money is divided among many projects, greatly prolonging completion of construction. The urgent task of the hour for local Soviets, ministries, and departments is the concentration of construction. The Party paper then declared that "this aspect of work must be placed under the special control of Party agencies."[22] Finally, the December 1969 Central Committee plenum instructed the Party and government organs

> to review within three months the list of administrative, entertainment, sports and large public buildings and structures, as well as apartment houses of more than nine stories (where these are not called for by city building requirements and are not economically expedient), now under construction and being designed, and to drop from the list those projects for which there is no necessity at the present time to channel the money and material resources that are thereby freed into housing and communal construction.

At the same time the Party directed the USSR People's Control Committee to intensify control over state discipline in urban construction and housing and "to give special attention to the impermissibility of diverting money and material resources to unplanned construction."[23] Economic reforms and Party statements seem to favor strengthening the local Soviets' hand in achieving greater centralization of control over construction at the local level, and at the same time increasing the central government's, particularly the Party's control over the activities of local Soviets in such matters. In the middle of 1969, in an attempt to provide greater centralization and control, the largest Soviet republic, the RSFSR, adopted a decree forming a Republic Ministry of Housing and Civil Construction, with Aleksandr Vasilyevich Gladyrevsky appointed its first head.[24]

ECONOMIC REFORMS AND INCENTIVES

We have seen that the Soviet construction industry has been characterized throughout its history by a low degree of skill and organization. Correspondingly, the Soviet construction worker has been of low status, earning low wages. Frequently the young construction worker was a recent arrival to the city or a man or woman entering the labor force for the first time. Because of the relatively low wages paid in the construction industry, he usually stayed for a short time in building trades and then quickly moved on to a more lucrative and often less strenuous job in other Soviet industries. As a result, the construction industry suffered badly from a lack of specialized skills and very high turnover. As early as 1957, the Moscow City Soviet Executive Committee took the unusual step of attempting to cope with this problem by adopting a special decision that provided an extra incentive to those who had switched to work in the construction industry. Housing space was to be provided in apartment buildings for those construction workers who were registered as residents of Moscow and who had worked conscientiously at construction sites for three years. Only within the last decade, however, have wage levels consistently risen in the industry, and only in 1969 did the decision to increase the wages of a large category of builders become effective. Poor finishing is usually the major complaint of both tenants and architects. Consequently, in 1969 the decision was also made to raise pay rates for finishing work. With a view to creating permanent cadres of skilled construction and finishing workers, the 1969 Party-state decree "On Measures for Improving the Quality of Housing and Civil Construction" assigned the Union Republic Councils of Ministers and the USSR Council of Ministers' State Vocational-Technical Education Committee, in conjunction with central construction ministries, the task of transforming, during 1969-1970, 132 schools accommodating 51,800 pupils into vocational-technical schools with a three-year course of instruction and of increasing the enrollment to 100,000 by 1973. The 1969-1970 reforms in the construction industry likewise pay special attention to the question of economic incentives. The workers, executives, engineers, and technicians of house construction enterprises, fulfilling production plans and developing for production new types of residential buildings, will be issued bonuses out of the above-plan profits of house construction combines. Several incentive funds have also been set up for construction and installation organizations: a material incentives fund, a fund for the development of production, and a fund for social and cultural measures and housing construction. These economic incentive funds are to be formed out of profits, "by means of the direct deduction of money from total profits received, as completed units or stages of work are turned over to the clients" (emphasis mine). Incentives, therefore, have been tied to profits and completed work. In order to cut down, and hopefully eliminate the great amount of partial completion of buildings that has meant great capital expenditures spread over many unfinished projects, the economic reform requires that housing contractors may receive payments only upon completion of the units or stages of the buildings. There are to be no intermediate payments between client and contractor. This new procedure of settling accounts was to take place for all construction projects whose estimated cost is less than 100,000 rubles by 1971. Complete changeover to this form of settling accounts was expected in 1972. As of January 1, 1970, a new procedure was also introduced for the planning of capital investments in housing construction and for the technical-economic evaluation of the apartment house. The new planning procedure is based on cost per square meter of total housing space and not, as in the past, on cost per square meter of living and useful space. Such a change in investment methods is intended to improve apartment designing and to make possible a more accurate evaluation of the actual construction work.[25] According to a Gosplan spokesman, the changeover to settling accounts for finished construction output had already yielded important results in trial runs before the 1969 reform decree. At projects built by the Leningrad Chief Administrator for Housing, Civil and Industrial Construction, before operating on the new procedure the volume of uncompleted construction was 40 percent. After the introduction of payments for completed projects, this figure fell to 21 percent. Moscow experienced similar results. In individual house construction combines, construction times decreased by an average of 25 percent to 30 percent per building, and expenditures on the operations of machines declined by 28 percent.[26] Another important incentive in effect Union-wide since 1967 is allotting to construction organizations 10 percent of all new housing constructed by their labor. The RSFSR has had a resolution since May 1962 providing a similar incentive. This practice is one of the clearest examples of housing's being used as a spur to greater labor productivity and hence greater economic efficiency.

Naturally the bonus system is to play a large role in achieving greater economic rationality. Currently the bonus payments system is in flux. In October 1968 a new "Statute on the Payment of Bonuses to Employees for the Commissioning of New Production Capacities and Units of Construction" replaced the previous statute, which had been in effect since 1964. Both the 1964 and 1968 statutes stipulated that a single bonus shall be paid for the commissioning of a facility to the contractor, the client, and the design organization and that they shall divide this bonus into shares. As critics of this bonus system point out, the statutes fail to define violations for which the clients and design organizations may be denied a bonus.[27] This situation served only to promote the lengthening of construction time, increased the growth of unfinished construction, in effect, frequent violations of contractual obligations. Obviously the most serious flaw in the bonus payments system has been the absence of any limit on the planned deadline for construction of a particular building. There have been a number of resolutions and regulations obliging ministries and departments to insure that construction projects are completed within limits of the norms established for the overall time of construction. However, as an Izvestia article clearly noted, the USSR State Construction Committee (Gosstroi), which approved the norms and "was one of the authors of the statute on bonuses," was guilty of completing only half the job. It made no provision in the statute for either inducements to meet the time norms or for sanctions in case of violations.[28] The 1969 reforms in the construction industry began to remedy this "oversight." The Party and government have ordered that construction duration norms (in conjunction with adherence to design and technical specifications and estimated costs) be taken as the basis for bonus payments. Bonuses will be raised by 50 percent when the time taken to put production capacities and construction units into operation is reduced by at least 30 percent of the established norm; by 25 percent when the time period is cut by 20 percent; and by 10 percent if a 10 percent time reduction is realized.[29] Supposedly such reforms will eventually affect the house construction industry as well. But as far as the bonus system for house commissioning goes, it is still subject to serious shortcomings. It is not the observance of construction time norms, or even of appointed deadlines for turning over dwellings for occupancy, but rather the fulfillment of the quarterly plan for the commissioning of housing space in square meters that has decided bonus payments. And who has established these quarterly plans? Not the client, but the contractor's parent organization, which itself receives a certain percentage of these bonuses. In practice this has resulted in cases of acute myopia, "too great tolerance of arbitrariness," and countless instances of altering assignments to conform to the amount of work actually performed.[30] Add to this the fact that dozens of the contract organizations are carrying out the house construction job for the major builders and that these contractors are under the jurisdiction of different trusts, and the resulting confused picture will at least aid our understanding of the difficulties in trying to untangle the bonus system. Writing in <u>Izvestia</u> in July 1970, the economist A. Boldyrev further noted a serious flaw in the bonus system. Article eight (paragraph seven) of Amendments and Addenda of the Construction Statute (1968) states:

> The amount of bonuses payable does not include bonuses for housing space commissioned during the quarter under consideration, but scheduled to be handed over for occupancy in preceding quarters of the current year.

The serious flaw is the lack of any mention of housing space scheduled for commissioning the previous year, but handed over for occupancy only in the current year. "As a result," Boldyrev relates, "housing can be carried over from one year's plan to another and included in the contractor's overall quarterly results for commissioning of housing space." In effect, the builder is denied any bonus if he delays the commissioning of a dwelling for a month or two, but is guaranteed a bonus if he hands the building over a year late! This condition, in turn, creates the current practice of working out a year's acceptance plan in which 50 to 80 percent of yearly planned housing is to be handed over for occupancy in the fourth quarter of the year, while the acceptance plan for the first three quarters consists mostly of housing that should have been handed over in earlier years.[31] Bonus statutes have likewise said very little about quality. Consequently, equal bonuses have been paid out for high-quality rated buildings and mediocre ones. Soviet leaders seem to be expressing greater and greater concern over the quality of construction. The 1969 resolutions and follow-up statements indicate a growing stress on quality in the granting of bonuses. At certain construction sites in the Russian, Ukrainian, Belorussian, and Kazakh republics, for instance, the so-called "fixed-assignment-and-bonus" system for paying workers has been tried out and officially declared successful. Under this system, a bonus amounting to 20 percent of earnings is granted for the fulfillment of an assignment with a "good" rating within the set deadline. A rating of "excellent" boosts the bonus to 40 percent.[32] The "fixed-assignment-and-bonus" system seems to have good prospects for Union-wide adoption. This new system, of course, puts a greater importance on inspection commissions that assign quality rating. In the past, such commissions have not been noted for their unswerving dedication to carrying out their jobs without undue influence or intimidation from parties with a direct financial interest in receiving high ratings. Thus, the proposed new bonus system may fall victim to the inspection system. The reforms seem to be wrestling gradually with these costly loopholes, which have shown an extraordinary ability to escape most previous reform efforts. It is obvious that progress in this field will be slow and uncertain. Even more obvious is the rocky, pit-filled road of entrenched interests, repetitive and conflicting authorities, and overly cautious officials. The present period is one of incremental transition. Success in establishing a more rational bonus system or overall general reform in the construction industry depends heavily on the Soviet Union's success in shifting its entire economy to the new economic system, based more on profitability, economic accountability, and a degree of market socialism and less on mere gross output "val." Just as the earliest Soviet experiments in Libermanism—which involved certain clothing enterprises—met particular difficulties in getting desired materials when needed, because of the isolation of the enterprises from the rest of the economy, so too, house construction combines have experienced troubles in acquiring or manufacturing complete sets of prefabricated parts required by new house building methods.

PROBLEMS OF QUALITY AND INSPECTION

Numerous articles, speeches, letters, and books have praised the increasing tempo of housing construction and more loudly decried the quality of that construction. "The Joys and Sorrows of Tenants in a New Building," "The Woes of the Newly Settled" are titles seen many times in the Soviet press. A cartoon in the Georgia Republic Press (Zaria Vostoka, October 28, 1970) clearly illustrates the problem that has so long plagued the entire nation. In the center of the cartoon drawing "stands" a newly completed apartment building, whose window frames have been set in at the most imaginative angles, whose walls are badly cracked, and whose roof allows a view of the heavens. Plaster and cement have already begun their ungraceful descent. The entire structure has the precarious look of a building slated for immediate demolition. Led by a very satisfied, cigarette-puffing brigade chief, the house construction workers happily march out of the "completed" building. In the same door, however, march the men of the repair organization—in a word, a capsule view of the two sides of the continuous-flow house construction process. The accompanying explanation and article note that in the struggle for the fulfillment of the annual plan for housing construction and for attaining a high tempo of construction work, there is no inclination to guarantee high quality of the dwelling being opened up for occupancy. In many cases the houses are put up with significant flaws and defects, and "even more often, as the picture observes, when the building has just been completed, it already requires repair." Krokodil also offers ample pictorial proof of the fact that quality of construction is often sacrificed on the altar of speed and plan fulfillment. The newly installed resident's first joy in moving into a new apartment house often turns to frustration and gloom within a very short time. A Kaluga tenant writes: "Immediately after the housewarming in my apartment, a leak was discovered in the ceiling, the reason for which has not been established to this day. And two years have now gone by." From Leningrad comes another letter. A twelve-story building was turned over for occupancy in December 1968. However, there were no celebrations for the tenants on the upper stories, because they had no water. "There was hardly a day that we didn't go to the Leningrad City Executive Committee and to the State Construction Inspectorate with requests, pleas and demands," write the exasperated residents. "There was then no water. There is none even now," that is, almost a year later.[33] Other tenants complain of rough cement blocks jutting out of corners "right into the living rooms." Old complaints of warped flooring, window frames, even warped walls go on. Another case is that of a new nine-story apartment house in Bolshevo (Moscow Province). In 1969 the State Commission accepted the unit and gave it an evaluation of "good." (Buildings are rated "satisfactory," "good," and "excellent.") A Pravda article "House out of Order" asked the question, "How could builders have offered the new building for tenancy with such flaws?" When it rained, water sometimes got into the rooms, and the whitewash dripped from the ceilings; wooden floors were poorly laid.[34] To judge from letters to Izvestia, Pravda, and republic newspapers, the special role assigned to quality control of construction work has been superficially carried out. The capital construction administrations (in cities that have them) and capital construction departments of city executive committees and enterprises and of the architectural and construction work inspection agencies have often been too eager to accept a new apartment building regardless of its quality of construction or unfinished condition. The press abounds in stories of officials accepting buildings for occupancy that are shockingly defective or incompleted. Local Soviets, as well as enterprises, it seems, are anxious to report great advances in the areas supposedly under their jurisdiction. One of the reasons for low quality, in addition to earlier noted reasons of low skill and poor organization, is the "pressure" from city or enterprise executives on builders to build as fast as possible, especially toward the end of a quarter or year, when results of competition are summed up and when prospects for bonuses take final shape. Builders themselves rush through their work when they are about to report on the accomplishments of their planning tasks. Leaky roofs, poor sound insulation, antiquated and defective locks and other useless hardware, and absence of proper amenities are more likely to be found in houses turned over for occupancy in the crash last quarters of the plan year or at the end of a plan quarter. As an example, in 1967, 41.2 percent of all new residential buildings for the RSFSR was put into use in the fourth quarter; for the Latvian and Kirghiz republics, 44.4 percent; the Ukraine, 45.1 percent; and for the ministries and departments of union subordination, 53.3 percent of the living area for the entire year was introduced in the fourth quarter.[35] Local Soviets and their executive committees have also pressured local inspection commissions and the city's chief architect into accepting inferior, partially completed dwellings. As a result of these damaging practices, residents sometimes ask the same builders who built the apartments to come back in and refinish their own work on a private basis.[36]

Control over the quality of housing and civil construction is supposed to be exercised by several parallel organizations—state architectural and construction-control agencies, client's technical inspection, design organizations' inspection, technical control departments of enterprises of the building material industry. Certain cities have also established public control commissions for housing and cultural-service construction. Party and trade union organs play additional roles in control and inspection of house construction. The State Architectural Building Inspectorate has responsibility for preventing the release of a residential building with defects. However, local Soviets have been able to have defective or unfinished houses opened up for occupancy in spite of state control agencies. Furthermore, architectural-construction control agencies at the construction sites have had insufficient authority to influence the building process. Reportedly there are not even very many such agencies in existence. In the past, inspectors of gosarkhstroikontrol' have not had the guaranteed right of participating in the step-by-step monitoring of a house under construction and of stopping construction when they have discovered deviations or violations of plans and technical specifications. This area of control and inspection of house construction is curiously the one area where even usually strong "home-rule" advocates suggest that there be more centralization and less local Soviet influence.[37] State architecture and construction control agencies, being subordinated to executive committees of local Soviets, have in the past lacked the ability to influence the quality of housing and civil construction, and, as we have seen, have often been forced to bow to the wishes of the ispolkoms in accepting buildings with major defects. Reforms in 1969 and 1970 seem to have recognized the problem. The 1969 resolutions granted USSR Gosstroi's State Civil Construction and Architecture Committee and Union-Republic Gosstrois the right to halt construction of buildings without confirmed designs or which deviate from or violate technical specifications.[38] A more recent resolution "On Procedure for Commissioning Completed Housing

Construction Projects" stresses the client's obligation to present completed housing construction or reconstruction to the state acceptance commission for occupancy only after fulfillment of all construction and installation work and after providing the premises with modern facilities. In addition, the buildings must be provided with equipment and stock in full conformity with approved plans and estimates. Before presenting the housing construction to the state commission for certification, the client, construction, and installation organizations are charged with conducting an inspection of quality of operations and their conformity with approved norms.[39] It remains to be seen whether these minor reforms will, in fact, improve inspection work. The client, which in an increasing number of cases is the local Soviet, seems to retain responsibility for much of the control work on construction projects it is anxious to add to its list of successful new openings. State inspection agencies still seem to lack necessary safeguards against pressures of local Soviets and enterprises.

With the official birth of the concept "State of the Whole People" in the late 1950s, there was a marked proliferation of semivoluntary public control and inspection groups. Trade unionists, along with other organizations, began to flood the reading public with articles, books, and pamphlets on the importance of trade union and "obshchestvennyi" control over housing and service construction. Activists of trade union committees and their Housing and Daily Living Subcommittees (Zhilishchnobytovye komissiia), supernumerary or nonstate inspectors, or control groups of the council of trade unions, as well as voluntary public controllers entered the fast growing field of inspection and control. Of course, this growth of public nonstate involvement in such matters was hailed as a great step forward in the transition and development of Soviet society into the era of communism, when state functions would be increasingly assumed by Party, public, and nongovernmental organizations. Leningrad oblast and the Lithuanian Republic apparently took the lead in motivating trade union participation in the job of construction inspection. In both places the Councils of Trade Unions created large groups of assistant (supernumerary) inspectors, assigned the job of daily public control over construction of every building, children's institution, club, and so on. Engineers, technical people in construction, students of construction institutes and of the technicums, experienced trade union workers, activists, workers, and pensioners were enlisted to serve as auxiliary inspectors. In some organizations an inspector of the state architecture-construction control was included. At construction sites and at enterprises of building materials, control posts were created, as well as brigades of activists for carrying out massive raids and public examinations over the tempo of construction. Under the guidance of the council of trade unions, these control posts conducted their public raids or reviews, whose results were usually widely publicized in the press and discussed with the builders at meetings of the oblast committees of the trade union. Once the trade union public control groups were set up, the cities formed city commissions of control to provide public surveillance over the work of large construction organizations and enterprises. Those at the on-site control posts could then turn to the city commissions as well as to the trade union groups.[40] These "public" control organizations were not the same as the party-state control committees (or later People's Control Committees), which maintained separate systems and conducted independent raids. Though sensational exposés of construction inefficiencies and incompetence were produced by the work of some of these activist semi-public construction control groups, their real effect is difficult to evaluate. In some cases, mistakes were discovered and corrected in the course of construction. In other cases, the builders viewed the public groups as unqualified interferors, hampering plan fulfillment. Since Khrushchev's ouster from leadership in October 1964 and subsequent toning down of the concept of the State of the Whole People, there has been less publicity about these public control commissions. We may assume that while still continuing to function, they most likely have been absorbed by more formal inspection agencies and have come under tighter governmental regulation.

HOUSING REPAIRS

Repairs in housing remain a major problem in the battle to overcome the Soviet housing shortage. As the December 1969 CC Plenum stated, "the solution of the housing problem depends not only on the construction of new houses. It also depends on a thrifty attitude to earlier buildings."[41] Dwellings in many towns are "decommissioned" prematurely because of inadequate maintenance and systematic underfulfillment of plans for capital repairs. Money allocated for capital repairs has sometimes been diverted at the local levels to new construction or to a multitude of different projects having nothing to do with repair work, or inefficiently scattered over many repair jobs.[42] Funds and materials allocated for capital repair of housing were used to build a restaurant and for city landscaping in Saratov. Repair sums were spent to build vehicle garages in Alma-Ata, Minsk, and Vil'nius.[43] At times the repair funds were not used at all. During the period from 1966 to 1969 for the Soviet Union as a whole, 115 million rubles earmarked for capital repairs on the housing stock went unused. Local Soviets of the Uzbek, Georgian, Lithuanian, and Estonian republics reportedly were lagging behind even more than other republics.[44] The situation is worse with repair of housing that belongs to and is operated by departments and enterprises. While enterprises and organizations were subordinated to sovnarkhozes (regional economic councils), matters of housing repair were still worse.[45] In some cities this led to a situation where housing repairs are dragged out over a long period of time. For example, in the town of Petrozavodsk, a certain house was under repair for fifteen months and was finally rented even before the roof was repaired. Another city turned up a house under repair for three years.[46] Because of the slowness in starting and completing repair work, many new buildings deteriorate quickly and housing space is lost before its time. For instance, between 1959 and 1961, 18 million square meters of housing became useless because repairs were not made on time.[47] Difficulties in getting house repairs have become notorious and the favorite subject of Krokodil. To a greater degree than the construction organizations, the repair organizations have experienced rapid turnover of laborers, very low level of skill, an inability to get necessary building materials, and a low technical production base. As we have seen, many of the causes of needed repairs are a result of faulty construction and unfinished buildings opened for occupancy. The entire repair process is further complicated by reluctance of many tenants to be "temporarily" relocated during capital repairs, or by the city's lack of relocation quarters. Because of the slowness in completing planned repairs, those who have been moved out for an expected six months' duration sometimes find that a year, two years, or three years have gone by before they can leave their "temporary" residences.[48] The question of housing repairs has frequently stirred up official wrath and set off a round of loud accusations and counter-accusations. While attending a meeting of the Executive Committee of the Leningrad District Soviet in Moscow (April 15, 1964), Henry W. Morton observed the passions aroused over the responsibility for repair work. The first item on the agenda, "on the progress of complex and constructive repairs and building of new housing," "unexpectedly fired a series of verbal explosions that seemed like an Izvestia feuilleton come to life." The chairman of the raiispolkom opened up the meeting by calling for the district housing engineer's report on the progress of capital repairs of housing. In reply to the call, the district housing engineer let loose accusing salvos against the Repair-Construction Trust for badly failing to meet the plan for capital repairs of the first quarter of 1964. The most serious lag in repairs was in the older buildings in the center of Moscow. Under attack, the Chairman of the Repair Trust vigorously defended himself and shifted the blame for delays to frustrating shortages of building materials and to the district's Department of Registration and Redistribution of Living Space. How can the Repair-Construction Trust possibly begin its work, he argued, before tenants are relocated?

According to Mr. Morton, the Chief of the Department of Registration and Redistribution of Living Space wearily admitted the Department's failure to move the tenants. But he went on to ask

> Where am I going to put them? Not in the new homes for which there are long waiting lists. We just don't have any empty space in the district. Even if we did, people living in the center of town don't want to be sent to the outskirts, particularly since the Repair-Construction Trust cannot guarantee their speedy return.

The Chairman of the raiispolkom then joined the fray. He reminded the Repair Trust that last year the district had only placed second in Moscow and said he hoped to do better this year. "'I don't care how the repairs get done,' he said, repeatedly jabbing his index finger in their direction. 'Just get them done. . .'"[49] Easier said than done. In May 1962 the Moscow City Soviet took the initiative in attempting to win the war against neglected repairs that speedily become major capital repair jobs. The Moscow City decree stipulated the transfer of permanent housing maintenance in houses of the raion executive committees, ministries, and departments to the inhabitants of the buildings. A special passport was then introduced for the use of state housing.[50] The passport booklet tells of the floor space in each room of the apartment, corridors, kitchen, what condition the premises are in, and whether they are in need of repair. The last few pages of the little booklet contain reference information for upkeep of the apartment—short rules about how to use the plumbing system, gas apparatus, refuse chute, advice on how to wash or polish the floors, how to take care of wall surfaces, and so on.[51] These instructions may be an indication of many new arrivals to the Soviet capital from the countryside where city amenities were unknown. For these persons, urban life is still a relatively new experience. Ignorance of use has been one more factor of rapid apartment house deterioration. Authorities are attempting to impress upon citizens the fact that the extent of repairs depends largely on how the houses are operated and how tenants treat them. Of course, much of the repair work, such as winter-proofing of doors with felt, fitting of locks, and replacing of baths, wash basins, and sinks is still done by the housing offices on request of the apartment dwellers at their expense. What the 1962 Moscow decree stresses is the responsibility of tenants for maintenance of areas of common use, the courtyard, landscaping, and naturally the interior of their own apartments. Furthermore, a person regularly destroying or spoiling housing and ignoring warnings and other public measures is liable to exile from Moscow without the assignment of housing. By September of 1962, Yerevan, Krasnodar, Volgograd, and

Leningrad had followed Moscow's example of shifting a greater burden for housing repairs on the shoulders of the tenants. Moscow also led the movement for popular repair brigades.[52] Finally in 1967 Moscow took another step in its struggle to hold the line on housing repairs. It set up the Moszhilremont (the Moscow Housing Repair) to deal with repairs. Hopefully the new organization would provide a greater degree of central coordination of repair work and enable the city's housing agencies to raise the level of skills among repair workers. Even so, by the end of 1969 shortage of good quality materials for repairs and lack of well-trained staff to do the work were hampering the local government's efforts to stem the tide of repairs and to improve dramatically the quality of the work performed.[53]

The costs of major repairs have likewise caused considerable official concern. The cost of these repairs in many cases approaches and in a number of cases even surpasses the expenditure for the new construction of one square meter of living space. Thus, in Kiev the cost of one square meter of new living space in a five-story apartment house amounts to between 112 and 125 rubles, and in a nine-story apartment house to 136 to 145 rubles. Data based on 1966 figures, however, demonstrate that expenditures for the complete repair of thirty Kiev apartment houses fluctuate within the limits of 102 to 140 rubles. The number of stories of the houses is a major determinant of the level of repair costs. Expenditures per square meter of living space for major repairs are higher in low-rise houses than in multistory ones. In Kiev, in 1966, this meant that the average cost of repair of four- to six-story houses amounted to forty rubles and for two- to three-story houses to seventy-six rubles per square meter of living space.[54] Analysis carried out by the Tsentral'nyi nauchnoissledovatel'skii institut eksperimental'nogo proyektirovaniia (Ts.N.I.I.E.P.) for Housing (The Central Scientific-Research Institute of Experimental Planning for Housing) resulted in the following correlation for expenditures per square meter of living space in masonry houses:

One Story 100 percent
Two stories 85 percent
Multistory 50 percent[55]

The conclusion of the analysis favors the demolition of many one- to three-story houses in need of substantial repairs and their replacement by new multistory dwellings.

Evaluations of the quality of Soviet house construction are extremely difficult to make from a great distance. From the Soviet press we have found that questions of quality remain at the forefront of the Soviet housing picture. As more attention is paid to raising specialization and the level of skills in the construction industry, a higher quality of construction seems most likely. Recent reforms seem to point in this direction. The matter of citizens' complaints about housing also reflects a change in the problem of the quality of construction. Overwhelmingly such complaints now express dismay over the poor finishing work, the monotony of standard designs, and operations of the building's utility services. In contrast to the past, when major concentration was on basic structural faults and on the building's questionable soundness, present criticism, taken as a whole, focuses more on the "luxury" of the building's appearance and interior conveniences. To A. Allan Bates, an American specialist on industrialized housing who has visited the Soviet Union repeatedly in the last decade, and who has had the opportunity to observe, as he says, "extensively, intimately and expertly" the construction work being done in that country, the improvements in the quality of that work over the period are "striking."[56] Though the average American visitor to a newly built Soviet apartment house would have a long list of criticisms in comparison to American structures, Bates feels that this would lead to invalid conclusions. He finds that in the period from 1958 to 1969 the quality of Soviet housing has improved steadily and that the residential buildings now being erected there would be acceptable as low-cost housing anywhere in the world, including the United States.[57] From all the evidence, we conclude that there has been a definite qualitative as well as quantitative rise in Soviet housing, particularly since 1957. That this has become the case is largely due to the leadership's decisions to reorganize the house construction industry with a view to making more rational use of limited resources and better-built, more durable dwellings. At the same time, speed and volume of housing construction and plan fulfillment have retained their place as primary concerns of Soviet policies. Only in the last several years have factors of quality seriously entered into the indices of success. Quality, however, still remains in second or third place in policy-makers' estimation. Progress in quality of construction, therefore, has been real. Nevertheless, the degree of that progress remains a question mark.

PEOPLE'S CONSTRUCTION MOVEMENT

Finally, we should mention a curious, but transitory phenomenon in the history of house construction in the USSR. In Chapter 2 reference was made to the People's Construction Movement (or Popular Construction Movement), popular in the latter half of the 1950s. The method of the "people's construction" of housing involved the labor participation of workers and employees who would occupy the finished building. At the time, the People's Construction Movement was given the widest publicity and cited as another example of Soviet society's transition into the State of the Whole People. The movement was encouraged as a major way to speed the end of the housing shortage. Those persons not having housing space or in need of an improvement could be enlisted to participate in the construction, on the approval of a joint decision of the enterprise administration and the trade union committee and with the agreement of the ispolkom. Usually the labor participant concluded a written agreement with the ispolkom of the local Soviet, indicating how many hours he must work for every square meter of living space issued to him. The agreement should (but did not always) indicate the number of rooms and the exact apartment in which assigned space was to be located.[58] Participation of workers unskilled in the arts of house construction did not add to the quality or longevity of the buildings. Most residential buildings built by the People's Construction Movement tended to be small. Though still employed here and there, the method is now largely forgotten and has lost the distinguished title of "movement." It obviously did not lend itself to the industrialized, conveyor-belt techniques by which policy-makers were hoping to revolutionize construction practices.

PARASITES IN ACTION:
ILLEGAL PRACTICES IN HOUSE CONSTRUCTION

Throughout the history of civilized man, whenever the essentials of life have been in short supply through legal channels, men have invented ingenious ways to obtain them through extralegal means. Periodically in the Soviet Union anticorruption campaigns are launched that inevitably dig up sensational cases of major scandals. While publicizing measures aimed against corruption in state organizations and speculation, the Soviet press in the spring of 1962 revealed the machinations of an extensive graft system fostered by the persistent housing shortage. At the same time, the campaign against social parasites—those who managed to avoid socially useful labor or who acquired property from unearned income—merged with the anticorruption crusade and swept up homes built with unearned income or by illegally acquired materials, as well as some officials who diverted funds and materials allocated for state housing to build their own homes.

SUMMARY

Faced with the emergency conditions of wartime destruction and accelerated urbanization, Soviet architects and builders were

forced to develop and introduce "radical" new industrialized techniques
and prefabrication into the house construction industry. In the process,
policy-makers had to overcome the building industry's severe disorganization and its reluctance to employ new methods. Success
required basic reorganization and reform of the construction industry,
which was characterized by a multitude of scattered, small, poorly
trained and equipped construction organizations subordinated to a
confusingly large number of different ministries, departments, and
agencies. Concentration of construction facilities and amalgamation
of the small, weak units into larger, construction organizations with
stronger technical production bases have been major tasks of the
last decade and a half. At the same time, beginning with the major
Party-state decrees on improving housing in 1957, attention was turned
to raising the level of skills of construction workers and, more recently, to improving the bonus-incentive system in the construction
industry. In 1959 the appearance of the house construction combine
(DSK) in Leningrad marked a major step forward in reorganizing
the Soviet house construction industry. Closely suited to requirements
of the new techniques of prefabrication and assembly-line methods of
building erection, the house construction combine assumes total responsibility for the entire process of house construction, from obtaining raw materials to presenting completed houses. In contrast to
the earlier highly diffuse, uncoordinated construction organizations,
the DSK appears to be a significant advance in the building industry
and seems to be proving a successful organizational form for the
achievement of lower construction time and higher labor productivity.
Unfortunately, the greater efficiency of the house construction combines does not always mean greater city-wide coordination of construction plans. Just as the smaller construction organizations (which
are still plentiful) are subject to many different masters, the house
construction combines not uncommonly find themselves in a similar
situation. As a consequence, the city Soviet still has to struggle with
numerous agencies and interests in its efforts to realize a city house
construction system. The larger cities with privileged positions,
such as Leningrad, Moscow, and Kiev have been more successful in
gaining control over house and civil construction organizations. In
recent years these cities have also been accomplishing the greater
centralization of funds for such construction and have been acting as
single clients for all housing, cultural, and service building.

Quality still remains a prominent issue in any evaluation of
the Soviet house construction industry. We have seen that there has
been an overall improvement in the quality of construction, as policies
have shown more concern with the organization, specialization, and
skill-level of the construction industry. Reforms of the last two years
indicate that quality must be taken more into account in determining

plan success and that bonus payments should be linked more closely with quality ratings. Improvements in quality, however, have been slow, and quality still takes a backseat to the demands of plan fulfillment in terms of square meters. The drive to "open up" new buildings has led construction organizations to the typical end-of-the-plan quarter and end-of-the-year frenzy of rushed assemblage of buildings, attended by questionable construction shortcuts and careless work. The same impulse of producing a good yearly record has spurred not a few local Soviets to pressure state and "public" inspection agencies to accept faulty or unfinished buildings for occupancy. Such practices have only served to lower the quality and life expectancy of the building. It is not unusual to find that an apartment house recently commissioned is already on the city's list for urgent capital repairs.

What begins to emerge from the earlier confused picture of many organizations and agencies with seemingly innumerable lines of subordination are the vague lines of a house construction system in the making. If a system is a well-coordinated, efficient process, involving various active and related parts aimed at the fulfillment of a specific goal, we must conclude that the Soviet Union has not yet developed such a house construction system. But given the recent reforms and actual reorganizations, particularly the creation of the house construction combine, the possibility of realizing an improved Soviet house construction system seems more likely today than a decade ago.

NOTES

1. Tutuchenko, Housing in the USSR, pp. 61-62, 69-70.
2. Ibid., p. 54.
3. Cited in Tutuchenko, op. cit., pp. 58-59.
4. Izvestia, September 20, 1949, and Sosnovy, op. cit., p. 86.
5. Pravda, April 19, 1964.
6. N. S. Khrushchev, "On Control Figures for Development of USSR National Economy in 1959-1965," Pravda, January 28, 1959 (CDSP XI, no. 3: 4).
7. A. S. Boldyrev, ed., Promyshlennost' stroitel'nykh materialov (Moscow, 1967), pp. 81, 83; Herman, "Urbanization and New Housing Construction in the USSR," Industrialized Housing, pp. 25, 26, 27.
8. Posokhin, op. cit., p. 13.
9. Iu. Ryaboshapko, "Builders Pool Their Experience," Zhilishchnoe Stroitel'stvo, no. 1 (1969): 30-31.
10. CC CPSU and USSR Council of Ministers, "On Measures for Improving the Quality of Housing and Civil Construction," Izvestia, June 20, 1969, p. 4.

11. Osnovy, op. cit., p. 70.
12. Tutuchenko, op. cit., p. 87.
13. See "Vsesouiznoe soveshchanie po striotel'stvu 30 noiabria-7 dekabria 1954 godu," Abridged Stenographic Report (Moscow, 1955), p. 386; A. E. Kharitonova, "Osnovy etapy zhilishchnogo stroitel'stva v SSSR," (Main Stages of Housing Construction in the USSR), Voprosy istorii, no. 5 (1965): 56.
14. Nezhny, op. cit., p. 204.
15. Kharitonova, op. cit., p. 58.
16. Volgogradskaia pravda, October 1, 1960 (Kharitonova, p. 59).
17. Stroitel'naia gazeta, December 26, 1962.
18. A. Illarionov, "From Nothing to the Key in the Door," Pravda, December 7, 1969, p. 3 (CDSP, XXI no. 49: 35-36).
19. Nezhny, op. cit., p. 204.
20. Izvestia, August 27, 1969, p. 3.
21. Gorodskoe khoziaistvo Moskvy, no. 6 (June 1968): 1-2.
22. "The Discipline of Urban Construction," Pravda, February 24, 1970, p. 1.
23. "Observe State Discipline in Urban Construction and Housing," Official Department, Izvestia, February 25, 1970, p. 3.
24. Izvestia, July 30, 1969, August 5, 1969.
25. "On Measures for Improving the Quality of Housing and Civil Construction," Izvestia, June 20, 1969, Pravda, June 21, 1969; "On Improving the Planning of Capital Construction and Increasing Economic Incentives in Construction Work," Pravda and Izvestia, June 20, 1969 (CDSP XXI, no. 25: 8-13); G. Fomin, "Our Home and City," Pravda, July 2, 1969.
26. V. Isayev, First Vice-Chairman of USSR State Planning Committee, "Make Good Preparations for the Economic Reform in Construction and Carry It Out Successfully," Ekonomicheskaia gazeta, no. 26, June 1969, pp. 3-4 (CDSP XXI, no. 25: 16).
27. A. Boldyrev, "Rewarding with Differentiated Bonuses—Why Has Construction Time on Buildings and Installment Been Increasing?" Izvestia, July 9, 1970, p. 5 (CDSP XXII, no. 27: 28-29).
28. Ibid.
29. "On Improving the Planning of Capital Construction and Increasing Economic Incentives in Construction Work," Pravda and Izvestia, June 20, 1969.
30. Boldyrev, op. cit.
31. Ibid.
32. Isayev, op. cit., pp. 3-4.
33. Letters to Izvestia: "The New Home," Izvestia, October 14, 1969, p. 4.

34. G. Maslennikov, "House out of Order," Pravda, July 31, 1969 (CDSP XXI, no. 31 [August 27, 1969]: 22, 24).

35. S. Krasnikov, "Build Excellently," Trud, February 15, 1969, p. 2 (JPRS—USSR Trade and Services, no. 2 [March 21, 1969]: 1-2).

36. Pravda, July 31, 1969.

37. Posokhin, op. cit.

38. "On Measures for Improving the Quality of Housing and Civil Construction," Izvestia, June 20, 1969, p. 4, Pravda, June 21, 1969, pp. 1-2.

39. Official Department: "Submitted for Occupancy," Izvestia, August 11, 1970, p. 3, (CDSP, XXII, 32, p. 19).

40. See P. Ladikov, Kontrol' profsoiuzov za zhilishchno-bytovym stroitel'stvom (Moscow: Profizdat, 1963); and Genrikh Iankoit', Obshchestvennyi kontrol' za zhilishchno-bytovym stroitel'stvom (Moscow: 1964).

41. Editorial, "The Discipline of Urban Construction," Pravda, February 24, 1970, p. 1 (CDSP XXII, no. 8: 23-24).

42. Izvestia, February 25, 1970, p. 3.

43. Pravda, July 22, 1962.

44. M. Vershinin, Sector Head CC CPSU Construction Department, "The Soviets and the City Economy: The Fate of a Residential Building," Izvestia, April 11, 1970 (CDSP XXII, no. 13: 19).

45. Pravda, July 22, 1962.

46. Pravda, March 19, 1960.

47. Pravda, July 22, 1962.

48. Izvestia, September 14, 1969.

49. Henry W. Morton, "The Leningrad District of Moscow—An Inside Look," Soviet Studies XX, no. 2 (October 1968): 206-208.

50. Pravda, July 22, 1962.

51. Vechernaia Moskva, October 8, 1962.

52. Lead editorial, Sovetskaia Rossiia, August 28, 1962; Kommunist (Erevan), August 21, 1962, p. 2.

53. Pravda, December 19, 1969.

54. Ye. Ye. Klyushnichenko, "Determining the Effectiveness of Renovation of Buildings with Consideration of Major Repairs of Housing," Kiev Stroitel'stvo i Arkhitektura, no. 1 (1969): 10-11 (JPRS, "USSR Trade and Services" series, no. 11 [April 22, 1969]: 20-21.

55. B. M. Kolotilkin, Dolgovechnost' zhilykh zdanii (The Useful Life of Housing) (Moscow: Construction Literature Publishing House, 1965), p. 105 (JPRS, "USSR Trade and Services" series, no. 11 [April 22, 1969]: 21).

56. Bates, op. cit., pp. 5-6.

57. Ibid.

58. For some of the legal implications of the People's Construction Movement, see Iurii K. Tolstoi, Sovetskoe zhilishchnoe pravo (Soviet Housing Law), Leningrad Univesity, 1967, pp. 27-30.

CHAPTER
5
DISTRIBUTION AND
TENANT'S USE OF HOUSING

Once the apartment house has been built, inspected, and certified for occupancy, the next task becomes allocation of living space for tenancy. As we enter a discussion of the allocation process and of the actual settlement of the apartments, we will come in close contact with the details of Soviet Housing Law. What are the characteristics and purposes of the housing law? In relation to an examination of the housing law, we will try to discover how allocation policies and practices tie in with other, broader leadership goals. Placement in a decent apartment is of vital concern to the Soviet citizen. How does the average citizen go about finding living quarters or improving his housing conditions? Are there any categories of persons entitled to special considerations and privileges in receiving housing and, if so, why? In previous chapters the difficulties of coordination have emerged as primary concerns in the planning, financing, and constructing of Soviet housing. Does the same problem occupy the center ground in the house allocation process, or has the refinement of the housing law and optimal citizen attention and self-interest produced a practical, city-wide allocation system? Who administers and controls the assigning of living space? Earlier phases of the housing story have revealed areas of confusion and sometimes great conflict among various local governmental, ministerial, departmental, and central governmental interests. Is there likewise such interinstitutional conflict when it comes time to place the tenants in completed quarters? Since the formulation of the concept "State of the Whole People," there has been a surge of emphasis on mass public participation in administering areas of everyday life. How has the public (obshchestvennost') participated in the allocation of living space and what forms have that participation taken? And has this public participation increased the citizen's control over this vital area of his life ? These are the basic questions we will try to answer in our presentation of the Soviet house allocation process. Another section of this chapter will deal with the tenant's rights and obligations and with Soviet rent policy.

ALLOCATION OF LIVING SPACE

Under conditions of a continued housing shortage, Soviet housing law is called upon to regulate the distribution of the limited housing commodity, to promote its rational use, and to minimize conflict. At the same time, Soviet housing law serves as a significant instrument of control over population mobility and as a valuable tool of the re-wards-incentive system. As one branch of Soviet law, the housing law likewise plays a crucial role in educating the people in the values defined by the central Party leadership and in instructing Soviet citizens (in this case the resident of an apartment house) of their rights and obligations or of changes in national and republic policies.

Soviet legislation recognizes several different "housing funds," depending on ownership or management affiliation. Briefly, the housing funds are called (1) the housing fund of the local Soviets, operated by the housing agencies of the local government's executive committee; (2) the housing fund of state, cooperative (except the ZhSK or housing construction cooperative), or social enterprises and organizations—so-called departmental houses or the departmental housing fund run by the various ministries, departments, and insti-tutions; (3) the fund of the housing construction cooperatives (ZhSK), or the cooperative housing fund; and finally (4) the individual housing fund—houses built by private builders and privately operated. In all but the last category, the state controls the distribution of living space, and even in the private sector, it sets limits on the amount of space. In addition to the four basic categories of housing, there are two special housing classifications—the "Maneuver or Mobile Fund" (Man-evrennyi fond) and the "Official or Service Fund" (Fond sluzhebnykh zhilykh pomeshchenii). Usually maintained by the ispolkoms of the local Soviets, the Maneuver or Mobile Fund contains the housing provided to a person who must vacate his premises during the time of major repairs or reconstruction. Apartments or dwellings classi-fied as part of the "official-service fund" are living quarters assigned to citizens for residency at their place of work or in official buildings connected with a particular job. For example, the nature of the job may require a person to live at his place of work, as in the case of the manager of a building, a caretaker or groundkeeper, janitor, or in an official building, as in the case of medical workers or educators (nursing homes, sanitoria, educational institutions, museums). The

"Official-Service Fund" also includes dwellings assigned to a defined category of workers established by union or republic legislation, such as specialists, directors, chief engineers.[1] The category embraces housing of important party and government people. Focus here will be on the allocation process in the housing fund of the local Soviets, with some discussion of the distribution procedure in departmental housing.

The main concern of the person in need of housing is to get his name put on the waiting list for housing maintained by the ispolkom. The fundamental principles for waiting lists are the same for the local Soviets and for the departments. First of all, the ispolkom establishes the list at the citizen's place of permanent residence or at his place of work. The individual seeking better living conditions starts out by filing an application with his local housing operations office (ZhEK). Attached to his application is a copy of his certificate of occupancy, which describes his present housing: its size, number of rooms, whether it is an individual apartment or shared, the number of persons occupying it. If the person is seeking space in a building owned by his work organization, he must also provide his personal file, which contains his labor record and recommendations from his work and social groups. From the housing operations office, papers are sent to the appropriate city agency on waiting lists or redistribution of living space. In an attempt to speed up the lengthy distribution process, a 1968 union law stipulates that applications for placing citizens on the registry for the receiving of dwelling space must be examined within one month, and within seven days for veteran's applications. The leadership of the ispolkom and of the enterprises may extend the period for deciding on an application by one more month, and by another fifteen days in the case of servicemen.[2] Only a decision of the ispolkom, or if the application is made at the place of work, the joint decision of the organization's administration and Factory-Plant or Local Committee (FZMK) of the trade union council, affirmed by the executive committee (ispolkom) of the local Soviet, can put a person's name on the waiting list. Violation of the general rule for placement on the waiting lists of enterprises providing housing through the place of work leads to a certain degree of confusion and a drawing out of time before apartments are occupied. Without the ispolkom checkup, it has been much easier for members of the same family to register in two places. Some republics have tried to close this loophole by establishing that every family may be registered for the assignment of living space only in one place, by choice of the family.[3] The need for housing or for an improvement in housing conditions must be clearly shown. Those citizens who own a house that is accessible and habitable are usually denied a place. On the other hand, those having no lodgings, extremely inadequate facilities less than the

minimal norm (in Leningrad in 1967, less than 4.5 square meters),
or poorly built housing are almost always given a place on the waiting
lists. Because of the housing shortage, thorough verification of the
applicant's present housing condition is a necessity. Several official,
semiofficial and semivoluntary agencies participate in investigating
the petitioner's situation. These organizations will be discussed below. In the larger cities citizens are placed on the waiting lists by a
decision of the raiispolkom (the district executive committee) on the
recommendation of a commission on housing questions. If the individual is unhappy with the raiispolkom's decision, he may appeal to
the higher city ispolkom. While attending a session of a raiispolkom
in Moscow, Henry Morton noted that one of the items on the agenda
was appeal cases by individuals who wanted to move into better living
quarters. Persons appealing before the raiispolkom had been turned
down by the district's commission on housing questions. In this case,
Morton observed that most petitioners came from the more privileged
strata of society and were seeking to bypass the longer priority system.[4] Soviet legal writers stress the fact that once citizens are on the
waiting lists, they are assigned living space strictly on the basis of
their turn, unless special resolutions apply to them.[5] The more important enterprises, however, have been known to exert pressure to
improve an employee's position on the city-wide waiting list. Party
membership or position may also influence the outcome of housing
decisions. Housing agencies are often in poor circumstances to resist
Party suggestions. V. Isaev, a Leningrad high official, has criticized
this practice, underlining that "if a person who has been waiting in
line for a long time suddenly finds out that someone has gotten ahead
of him, this will undermine his faith in justice."[6] The allocation process once again points out the contradiction between a policy that
views housing as a public service and the right of all citizens and at
the same time ties housing to the rewards system. In the same article
in which he expressed concern for undermining faith in justice, Isaev
also expressed approval of the national policy of giving priority in
housing "to those who do excellent work." In the years 1962 to 1964,
and once again since the end of 1969, government, Party, and trade
union officials and lawyers have been reminding those involved in
the distribution of housing that the socialist principle "to each according to his labor" must be a primary consideration in housing
decisions. At the November 1962 Central Committee Plenum, for
example, Khrushchev launched a campaign against all manner of labor
shirkers. The Party Chief pointed out the necessity of making the
distribution of apartments "dependent on the uninterrupted length of
work at the enterprise and building."[7] The publication of letters from
many workers' collectives in Pravda followed during July and August
1963. Turnover of labor personnel was pointed to as a genuine scourge

of production, and all letters enthusiastically supported Khrushchev's suggestion of linking the distribution of living quarters to an estimation of the applicant's socially useful work.[8] Even after Khrushchev's ouster, labor leaders continued to denounce the practice of giving the same preference for housing assignments to workers with different work records and lengths of service.[9] The conflict here seems to be greater than that between housing as a public service or incentive. It seems to be a peculiar manifestation of the ambiguities of the transition period to communism. With the official declaration that the Soviet Union had entered that transition period to communism, the goals of communism seemed closer. Yet, the banner of communism— "from each according to his ability, to each according to his need"— appeared to be interfering with the banner of socialism— "to each according to his labor." During the last five years (1969-73), Comrade Brezhnev has reiterated more than once the importance of linking the assignment of good housing with a record of good labor discipline and productivity, and of placing a worker's name further down the waiting list for housing if his record shows weak labor discipline. The transition period to communism is proving a very long one indeed.

Naturally a change in one's housing condition or job may mean loss of the right to remain on the waiting list. Those who have improved their housing condition or been dismissed from their enterprise or organization most likely will be removed from the lists, which are supposed to be checked annually. Since 1966 a person's place on the waiting list may be altered as a result of the ukaz of the Presidium of the Supreme Soviet of the USSR "On Strengthening the Responsibility for Hooliganism." According to this law, those persons committing hooliganistic acts may lose their turn on the waiting lists for housing.[10] The vague meaning of the term "hooliganistic act" opens this law up to potential abuse and arbitrary application.

The search for good housing occasionally leads citizens to employ highly unscrupulous means, in addition to the usual one of bribery. While repairing a recently vacated apartment, for example, workmen discovered an old letter. After a very brief battle with their collective conscience, the workers gave in to their burning curiosity. And, naturally, they were horrified with what they learned. The letter turned out to be a bit of practical, but unofficial advice on how to get housing:

I am writing an answer and a little advice right away. When you are demobilized, hang onto your various documents. They will come in handy because then they will take you right away in the city executive committee. . . .
     You will go to Voronezh or some other such city, and the military commissar will ask you right away:

What did you come here for? So you beat him over the
head. Not literally, of course, but start yelling that you
are suffering from headaches and also that you have received large doses of radiation. Try to yell as much as
possible. Let them think that you are insane. He will sit
in the commission for allotting apartments to officers in
the city executive committee and he will tell the members
of the commission that you are not well and that they should
give you an apartment without waiting.

Then go every day to the military commissariat and
the city executive committee and demand an apartment.
If you go every day, believe me, they will get the idea that
you are sick and that you will not leave them alone, and
they will give you an apartment if you will just leave them
alone.

The letter writer goes on to describe other devious means for receiving an apartment and essential commodities such as a refrigerator.
Because of the harsh penalties, including the retroactive use of the
death penalty for economic crimes (bribery), in 1962, the author
issues a clear warning to the demobilized officer. "If, however, you
think about giving someone a small bribe, be careful. It is very hard
and dangerous now." Should the city and military authorities tell the
officer to go to the virgin lands, to Siberia, or to the Altai, the advice
giver supplies a ready reply:

Answer them politely that the army deprived you of your
health, made you a cripple, an invalid, and that you must
get well and be under the care of doctors, and that you do
not wish to die in Siberia, where the climate is so harsh.
So this is my message. Not a word to anybody in your
unit about this.

Apparently the advice was well received.[11]

Accusations of parasitism under the notorious Anti-Parasite
Laws of the early 1960s, which allowed for administrative exile, provided another way to obtain housing.[12] One distraught woman, for
example, wrote the following letter to Izvestia:

Something terrible happened to me. On July 31 I was
awakened at 6 o'clock in the morning and driven to the
militia station. Without any explanation I was kept there,
hungry and hastily dressed, until 5 o'clock in the evening
and was then sent to court. There it was decided in ten
minutes that I should be deported from Kiev for two years.

I cannot understand why I have been placed in the situation of a criminal. . . .[13]

The letter writer was deported from Kiev on the grounds of her neighbor's letters, which asserted that she was a typical loafer. Immediately after the woman's conviction, the "good neighbor" Smertenko applied for her room![14]

In most cases, however, the person in need of housing takes the longer, but safer route of applying through regular channels and of waiting patiently for an assignment. The length of his wait and the size of the allotted housing space will depend on several factors in addition to his need, work, and social record. If the apartment hunter belongs to a privileged category, he will be entitled to special consideration on the priority list or to extra housing space. In the RSFSR the right to additional living space for privileged categories of persons was established in 1930. Obviously, the five-year plans for industrialization demanded the enlistment and active cooperation of specialized workers and leaders and scientific and technical personnel. Creative artists—writers, composers, artists, architects, and sculptors—scientists, certain professors, and military men above the rank of colonel are among the privileged categories. In addition, higher-level Party and government workers, as well as persons suffering from certain illnesses, are eligible for increased living quarters or advantages in housing assignments. In general, the policy insures housing to "advanced cadres" of constructors and workers of transport and communications. This practice is explained by the fact that since the creation of communism depends on the creation of society's full material technical base, industry holds a special place and workers of certain main industries should be given preference in the receipt of housing.[15] Those entitled to the use of additional living space include (1) leading workers of state, party, professional, cooperative, and other social organizations, and executives (otvetstvennye rabotniki) of state institutions and enterprises, according to a list of posts established by the ispolkoms jointly with the interested organizations. Included in this list are engineers and technical people. This category seems to include the elite corps of most Party, state, and economic organizations; (2) persons suffering from diseases enumerated by the republic ministry of health—particularly contagious tuberculosis; (3) members and corresponding members of the Academy of Sciences, scientific workers who have received a higher degree or an academic title. The scientific worker's right to additonal space was insured by a decree dating back to March 1933; (4) persons who have received honorific titles for services—Heroes of Labor, Heroes of the Soviet Union, and Heroes of Socialist Labor; Honored Scientists, Honored Art Workers, Honored Technical Workers, People's and Honored Artists of the Republic, Honored Teachers,

Honored Doctors, and so on; (5) artists, sculptors, architects, writers, and composers who are members of their respective creative unions; (6) inventors, discoverers, and "rationalizers," those who have given valuable suggestions to the state; (7) as noted above, military men of the commanding or directing staff with the rank of colonel or higher; (8) lawyers who are fulfilling tasks of the collegium of lawyers and of social organizations, on application of the collegium's Presidium; (9) medical and dental doctors approved by the Department of Health who practice in residential buildings. It should be noted that those medical men who are engaged in "private practice" are entitled to additional space for an office, but at a rent level above the rates for basic living space; (10) individual or personal pensioners (those granted special, personal pensions as a result of particular service.)[16] In individual republics, deputies of the USSR Supreme Soviet and of Union Republic Soviets have the right to use additional housing space. Highly qualified artists, performing musicians, and pedagogues likewise receive housing privileges. Those women in the RSFSR who are fortunate and fertile enough to be called "Mother-Heroine" (having given birth to ten or more children) or have been awarded either the order of "Maternal Glory" (seven to nine children) or the "Medal of Motherhood" (five to six children) also receive special consideration for improved living conditions.[17] Large families, however, have been finding it difficult to improve their housing when needed. Searching for a policy to stimulate the sagging birth rate, Soviet economists and demographers have been calling for legislation providing preferences in obtaining housing for families with a certain number of children. The economist D. Valentei, for example, suggests that an important measure to increase the birth rate would be "a decision on the priority allocation to families with two, three or more youngsters."[18] The category of persons eligible for additional housing may be changed, depending upon local housing conditions. The RSFSR, for example, allows the ispolkoms of the local Soviets to broaden the circle of persons who may be assigned additional space, if local conditions warrant this action.

The additional housing assigned may consist of a separate room, regardless of size. If a separate room is not available, the norm for additional space is ten square meters (nine square meters in the BSSR, ten to twelve square meters in the Georgian Republic, fifteen square meters in Latvia, ten to twelve in the Uzbek Republic, 13.65 in the Ukraine) and where indicated by law, twenty square meters (for example, creative artists and scientific workers).[19] If more than one member of the same family has the right to use extra space, the total additional space cannot be more than twenty square meters or one separate room.[20] This additional housing is subject to the same rent level as basic housing space. Consequently, there is a

real, though modest advantage in being designated eligible for such
housing privileges. Living space that goes beyond the limits of the
basic norms with the right to additional space taken into account is
labeled "superfluous" and is subject either to a higher rent payment
or withdrawal from the tenant's use.

Special priority waiting lists (though not necessarily privileges
of additional space) have also been established for invalids of World
War II, families of servicemen killed or lost in defense of the USSR,
tenants living in cellars, wrecked or dilapidated houses and barracks,
or in housing to be torn down, troops of the Committee of State Security
(KGB), and finally persons singled out by the government.[21] Part of
the living space in newly erected buildings is set aside for invalids
and families of participants of World War II. According to a 1945
union resolution, ministries and departments are to turn over to ispolkoms 10 percent of all the living space of buildings they have erected
(more recently, excluding any housing space built by enterprise incentive funds). In this space the executive committees are obliged
to settle exclusively those invalids, families of soldiers lost in the
Great Patriotic War, as well as families of servicemen and demobilized
soldiers.[22] There are now housing privileges to induce workers to
move to regions of the Far North or to localities equivalent to regions
of the Far North. According to a February 10, 1960, ukaz, living
space in accord with the standard of the area is guaranteed such workers and their families. These workers have even been granted the
right to require housing from the enterprise. In the event the enterprise should not insure the worker living space, he has the right to
break the labor agreement.[23] Recalling Alexander Solzhenitysn's
short story "Matyrona's House," we also find that teachers in village
localities have special housing "privileges"—gratis living space.

In the early 1950s and again in 1959, Timothy Sosnovy found that
the characteristic feature of the Soviet housing economy was the unequal distribution of living space among various social groups.[24] We
have seen that since 1930 the specialist, the Party and government
bureaucrats, the labor aristocracy—the professional intelligentsia—
have been beneficiaries of privilege-bearing policies. Besides the
overt policy of increasing labor productivity, Soviet policy has sought
to use housing as a means for enlisting the political support and loyalty
of those groups the leadership views as essential to the maintenance
of their own power, as well as to the continued economic and social
advancement of the nation. In contrast to the housing of average citizens, the housing of members of the elite professional intellegentsia
has often been of superior quality and a more attractive style. Receiving space in the House of Soviet Writers or the House of Scientists
is a significant reward in a society where the housing shortage remains a major problem. Landing an apartment in such a building is

not always a reward for distinguished service. It may be an indication
of political reliability plus a little political "know who." Clauses in
the housing privilege laws, such as ". . . and any person specifically
designated by the government," give a high degree of flexibility to
those in positions of influence to use housing for patronage purposes.
Just as this privileged housing rewards the faithful as well as the
skillful and outstanding, it may also be used to punish the less reliable.
In such a way, housing becomes part of the informal control system
available to Party and governmental leaders. Top members of the
government, the Central Committee and Politburo, the secret police,
and military have the opportunity to live in specially constructed residences in Moscow. At the same time, too much should not be made
of these housing privileges. In many cases they are small advantages.
It is still not uncommon to find a higher paid professional living next
to a lower paid semiskilled worker. A housing study of most noncommunist countries would naturally reveal vast differences between
the housing of the average citizen and that of the country's elite strata.
When focusing on the Soviet Union, the promises of the Revolution and
the subsequent years of leadership in the name of the toiling masses
provide automatic yardsticks with which to criticize actual practices.
These promises of a more just society and claims of a classless
society cause the Western student of contemporary Soviet society and
politics to look for and emphasize its inequalities. The danger of this
reaction is the tendency to overemphasize and overconcentrate on the
system's inequities, and hence to underestimate solid achievements.
Such an approach may try to make unique a situation that exists throughout the world and so present a distorted picture. All societies reward
those persons they feel are most essential for survival or advancement. One society may allow draft deferments to certain occupational
categories and provide very high salaries to particular groups; another
may offer those persons better shelter. The main difference in this
case between Soviet and American society lies not in the fact that inequalities and privileges exist in one or the other society, but rather
in the fact that each society has a very different way of determining
national purposes and of formulating its values. Criticism should
not be leveled at the policy that insures housing privileges for some.
It should be directed at the decision-making process, concentrated
in relatively few hands, that ultimately define the values of Soviet
society.

Since the mid-1950s, the local Soviets have been increasingly
allocating the bulk of all housing. Dating from the same period, executive committees (ispolkoms) have been officially encouraged to
enlist the deputies, housing commisssion, and representatives of
trade unions, the Komsomol, and other "public" organizations in
drawing up lists of those who need better housing. But complaints in

the Soviet press indicate that there are still quite a few cities where new apartments are allocated behind closed doors, without the participation of representatives of the public. In any case, the ispolkom and its agencies remain the center of focus in the house allocation process. Great stress is placed on workers' participation in certain phases of housing distribution. In effect, the increased role of citizens in investigating housing conditions of applicants for improved living quarters, and the local Soviet's degree of control over allocation, facilitate the participant's readiness to accept the ispolkom's final decisions on housing questions and improve the local Soviet's work in implementing the national and local housing policy.

Standing housing committees of the city and raion Soviets (composed of from three to fifty city or raion deputies) and of housing and technical experts and citizen volunteers, have been organized to examine applications for the assignment of housing, decide questions of the distribution of new living space, and pass on recommendations to the ispolkom. One of their main functions is to see that the executive committee's decisions are being carried out. The raion Standing Committee on Waiting Lists and Distribution of Living Space may check the work of the departments involved with those aspects of the housing problem. It may conduct an investigation of the housing operations offices (ZhEK) of the raion to discover any weaknesses or areas for improvement. In one such check, for example, the Standing Committee that set out to discover how much superfluous or vacant space was available in its district found that the housing offices were doing a poor job in carrying out the Leningrad city decision on improving information on vacant housing spaces. The committee members found cases in which rooms had been unoccupied for an entire year. As a result, the local Soviet deputies who sat on the committee decided to pay more attention to controlling the work of the housing offices and house management. Each deputy on the committee was assigned to a particular housing office to insure the desired improved control. At the same time, in an effort to increase efficient operations of the housing fund, committee members undertook a tightening of connections with the organs of police and department of waiting lists.[25] In addition to deputy members, the standing committees enlist the help of citizen activists. These committees act as hearing committees on various aspects of the housing situation. Their investigations and exposés bring pressure to bear on incompetent bureaucrats or on officials reluctant to carry out the latest state directives. They also provide valuable channels for the collection of important information on city problems and for airing citizens' grievances. (In Moscow there are some seventeen standing committees covering all aspects of city life, including housing. They enlist the services of 4,000 deputies and some 7,000 activists.)

Even more in keeping with the development of the State of the Whole People has been the appearance of commissions on housing problems. These commissions are, in reality, societal (that is, nongovernmental) organs under the ispolkoms, operating at the raion level. The commission on housing problems consists of a chairman (who is so usually a deputy chairman of the ispolkom), a deputy chairman (who is the chairman of either the council of trade unions or the city's house distribution agency), and members—deputies of the Soviet, representatives of social organizations, workers from housing and municipal organs, representatives of the party and trade union organizations, workers, and pensioners. The commission's composition is approved by the corresponding ispolkom. Leadership positions clearly indicate that these housing commissions are not loosely controlled "public" organizations. Instead, they are led by the same men who direct most of the city's activities. The major task of the commission is the verification of the applicant's living conditions. The so-called voluntary housing commissions have the job of carefully examining every petition (including the appropriate documents) for the assignment of housing. Then the commission prepares materials and makes its suggested decisions on distribution and exchange of living space for the ispolkom. In the Leningrad District of Moscow, for example, a housing commission composed of eleven members decided 90 percent of the housing cases, and its recommendations were automatically approved by the raiispolkom.[26] On the housing commission's recommendations, the ispolkom decides who should be placed on the waiting lists, what space to assign, and whether to allow an exchange of apartments. In addition to these commissions, there are also auxiliary social-voluntary inspectors in the field of waiting lists and the distribution of housing space. These societal inspectors—often activist workers, officers in the reserves, retired old Bolsheviks, or pensioners—do much of the leg and paperwork in checking out the living conditions of petitioners.[27]

A recent development in local government, having its origins in early Soviet experience, is the deputies' council (deputatskie sovety or sovet deputatov), in some cities called the deputies' group. Created in Moscow in the early 1960s, the deputies' council is composed of all deputies whose districts are within the limits of the house operations office. There are now more than 440 such councils in Moscow, composed of from eight to thirty deputies, depending on the size of the microraion. In Moscow and Leningrad, besides its other functions (discussed in a later section) the deputies' council examines citizens' applications for the improvement of living conditions and for the assignment of vacant space. Before the formation of the deputies' councils, all vacant (not new) living space had been assigned by the boards of the raiispolkom. In certain districts of Moscow, the deputies' councils have even assumed the job of distributing living space in newly constructed buildings. Members of the councils hold regular hours on set days for receiving the population. As a rule, citizens turn to the deputy if they have been refused a place on the waiting list, or if they want to give the distribution process a push. At least the deputy's appeal can bring the question of allocation once again before the raiispolkom's commission on housing problems.[28] Thus the deputy and the deputies' councils provide important channels for citizens' petitions and often operate as ombudsmen to help citizens through the bureaucratic housing tangle. Since the deputies' council is formed at the House Operations Office (ZhEK), it is in close proximity to the housing fund. According to Soviet writers, this was done to insure the development of a new form of public participation in the distribution of living space. Particularly in the distribution of vacant living space, the Moscow deputies' councils have assumed the leading role. This fact leads us to conclude that one of the original aims in setting up the councils was to keep an eye on the housing offices and to root out the inefficiency of unlived-in housing space.

The distribution of dwellings in departmental housing involves a procedure different from that of housing under the local Soviets. In the case of departmental housing, trade union committees do much of the preliminary checking of living conditions—verifying the applicant's documents. But as happens so often in Soviet life, those committees charged with enlisting the broad participation of the masses in deciding questions of daily living, are bypassed by a small group of persons holding real executive power in the enterprise, namely, the Party and economic leaders. Such leaders use the trade union committees to put the public seal of approval on their decisions. Even Pravda has criticized the practice of certain factory managers, or of small groups selected by the management, in the distribution of housing without the participation of trade union committees.[29] These small groups, known as "triangles" or special commissions, as a rule consist of management's men in the majority, in violation of the Party-state decree of joint administration-trade union decision in the distribution of housing.[30] The regular procedure for seeking living space in departmental housing involves applying to the Housing and Daily Life Commission of the trade union's shop committee. The procedure is very similar to that involving the ispolkom's commissions. After examining the application and verifying the applicant's living conditions, the commission gives its recommendation to the shop committee. When need, length of service, and even labor productivity of two applicants are equal, the commissions are instructed to learn of the applicant's general attitude toward labor, as well as his participation in the collective's life. Here is an interesting illustration of the policy that places a premium on the value of labor and

community involvement. In the case of a certain A. Riabinin and one
V. Voronov, Riabinin was placed eighteenth on the waiting list and
Voronov twenty-sixth. But when the shop received twenty-one apartments, it decided to move Voronov into eleventh place, and not to
assign Riabinin a new apartment. It seems that the shop administration learned that Voronov—a leading production worker—leads a brigade of Communist labor (echoes of Stakhanov). Furthermore, Voronov
turns out to be an active "rationalizer" (that is, strives to economize
the process of work) and devotes much time to communal work. The
other man, Riabinin, in the meantime, has become famous for drunk-
enness, truancy, and loafing.[31] One wonders how the two men's true
natures were so badly represented in the first place. Besides indicating the values seen of worthy of reward, the case brings up questions of why the original positions on the waiting list? Did one worker
have the right "know who" or was it simply an oversight of an overburdened commission? In another case, the decision was much clearer.
One worker did not receive a higher place because he shied away from
communal work.[32]

It is difficult to conclude that the greater involvement of the
public in the house allocation process has actually increased the citizen's control over his basic housing needs. The so-called "nonstate"
voluntary committees and commissions set up to handle housing questions are carefully led by state and Party officials, and their activities
closely watched and reviewed by regular state organs of government.
Public participation in the distribution of living space has exposed
a greater number of people to the complexities of the housing situation
and has relieved official city agencies of some of the burdens of inspecting housing conditions. At the same time, mobilizing retired
or pensioned citizens for the job of public inspectors has meant
renewed purpose for those involved and extended service to the community—both highly desirable goals. Increased public involvement
has also broadened the flow of information from the bottom up and
further defined the process of legislation in social policies affecting
the daily lives of citizens through expanded consultation.

On the whole, the house allocation process appears to be under-
standable and manageable for most citizens. It is clear, however,
that the practice of assigning living space is not always uniform throughout the USSR. At the Twenty-Third Party Congress in March 1966,
for example, Leonid Brezhnev exhorted the Party, the Soviets, economic and trade union agencies to provide a clear-cut and strict procedure for the distribution of living space, "giving widespread publicity
to this matter."[33] Brezhnev's comments, as well as those of Soviet
lawyers specializing in housing law, indicate that in some local areas
persons responsible for the assignment of housing are ignorant of
the laws and that such a condition leads to injustices and citizen complaints.

Neither is the allocation process always a smooth operation, left to local Soviet control. Interference from "above" has at times determined distribution and disrupted local Soviet allocation plans. For example, in November 1964 the First Secretary of the Khabarovsk City Party Committee (who was also Mayor, Chairman of the City Executive Committee) wrote to Izvestia, complaining of unwarranted Gosplan meddling. In 1964 the city had obtained a plan for the erection of new housing. Suddenly an order arrived from the RSFSR Gosplan to establish 35,000 square meters for sovnarkhoz enterprises. The Party Chief-Mayor wanted to know why Gosplan was involved with allocating housing within a city. At times, some enterprises wind up with great housing preferences over other enterprises and the ispolkom has little to say. "The leaders (of the enterprises) write 'pitiful' letters. They apply to Gosplan in person, and wrest, so to speak, a few extra thousand meters," relates the Mayor. And what is derived as a result of such "centralized" housing allocation? Certain industrial enterprises in Khabarovsk received housing space per worker many times greater than that received by students, physicians, and other workers. Finally, the letter writer advocated that the right of housing allocation be transferred to the Soviets—that the Soviets' traditional function, the allocation of the housing fund, be restored. Izvestia's editors agreed, adding that the condition in Khabarovsk was not an isolated one.[34] The loss of this traditional function may have been the result of the economic-administrative reforms creating the system of regional economic councils and of the November 1962 reforms producing bifurcation of certain Party and government organs into agricultural and industrial branches. It is significant that the complaint was published in Izvestia on November 24, 1964, a month after Khrushchev's ouster. With the elimination of the sovnarkhoz system in 1965, there seems to have been a lessening of complaints about such interference from above. While the allocation process is still not totally free from Party, ministerial, and enterprisal pressures on local Soviets, the Soviets seem to have succeeded in recapturing their "traditional function" for the time being. Unlike planning and financing, the distribution of living space has, by and large, escaped "centralization" and remained part of the local administrative system.

Because of shortages, housing has not managed to escape the temptations of bribery. Earlier we read the advice to a demobilized officer on seeking an apartment by somewhat outlandish, though cautious, means. Others have not always shown such caution. In 1962 the Soviet press uncovered several sensational cases of bribery. Attention focused on Dushanbe, where a certain N. Babadzhanov, who had formerly been a member of the Tadzhik Bureau, a member of the Presidium of the Tadzhik Supreme Soviet, and First Secretary

of the Dushanbe City Party Committee, was exposed as the kingpin in
a widespread network of bribe-taking and usury. He and his associates
"stopped at nothing;" they took teaspoons, bracelets, linen, bolts of
cloth, shirts and shoes, meat and watches, and, of course, "money
and more money." Only by a bribe could one be listed on the apartment distribution register. The commission on housing questions,
which was supposed to check housing conditions and recommend
assignments, existed in name only. Its Chairman was none other than
Babadzhanov. Waiting lists were deliberately confused, citizens'
statements not examined, and no priority observed in assigning housing. With the collaboration and protection of his friend, A. Khasanov,
First Secretary of the Dushanbe City Party Committee, Babadzhanov
regularly bypassed the commission and assigned apartments at his
own discretion. Apartments were not only distributed by bribes, but
also on the basis of association and personal friendships. It seems
that the corruption had spread to many top leaders, including the
former procurator of Dushanbe City. The bribe-takers set up a regular "schedule" of fees for their services: 3,000 rubles for a one-
room apartment, 5,000 for a two-room dwelling, and 8,000 for three
rooms. The "clients" paid half the sum in advance and the rest when
they received their order of occupancy. Just to give the whole procedure a legal appearance, for a fee the officials sent false documents
to the raiispolkom stating that their clients had been on the waiting
lists for many years. Sentences for such illegal actions were very
severe; Babadzhanov was executed.[35] Though reports of this kind
are relatively rare in the press, they are instructive. Once again
they show the positions that major Party and local government figures
of a particular city occupy on so-called "nongovernmental," "voluntary-
public" organizations, and the connection between Party and government offices at the local level.

THE TENANT: RIGHTS AND OBLIGATIONS

One of the most important problems in Soviet housing law is
defining the "family member," which determines who is or is not
entitled to occupy a particular dwelling. This section will discuss
the tenant's receipt of the certificate or order of occupancy, the
definition of "family member," the lease, and the tenant's rights and
obligations, including exchanges, evictions, and housing disputes.

As the Soviet specialist on housing law Iurii Tolstoi notes, the
order of occupancy is an administrative act. It is issued by the ispolkom to the person being assigned housing space. At the moment
of its issuance to the citizen it conveys to the citizen the right to
occupy a particular living space.[36] Upon receipt of his order of

131

occupancy (orderoderzhatel'), the individual has, depending on his locale, from there to ten days to move into the assigned quarters. It is very rare, however, for housing agencies to raise the question of declaring an order invalid on the grounds that the assigned occupant went beyond the period for presenting the order to the housing office.[37] In addition to the court's right to declare an "order" invalid when housing was obtained by illegal methods, several legalists have been arguing that in the present improved conditions any order given for the occupancy of space that is not isolated, that is, space that forms part of a room, or a room connected with another room by a common exit, should be declared invalid.[38] After the tenant presents his order of occupancy to the housing management, a lease officially formalizing the use of the living quarters may then be concluded. The lease or tenancy agreement (dogovor naima zhilogo pomeschcheniia) defines the rights and obligations of both the house management (domoupravlenie or zhilishchnoekspluatatsionnye kontory—House Operations Offices or ZhEK) and the tenant. While the lease may be for a definite period of time, or may have no time limit, in most republics the lease stipulates a five-year period in houses of the local Soviet and departments. In most cases, this time limit is a mere formality, since expiration of the period of the agreement does not at all mean that the right to use the housing ceases to exist. Renewal right is guaranteed by law and is almost always automatic. Only systematic tenant refusal to fulfill his obligations or systematic violations of the lease's terms can lead to a court action withdrawing the right to occupancy (that is, eviction) (Article 328, Civil Code, RSFSR, 1964). The tenant has the right to terminate the lease at any time (Article 329, RSFSR Civil Code). In contrast to earlier legislation, Article 300 of the Civil Code of RSFSR (1964) establishes that in houses of the local Soviets and departments, the object of the lease may be only an isolated living space, consisting of an apartment either of one or several adjacent rooms.[39] That practice does not always conform to desired policy as expressed in the law may be seen by the need for lawyers to argue that the courts should declare invalid those orders of occupancy granted for housing space not considered isolated. Once again policy mixes both present and expected improved conditions and does not necessarily provide a practical guide for actual shortage circumstances.

Soviet housing laws and model leases make clear that the housing management (which may be the housing office or an agency of an institution or enterprise), known as the leasing agent (naimodatel'), is responsible for taking care of necessary capital repairs, which usually include replacement as a result of normal use of the basic structural parts of the building, doors, windows, floors, stoves, repair of central heating, plumbing, bathroom equipment, and of garbage disposal. For his part, the tenant (nanimatel') must pay for current repairs of living spaces and places of common use in the apartments. "Current repairs" include the following type of work: whitewashing ceilings, painting or wallpapering walls, painting floors, doors, and inside window sashes, replacing the glass of broken windows, replacing window and door fittings, and repairing electrical wiring inside the apartment.[40] It is this area of current repairs where most housing disputes occur. Besides the obligations for current repairs, the tenant is also held responsible for keeping his apartment in good order, for using electricity, water, and gas as economically as possible, for observing the rules of socialist conduct, and for paying rent.

One of the resident's most important obligations, imposed "not only by the norms of the law, but also by the norms of communist morality," is the strict observance of the rules of everyday order. Tenants must maintain absolutely quiet in their apartments from eleven o'clock p.m. until seven o'clock a.m. During these "quiet hours" the playing of musical instruments, singing, dancing, loud telephone conversations, and noise are "categorically forbidden." Other residents' requests to lower the sound of the radio or instruments during the restricted period must be met. In addition, when the tenant leaves his apartment, he must turn off all his loudspeaker systems. Use of record players, radios, or loudspeakers on the balconies or on window-sills with opened windows is also against the regulations governing socialist conduct. These rules are absolutely essential to make living possible under conditions of a housing shortage.

Inevitably, disputes also arise between inhabitants about the responsibility for cleaning places of common use, payment for municipal facilities, and use of auxiliary spaces. Depending on the degree and frequency of a person's violation of the rules of everyday order, the offending party may be answerable to a social housing committee, a comrades' court, or even to a regular court. The offender is morally answerable and subject to the judgment of the Kollektiv in which he lives and works.[41]

As far as rights go, in addition to the right to housing, the tenant has the right to sublet, exchange, or have his dwelling space held in reserve for a definite period of time. All legal commentaries, as well as the laws themselves, stress that the tenant is given living quarters for his and his family's living in. But the tenant does not have the right to use the dwelling as a secondary or extra living space, nor the right to sublet the apartment systematically, thereby creating a source of unearned income. Thus, payment for the use of a subleased dwelling is agreed upon by both parties involved, but it cannot be more than the amount of the apartment rent the leasee pays for this lodging. If the subleasee uses household articles and utensils, the general sum paid to the tenant cannot be more than twice the amount of the apartment rent.[42]

Member of the Family

Housing rights and obligations are directly related to the definition of a member of the family. In Soviet housing law the closeness of the relation does not have a decisive meaning. For example, Article 301 of the RSFSR Civil Code includes as members of the family not only the tenant's children and parents, but also other relations, without establishing the limits in the degree of their closeness. In assigning living space, the executive committees often include relatives by marriage of the tenant in determining members of his family.[43] Inevitably, serious conflicts arise when the legal definition of such intimate relations is a prerequisite for the right of occupancy. Part III of Article 301 of the RSFSR Civil Code defines members of the tenant's family as his spouse, children, and parents, with the right of living space if they meet a major condition—they must live together with the tenant. Other relatives (through marriage, as well as dependents unable to work) can be considered members of the tenant's family if they live with him and have a common household economy with the tenant.[44] The "housing closeness," particularly in the past, frequently led to hastily formed romances and marriages. Mikhail Zoschenko's satires are often directed to the peculiar relations arising out of the housing shortage. One such story depicts the trials of a certain young man who undergoes the grueling task of attempting to woo a charming comrade under the cautious eyes and loud mouths of her many roommates. The young woman lives on top of an old trunk, and that is where the timid Ivan asks her to become his wife. "No," screams one outraged toiler from behind a hot water tank. "Tell him NO, Maria Petrovna," cries another mortified fellow, who quickly estimates the potential damage in square meters. "How could you do this to us?" "It's all a trick to get a place to live." "Never!" "He's just marrying you for your square meters!"—are all shouted at once. Overwhelmed by the sudden outburst of sentiment and about to crawl away in utter defeat, the suitor lets slip his intention to take his beloved off her trunk to live in his apartment. With a lightning reversal the girl's "friends" now wish her the best of luck, heap a million blessings on the dear couple, and wish them many happy years together—in the groom's apartment. One wonders what the scene would be like at Ivan's apartment.

Because of the connection between housing and family relations, marriage was and is sometimes seen as the speediest means to attain the desired end—a place to live. The interviews of the Harvard Project on the Soviet social system clearly illustrate the practice:

> The apartment situation often forced people into marriage
> —that is, girls married men with a suitable room and

vice-versa. They could then divorce and claim a part of
the room they had married. It could often be heard said
that someone had married a twenty square meter room.
Then after two weeks or a month of marriage, the person concerned would divorce. The room would then remain in the possession of the least scrupulous one with
the strongest nerves. He or she would proceed to organize parties every night in his or her section of the
room. These parties would usually be very noisy, smoky
and drink-filled. As a final recourse, if his ex-wife had
by that time not yet decided to move out, the man would
bring in women. The ex-owner of the room would then
attempt to find another man with a suitable room and the
cycle would begin all over again.[45]

Although under the improved conditions of housing in the Soviet
Union the need for "marrying a room" has lessened considerably,
there are still some cases where the right to several square meters
is the basic relation-forming factor. Jurists argue that a person who
enters into a registered marriage with the aim of getting a living
space cannot be considered a member of the family and thus may be
evicted through a court suit. The greatest difficulty becomes proving
the person's intention at the time of marriage—a near impossibility.[46]
Divorce, then, does not usually do away with the right to occupy living
space. The former spouse continues to exercise that right. Even if
the marriage is declared invalid by the court, the right to living space
of the former spouse is preserved if the marriage is invalid through
no fault of the former spouse.[47] These housing laws that concern
the rights of the family member are not only safeguards for the individual family members but, more importantly, are intended to provide
a stabilizing influence in family relations and to cut down on the degree
of tenant mobility and turnover. Presumably, less turnover also means
better care of the apartment. Whether they actually achieve the goal
of stabilizing complicated family relations remains in doubt. More
than a few violent crimes have been reported relating to housing disputes between married or divorced persons, in-laws, and other relatives. The housing laws may contribute to the slowing down of tenant
turnover, but they may also contribute to the tenseness of family relations. Furthermore, it is not difficult to understand why some commissions on housing and some ispolkoms have been accused of "ignorance" of the housing law. The law dealing with the "family member" is both extremely detailed and yet vague. The RSFSR Civil Code
(Article 301, Part III), for example, speaks of the housing rights of
children and parents, but does not say that it is a question only of the
tenant's (leasee's) children and parents. This law is widely interpreted

as meaning the children and parents of any member of the family.
We saw that the law speaks of "other relatives" as part of the family
without establishing the degree of this relationship. Yet, when it
speaks of dependents "unable to work" as part of the family, the law
is very precise. "Unable to work" means those who have not reached
the age of 16, students under 18, women older than 55, men older
than 60, and invalids. In almost all cases, including change of the
dependent's status, the right to housing is preserved if the person
continues to live in the leased dwelling.[48] Once an individual has his
foot in the door, legally that is, as Nikita Khrushchev might put it,
"you can't smoke him out, no matter what kind of gas you use." One
situation involving housing rights and family membership has been
definitely cleared up by the Collegium of the Supreme Court of the
RSFSR—to the relief of many Soviet papas. The higher court decided
that the republic Supreme Court wrongly recognized as a member of
the family with the right to occupy living space the tenant's daughter
who had gone to live in a different place as a result of marriage,
lived there for some time, and then returned with her husband to her
father's place with the understanding that it would be a temporary
stay.[49] By freely leaving one residence and settling in another, the
right to occupy the former is lost.

The law also provides for the inclusion of new members of the
family. In doing so, it strives for the least amount of internal friction
or upheaval. According to the RSFSR Civil Code (Article 302), if a
person is seeking to enter an apartment as a new resident with the
rights of a member of the family, he must be able to produce a written
agreement with the consent of all adult members of the given family.
This rule does not apply to minor children who are moving into their
parents' residence In all other cases, however, if just one member
of the family does not give his consent, the new resident cannot be
installed on the basis of rights of a member of the family. The law
allows for a considerable amount of leeway when it comes to making
living arrangements with those who do not move in. Even if they are
accepted as members of the family with an equal right to living space,
the law is flexible in permitting specific agreements between the
newly arrived residents and the old members of the family. Such
arrangements may provide the new arrival with the right to a defined
space or part of the apartment. The parents may decide to let their
son's wife move into their apartment, but give the son and his wife
a room of sixteen square meters, while keeping another room of twenty
square meters for themselves. It is likewise possible to conclude
an agreement whereby a member of the family (say a son's wife) moves
in without the right to living space, that is, moves in only as a temporary resident. In this case, the person may be evicted at any time.[50]
No matter what the arrangement, in order to avoid conflict, all Soviet

legal authors strongly advise that the conditions of residency be clearly written down, and even better, registered with the housing management.

The Reservation of Living Space

Another mechanism geared for achieving both the rational use of the housing fund and a degree of stability in housing affairs is the reservation of the right to living space for those temporarily absent. A tenant is entitled to sublet the reserved living accommodation or to settle temporary occupants for the length of the period of reservation (Article 309, RSFSR Civil Code). Generally, there is a six months' reservation of the space (Article 306, Civil Code of the RSFSR). But an absence above the six-month period does not mean an automatic loss of the right to use the premises. As Korneev and Kon'kov point out, expiration of the time period can serve only as grounds for the house management's request to break the lease. A good example is given for this ruling. In the case of Tarashkevich v. Orlova, the Collegium on Civil Affairs of the Supreme Court of the USSR indicated that a certain Orlova never left the disputed housing space. True, Orlova did not occupy this space for a long period of time, far in excess of the six-month limit, but only because comrade Tarashkevich and his wife Romanova did not let her into the apartment. Thus, the circumstances of Orlova's not living in the disputed premises for more than six months cannot be grounds for declaring that her right to occupy this space has been lost.[51]
There are likewise special cases for the extended reservation of the right of occupancy applying to those in the military service, those whose jobs require absences from their permanent place of residency (crews of ships, workers on geological surveys and expeditions), and students or postgraduates away for educational reasons.[52] Citizens officially "sent abroad" or leaving to work in the regions of the Far North, or in a locality equivalent to the regions of the Far North, as well as in other cases stipulated by the Council of Ministers, have their housing reserved for the entire stay abroad or away from their permanent residence.[53] Because house rationing has been so important, the law even deals with those arrested for crimes. A defendant's premises are reserved during the entire time he is held for investigation or is on trial. Most of the republics (RSFSR, Ukrainian, Belorussian, Kirgizian, Armenian, and a number of others) provide that in the event of a conviction involving imprisonment, exile, or being sent away for more than six months and where no members of the convicted man's family remain in the lodgings, the lease is considered broken from the moment the sentence is executed. If the

convicted man's family does occupy the dwelling, his place is reserved for the first six months of his sentence.[54]

Exchanging Apartments

An important right granted to the Soviet tenant by the law of October 17, 1937, is the right to exchange one's living space with other tenants in buildings of the local Soviets and departments. The right of exchange introduced a necessary degree of flexibility into Soviet housing, increasing the rational use of a limited housing fund. Exchanges often allow a quicker relief of changed housing needs stemming from changes in the size of the family than does the longer procedure of applying to be placed on the city-wide waiting lists for living space. In addition to the written agreement of the tenant and all the adult members of his family living with him, permission of the housing organs involved is necessary to legalize the exchange.[55] Regardless of which department may own the premises, official registration of the exchange takes place in the local Soviet's ispolkom. The housing organs of the raion where one of the premises involved in the exchange is located actually issue the "exchange order." Those anxious citizens who consummate an exchange on their own initiative without exchange orders are subject to eviction. This last provision provides city housing authorities with an instrument for maintaining control over the housing fund, and especially over the distribution of living space. According to the 1967 Instructions on the Procedure for the Exchange of Living Quarters and the 1964 RSFSR Civil Code, exchanges are not allowed in the following cases: (1) If the tenant is under a suit for the breaking or changing of his lease; (2) if the exchange has a speculative or fictitious nature; (3) If one of the premises involved in the exchange is located in a building of an enterprise or institution included in a list of the most important branches of the national economy, from whose houses eviction is permitted without the assignment of another living space (Article 334, Civil Code of the RSFSR), and the tenant of the other dwelling does not have a labor relationship with this enterprise or institution. (In general, if a tenant's right to living space depends on the preservation of labor relations with the organization that assigned the space, the tenant does not have the right to exchange the space.) (4) If the house threatens to collapse or is subject to being torn down; and (5) If the living quarters are a service tenancy or located in a dormitory.[56] Intercity exchanges involving Moscow, Leningrad, and health resorts require that the exchange orders be issued only in those cities, and only where the exchange observes the rules of those cities' passport-registration system.[57]

Most large Soviet cities maintain a Bureau of Exchanges of Living Quarters, which is usually subordinated to the city's Board on the Waiting List and Distribution of Living Space. It is this bureau that has the job of keeping an exchange directory or bulletin up to date and of processing and controlling apartment exchanges. The exchange bulletin acts as a want ad, listing persons desiring to make an exchange, describing their apartments, and their particular needs. The Moscow bulletin appears weekly and contains several hundred notices. In 1956 the Moscow City Executive Committee sharply criticized the work of its Bureau of Exchanges. The Mosgorispolkom pointed out that as as a result of the bureau's ineffective work, citizens were turning to the services of speculators in living space. In an attempt to gain tighter control over the exchange process, the City Government ordered the Bureau of Exchanges to establish a close tie with the standing committees of the Moscow Soviet. The Moscow Standing Housing Committee was asked to take a more active part in the work of exchanges. Eventually, special groups under the departments of waiting lists and the distribution of living space were set up in the raions to facilitate exchanges and keep them within legal channels.[58]

From the numerous articles in the Soviet legal journals, it is obvious that the exchange right is actively and frequently exercised. Exchanges can become bogged down in a network of very detailed laws and conflicting legal opinions.[59] When exchanges concern quarters from different housing funds (local Soviet, departmental, cooperative, and private), located in different cities, and of unequal size, the complexities of the law are indeed frightening for the average citizen. On the whole, however, the exchange process offers the person in search of new living conditions an important channel for satisfying his needs, and the housing authorities a handy tool for making better use of the housing fund.

Evictions and the Problem of Resettlement

Perhaps the most outstanding feature of Soviet housing law is the great protection it affords those persons who are evicted from their apartments through no fault of their own. Eviction by court order with the provision of another living space takes place, in practice, only in connection with the tearing down of a building (or with earmarking the building) for production or social needs, that is, by eminent domain.[60] In sharp contrast to the practices of most other legal systems, Soviet law makes it the duty of the owner or lessor of the building from which a tenant is being evicted to provide the tenant and those living with him another suitable dwelling (Article 331, RSFSR Civil Code). Furthermore, this dwelling must be at least comparable to the one the evicted tenant formerly occupied. It must be situated within the limits of the same inhabited place, in a permanent building, well-built and appointed in conformity with the conditions of the locale, and no smaller than the tenant's previous apartment. "Permanent building" or building of a "capital type," means that the building has been designed for long-term use and is suitable for habitation during the entire year. "Well-built and appointed" in regard to the circumstances of the given populated place means that the building should meet the current sanitary norms and be provided with the municipal amenities (comforts and services) that are in operation as a rule in the given town, regardless of the state of the premises from which the person is being evicted. In other words, while the tenant cannot be assigned a dwelling that is dark, damp, and generally unfit for habitation, or a dwelling without running water, plumbing, and other comforts if the majority of residences in the given place have such amenities, he cannot insist on being assigned to an apartment with a bath, telephone, hot water, and other comforts if only a few houses have these facilities.[61] If the tenant used to have a separate apartment or more than one room, he must accordingly be provided with a separate apartment or dwelling of the same number of rooms (Article 331, RSFSR Civil Code, 1964). Upon eviction with the assignment of another living space, the tenant may not be put in with another family in a small apartment intended for only one family.[62] Compared to earlier legislation that provided the assignment to the evicted tenant of "another dwelling space, suitable for living," the new Civil Codes talk about the assignment of a "well-built and appointed" (blagoustroennoe) living space. In doing so, the laws attempt to insure the tenant against a worsening of his living conditions as a result of eviction from houses slated for demolition.[63] A study conducted by the RSFSR Supreme Court, however, revealed that many mistakes and injustices were made in cases of evictions with the assignment of living space. The court cited as examples, cases in the Zhukov City People's Court of Moscow oblast, and the Nizhneturin Court of Sverdlovsk oblast, where families were evicted from their communal housing and reassigned to barracks, and another family evicted from housing connected with its labor relationship, then assigned a room in a ramshackle, cold building.[64]

If a residential building must undergo capital repairs, or substantial remodeling, a family may be temporarily evicted. In such a case, the leasing agent is required to resettle the tenant in other living accommodations for the duration of the repairs (Article 318, RSFSR Civil Code). For such purposes, the ispolkoms operate a special housing fund called the Maneuver or Mobile Fund (manevrennyi fond). From time to time, there is a rash of stories in the Soviet press telling of the difficulties encountered in permanently resettling reluctant tenants. These stories speak of the "hold outs" and "squeezers" who manage to squeeze out more and more square meters and extra conveniences, while setting back the deadlines for the construction of new developments. The squeezers are more than willing to sit it out until the state gives in. Upon learning of their intended relocation, these stubborn individuals often develop medical complications, requiring special housing features. Their housing needs seem to proliferate as the days pass. In one case reported by Vechernaia Moskva, "Capitulation took place on the 230th day. Only not by the extortioners."[65] Some cases drag on for eight, nine, or more months. Moscow cited a record hold out of two years! Not all of the reluctance is on account of avarice. Many tenants may be hesitant to move to the new apartment buildings located in the outskirts of the city for very practical considerations—namely, longer time spent in transportation and incomplete public services.[66]

Conditions of eviction without the provision of another dwelling are very explicit. Such evictions are also very rare and are extreme measures. An occupant of the apartment may be evicted without the assignment of another living space (1) If he systematically destroys or damages the dwelling. (In court practice there are almost no evictions for this reason.) (2) If he systematically violates the rules of socialist community life, making it impossible for others to live in the same apartment or house with him. Eviction can only take place after the tenant's conduct has already been examined by the police, the procurator, or by social organizations, such as the Comrades' Courts, but all warnings and public persuasion have failed to have any effect; (3) If the tenant and members of his family are absent without good reasons for longer periods of time than legally sanctioned; (4) Eviction is possible if the tenant owns a dwelling situated in the same populated place that is suitable for permanent residence and he has an opportunity to move into it. At the end of the 1950s and the beginning of the 1960s cases of eviction of tenants who had their own homes were widespread. In the last few years, particularly since Khrushchev's ouster, they have clearly decreased; (5) Finally, the tenant may be evicted if he fails to pay rent for more than three months.[67] When an individual's behavior is deviant, the collective is first called upon to influence, reform, and re-educate the culprit. Eviction is the ultimate sanction, the final step. Rather than imposing that sanction, the court stresses the importance of the community's warnings and discussions in the Comrades' Court. In its turn, the Comrades' Court has the right to bring the question of eviction before the People's Court. In fact, where there is an absence of sufficient evidence that social action and warnings were undertaken by the community either in the Comrades' Courts or in general meetings of the building's residents, the RSFSR Supreme Court has reversed lower rulings for eviction.[68] Though there have been practically no

141

cases of eviction as a result of the systematic destroying or damaging of dwellings, this does not mean that such damage has not occurred. In truth, there is an almost indistinguishable line between the poor maintenance of living quarters and the systematic damaging of the housing fund. In 1962 a Pravda article exposed the "far from unique facts" of Muscovite tenants' destroying and damaging living quarters and places of common use, systematically not fulfilling their obligations in regard to repairs, and even transforming living quarters into auxiliary places for the raising of animals.

> Housing maintenance depends largely on the inhabitants
> themselves. Unfortunately, we still have people who treat
> badly both their own housing and areas of common use.
> The rules of housing maintenance are frequently ignored,
> and current repairs at the expense of the inhabitants is not
> done for years on end. Cases also happen of deliberate
> spoilage of housing and areas of common use. Unfortu-
> nately, such barbaric incidents do not always meet the
> proper rebuff and condemnation which they deserve.[69]

The Moscow City Government went so far as to make the person who regularly destroys or spoils housing liable to exile from Moscow without assigning him housing.[70] Most disturbing to housing authorities are the reports of careless citizens who render unfit for habitation living space in a newly constructed building. The jurist Iurii Tolstoi advocates the court's vigorous examination of such persons for eviction in well-publicized traveling or circuit sessions with the active participation of the community.[71] One reason for the lack of evictions in instances of damaging or destroying apartments may be the widespread nature of such abuses and the average citizen's detached attitude toward property. The building's equipment is often used incorrectly or very carelessly. The tenant appears to have little or no sense that the apartment assigned him is his, and that even he and his family have a direct interest in the building's upkeep. The laws, decrees, instructions, and rules warn of harsh penalties and eviction for the misuse of living quarters and buildings, but the social organizations charged with enforcing those rules are made up of the very citizens who hold a cavalier attitude toward property. Low quality housing construction and lengthy delays in obtaining minor repairs only reinforce the attitude that it is not worth the effort to be careful with the building's equipment, and encourages inhabitants to use the building's facilities recklessly or improperly.

The Fundamentals of Civil Legislation and the RSFSR Civil Code enumerate special cases of eviction from departmental housing (housing operated by the ministries, enterprises, or organizations) without the offer of another living space. Article 62 of the Fundamentals and Article 334 of the RSFSR Civil Code stipulate that the USSR Council of Ministers and the Council of Ministers of the union republics may establish lists of enterprises and establishments of the most important branches of the economy and of particular departments from whose houses workers may be evicted by court action without provision for the assignment of living space, where their employment has terminated if they had (1) received their dwelling as a result of their job; (2) have left their job by their own wish or because of violations of labor discipline; (3) or left as a result of committing a crime. Evictions under this category "because of violations of labor discipline" are subject to abuse, since the labor "violations" are not precisely spelled out and are subject to quick redefinition during periodic campaigns to strengthen labor discipline. But even in the cases set down in Article 334, eviction without the reassignment of housing is not allowed for war and labor invalids, old age and personal pensioners, families of armed forces personnel, and also for families of servicemen and partisans who perished or disappeared while defending the USSR or in the performance of other military duties (Article 334, RSFSR Civil Code). Application of these laws offers an excellent example of housing law employed to stabilize the labor force, and of housing as an incentive. When a worker ceases his labor relations by his own wish, he may be evicted on the basis of Article 334 if he cannot offer the court important reasons for refusing to return to his former place of employ. In other words, the court should make clear to the person his right to return to his former place of work. Once he declares his intention to return to his former work, the person may not be evicted without the reassignment of living quarters.[72] Furthermore, if the management refuses to take him back, refuses to give him a job suited to his specialty, or refuses to assign him work corresponding to his new or higher qualifications, the worker cannot be put out in the cold before he is assigned another home.[73] The obvious aim of such court practices is to keep men on the job and to slow down labor turnover.

Even when out-and-out eviction, without provision for any other dwelling seems warranted, for example, because of a suit brought by one tenant against another whose disruptive conduct has been proven, the misbehaving tenant may escape the ultimate sanction. One of the most effective measures for mitigating such housing conflicts and for returning life to "normal" for all tenants is the mandatory exchange of living quarters. The person who has created a situation making it impossible to live with him may be ordered by the court to carry out an exchange of living quarters with a person interested in such an exchange. If the guilty person refuses to make the exchange, he may be evicted without the assignment of another place.[74]

Besides the desire for labor and population stability, the great reluctance to impose evictions may stem from early Soviet traditions that condemned the inhumane use of evictions by greedy bourgeois landlords in search of profits. Soviet critics point to the eviction laws of most nonsocialist countries as splendid examples of bourgeois law protecting the private property interests of the society, while offering little or no real protection of the interests of the general public. Clearly the necessity for evictions under certain conditions is recognized. But in Soviet legal and popular thinking, the right of every citizen to housing is very strong. It is the extraordinary provision for another living space in the event of eviction by eminent domain and the extremely restricted uses of eviction without reassignment of housing that underline the citizen's right to housing. These same conditions provide Soviet spokesmen with persuasive and powerful examples to back up their contentions that Soviet society is the most humane in the world.

RENT AND RENT POLICIES

In the course of the second decade housing will gradually become rent-free for all citizens.
—The 1961 Program of the Communist Party of
  the Soviet Union.
        Until the introduction of a system of rent-free living accommodation the tenant must pay his rent and pay it promptly.
—Article 303, RSFSR Civil Code (1964)

In an attempt to herald the arrival of the "New Way of Life," all rents were abolished in January 1921. The realities of a deteriorating housing fund, the rush to the cities of thousands of citizens, and the desperate need for capital soon caused the re-establishment of rent as part of the housing policy under the New Economic Policy. On June 4, 1926, an all-Union rent law was adopted. This law, which is still in force today, set rates at very low levels and, in effect, guaranteed that rent revenue could not cover most of the cost of building repairs and maintenance. Substantial government subsidies would still be essential for keeping the housing fund in any livable condition. It is important to note that the amount of apartment rent in the USSR has never been raised since the issuance of the 1926 law. Rent averages about 4 to 5 percent of the family's income, and covers only about 40 percent of the operational and repair costs of the housing fund. In discussing the completed 1966-1970 Economic Plan, Pravda re-emphasized the fact that Soviet rents remain the lowest in the world,

144

on the average between 4-5 rubles of every 100 rubles of family income.[75] Most Soviet commentators point out that in capitalist countries, where housing is a source of profit, rent accounts for 25 to 30 percent of the working family's income. Hence, the rent policy in the Soviet Union is put forward as another example of that society's progressive humanism.

There are several factors that determine the individual's rent level, including his ability to pay. Size of income, number of dependents, condition and locale of the building, the presence or absence of municipal services and amenities, special privileges, and, of course, the size of the living space are all considered in calculating the tenant's rent. Only living space is subject to rent. As a reflection of the changed housing situation and of a housing policy stressing individual apartments, in 1962 the Moscow Soviet published a decree stipulating that certificates of occupancy must indicate living space according to Gosstroi standards for separate apartments, from which rent should be calculated. Gosstroi established that in apartments intended for one family, the kitchens are considered auxiliary (that is, nonliving) space, if the size of the kitchen is no more than six square meters. If the kitchen is more than six square meters, the amount of kitchen space in excess of six square meters is to be included in the apartment's living space for allocation and rent purposes.[76] As a general rule, "superfluous" living space, that is, living space in excess of the established norm per person (usually nine square meters), is paid for at three times the rate for basic living space. However, tenants paying rent at the workers' and employees' rate may pay the same rate for up to 4.5 square meters of their superfluous living space. The basic rate of apartment rent (osnovnaia stavka kvartirnoi platy) is the rate of one square meter of living space per month in a given town. Established by the local Soviet, the basic rate ranges from a low of three to a high of 4.4 kopecks, depending upon the local conditions for operating and repairing the housing fund as well as for its amortization. In towns with a population of 40,000 or less the basic rate can be below 3.5 kopecks per square meter, but no lower than three kopecks. In towns with more than 40,000 persons, the rate is between 3.5 and 4.4 kopecks.[77] There can be only one basic rate for any given town.

The second element one must know in calculating rents is the rate of one square meter of living space in a given building (rastsenka zhilogo pomeshcheniia), determined by applying deductions and increments to the basic rate. These deductions and increments depend on the location of the house (its distance from the center of the city), the degree of its upkeep, the quality of construction, and its modern conveniences.[78] If the building has no electricity, there is a 5 percent reduction of the basic rate. A long distance from the urban center may mean a reduction of up to 10 percent, no running water, up to 10 percent, no plumbing, 10 percent. If the building has special conveniences, there may be an increase of the basic rate in the amount needed to amortize the equipment, but not higher than 10 percent, regardless of the number of conveniences.[79]

The apartment tax (kvartirnaia taksa) is the third necessary figure for calculating rents. The apartment tax is the rate of one square meter of living space in a given apartment, regardless of who occupies the apartment. Any "defects" in the apartment—for example, low ceilings, poor ventilation and dampness, lack of natural lighting, its location in the building—or the apartment's special conveniences are the considerations that make up the apartment tax. If the apartment has no defects or special amenities, the apartment tax is the same as the rate of one square meter of living space in the given building. The apartment tax then is the standard rate for the particular living quarters, based exclusively on the quality of the apartment.

After the apartment tax has been calculated, the income of the family member having the largest earnings, considerations of the number of dependents, and special housing privileges combine to produce the individual tenant's rate of rent (stavka kvartirnoi platy) for the use of one square meter of living space per month in the given apartment. For workers and employees, 0.33 kopecks for every full ruble of earnings above 14 rubles 50 kopecks is added to the apartment tax to determine the rate of rent. However, for workers and employees, the rent rate cannot be higher than 13.2 kopecks per square meter per month.[80] In buildings constructed after January 1, 1924, increments of up to 25 percent may be added to the rent rate when necessary to cover operational expenses.[81] A December 19, 1960, ruling of the RSFSR Ministry of the Communal Economy kept this rent increment of up to 25 percent in those buildings for which the increase had already been calculated. In the future, however, such increments can only be added by an ispolkom decision, but only as a temporary measure, and only if the social house committee of tenants supports the action. Since all monthly earnings are well above the 14 rubles 50 kopecks level, the majority of tenants pay the maximum rate of 13.2 kopecks per square meter. (In tall buildings the maximum rate is thirty kopecks.)

For a certain category of people there are special rent rates. For example, personal or individual pensioners and members of their families pay rent on the basis of only 50 percent of the rate paid by workers. In addition, the individual pensioner pays ordinary rates for superfluous space up to fifteen square meters. Military personnel in commanding positions, KGB personnel on the commanding staff, and officers in police organs pay a special fixed rent rate of eight kopecks per square meter if their pay is seventy-five rubles or more.[82]

There are other categories of persons receiving rent privileges, similar to those entitled to privileges in housing allocation.[83]

On the other hand, certain categories of people have distinct disadvantages when it comes to paying rent. Members of the so-called "free professions," the self-employed engineers, doctors, artists, handicraftsmen, writers, and the clergy must pay for all additional space above the basic norm of nine square meters at three times the basic rent rate. In other words, they do not enjoy the privilege of paying for up to 4.5 square meters of superfluous living space at the same rate as the "norm" space. Furthermore, these self-employed persons, especially religious ministers, pay for the living space they occupy on the basis of their incomes. For example, if the average annual income of the minister does not exceed 300 rubles, his rate of rent is established at 19.8 kopecks per square meter per month. If his income is more than 300 rubles, for every twenty rubles of income above the first 300 there is an addition of 1.1 kopecks to the set rate of 19.8 kopecks up to the maximum rate of forty-four kopecks per square meter per month. Moscow has become even more expensive for the clergyman. There the beginning rate of 19.8 kopecks is applied to the minister's first 120 rubles of annual income, with an addition of 1.1 kopecks for every twenty rubles above the first 120 rubles, up to a maximum rate of eighty-eight kopecks per square meter per month.[84] What this policy means is that the priest in Moscow might be paying from five to over six times more for his living accommodations than his fellow Soviet citizens. Clearly, rent policy is an accurate reflection of official antireligious and antiprivate enterprise attitudes.

To summarize, in order to calculate a tenant's rent rate we must first know the basic rate of rent for one square meter of living space in the given city. From this we can determine (1) the rate of one square meter of living space in the given building, (2) the rate of one square meter of living space for the given apartment (the apartment tax), and (3) the rate of rent for one square meter of living space for a given tenant.

By way of example, let us calculate the rent of a family of four, two adults and two children, who occupy a two-room apartment of a total of thirty square meters of living space. Since the building and apartment are equipped with amenities standard for the town, and the tenant's earnings are well above 14 rubles 50 kopecks, his rent rate is the maximum 13.2 kopecks per square meter of living space per month. Thus, this tenant's rent for one month is 13.2 kopecks x 30 = 3 rubles 96 kopecks.

Another example finds a family of four, again a husband, wife, and two children, who occupy three rooms or forty-eight square meters of living space. Since the sanitary norm is nine square meters per

person, the family is entitled to thirty-six square meters. Obviously, the family enjoys a small amount of superfluous living space. Classified as a worker-employee, the tenant has the privilege of paying the usual rate for excess or superfluous space not exceeding 4.5 square meters. For the superfluous space above the allowance of 4.5 square meters, he must pay three times the usual rate. The rent rate for this tenant is set at the maximum 13.2 kopecks per square meter of living space. For 40.5 square meters the rate is 13.2 kopecks (that is, 9 square meters x 4 + 4.5 square meters = 40.5 square meters). But this lucky family has an extra 7.5 square meters that is subject to payment at three times the regular rent rate. To calculate the rent:
(1) 13.2 kopecks x 40.5 = 5 rubles 35 kopecks
(2) for 7.5 square meters of superfluous space, he pays an additional
        13.2 x 3 x 7.5 = 2 rubles 97 kopecks
This tenant's apartment rent for one month comes to 8 rubles 32 kopecks.

In addition to their rent for living quarters, tenants also have the duty to pay for central heating. The annual cost of central heating is distributed proportionally among the users in relation to their rent, but may not be higher than 40 percent of the rent. If the cost of central heating rises above 40 percent of the total sum of rents, the excess cost is shared among all users on the basis of the amount of useful space they occupy.[85] Payment for municipal or communal services, such as electricity, gas, water, and maintenance of plumbing or cleaning of septic tanks is also part of the tenant's obligation.

From a purely economic view, it is clear that the Soviet rent policy does not provide a realistic means for maintaining the housing fund. Vast amounts of state subsidies are required to insure housing operations. From a strictly political view, however, Soviet rent policy is a very sensible and effective instrument. Soviet leaders confidently ask where else in the noncommunist world is the right to housing guaranteed to all citizens, regardless of their ability to pay? Furthermore, the low rent levels act as safety valves, taking much of the steam out of potential tenant complaints about poor quality, crowded conditions, and lack of services. Any sudden rent increases would be accompanied by an increase in the citizen's expectations for an immediate improvement in housing and services. The state would have to be sure to meet or restrict those expectations. If the need for large government subsidies to maintain low rent levels is taken into account, the real rent paid by tenants is not as low as the monthly rent handed over to the housing offices. High prices on most consumer goods and services tend to balance off the low official rents. Since the funds needed to maintain the socialist sector of housing come from the state, in the long run the tenants are actually the primary source of the funds, through wage-labor and consumer policies rather than direct rent payments.

For the last ten years there have been voices calling for a more realistic approach to the Soviet rent policy with the aim of making the housing fund more economically self-sufficient. Even Khrushchev hinted at the need for a readjustment of the rent levels set back in 1926. The violent reaction in certain Soviet towns to price increases for food in the early 1960s probably gave the Soviet leaders second thoughts about tampering with the long-standing, though economically inadequate, rent system. The Polish riots (December 1970) over price increases for food and fuel may serve to postpone for an indefinite period any contemplated Soviet rent increases. Those Soviet citizens who appear ready and willing to accept increases in their rent rates are most likely still in the minority. Surveys of the Soviet courts indicate that, while housing disputes have gone down in numbers from year to year, they still constitute a significant part of the civil cases examined by the courts.[86] Many of these disputes are arguments concerning payment for municipal services. The tenants involved fight over every ruble down to the last kopeck. This evidence may reflect the average citizen's cautiousness and reluctance when it comes to questions of paying for the necessities of life. Any revision of the rent system would have to be linked with readjustments of the wage system. Consequently, it appears that the current rent policy, which politically serves the Soviet leadership so well, and which has come to be the expected way of life for the Soviet man in the street, will remain essentially intact for a long period of time. Indeed, if any change should occur, it will probably be toward the Party Program's stated goal of rent-free housing for all citizens. Whether this policy can be realized during the 1970s remains to be seen.

NOTES

1. Iu. K. Tolstoi, op. cit., p. 56; Article 297, Civil Code of the RSFSR, 1964.

"Service tenancies are provided for citizens to live at their place of work or office building on the basis of the character of their terms of employment, and for defined classes of workers in accordance with the legislation of the USSR and the decrees of the Council of Ministries of the RSFSR.

"Living accomodation, regardless of the ownership of the building in which it is situated, is included in the category of service buildings by a decision of the regional or town Soviet of workers' deputies and is made available for use by a special warrant issued by such committee."

2. Ukaz of the Presidium of the Supreme Soviet of the USSR, "On the Procedure of Examining Proposals, Applications and Complaints of Workers," April 12, 1968, Vedomosti Verkhovnogo Soveta SSSR, no. 17: 144.

3. Vedomosti Verkhovnogo Soveta ESSR, 1967, no. 16, p. 214, cited in Sovetskoe gosudarstvo i pravo, no. 10 (October 1968): 143-144.

4. Morton, op. cit., p. 209.

5. See especially Iu. K. Tolstoi, op. cit., p. 10; S. M. Korneev and Iu. M. Kon'kov, Pravo na zhiluiu ploshchad' v SSSR (Right to Living Quarters in the USSR), (Moscow, Znanie, 1968). Seriia: gosudarstvo i pravo no. 8.

6. V. Izvestia, June 12, 1963.

7. Pravda, November 20, 1962.

8. Pravda, July 18, July 24, August 10, August 19, 1963; lead editorial, August 29, 1963.

9. See, for example, G. Makarov, "Komu byt' novoselom?" (Who Should Get a New Apartment?) Sovetskoe profsoiuzy, no. 16 (August 1966): 28-29.

10. Vedomosti verkhovnogo soveta SSSR, 1966, no. 30, p. 595.

11. Izvestia, September 22, 1963.

12. The Anti-Parasite Law was officially aimed at those who do not wish "to work honestly, according to their abilities, and who avoid socially useful work, derive unearned income "from the exploitation of private property," or "commit other antisocial acts which enable them to lead a parasitic way of life." Before a September 1965 amendment that limited the decree's exile provisions, such people were "subject . . . to resettlement in specially designated localities for a period of from two to five years, with confiscation of the property acquired by nonlabor means. . . ." Those who took jobs "only for the sake of appearances" were also subject to exile. May 4, 1961, "Decree of the Presidium of the Russian Supreme Soviet: On Intensifying the Struggle Against Persons Who Avoid Socially Useful Work and Lead an Antisocial, Parasitic Way of Life," Sovetskaia Rossiia, May 5, 1961, p. 3 (CDSP XIII, no. 17: 8-9).

13. Ye. Rybina, "A Malicious Charge of 'Parasitism': Slanderer's Helpers," Izvestia, February 21, 1962 (CDSP XIV, 9: 16).

14. Ibid., pp. 15-16.

15. Tikhon D. Alekseev, Zhilishchnye l'goty grazhdan SSSR (Housing Privileges of Citizens of the USSR) (Moscow: Gosiurizdat, 1962), pp. 12-13.

16. Ibid., pp. 44-45, Iu. K. Tolstoi, op. cit, pp. 78-80; Sbornik zhilishchnogo zakonodatel'stva, Moscow: Iuridicheskaia Literatura, 1963), pp. 297-304; Zhilishchno-bytovye voprosy (sbornik) (Moscow: Profizdat, 1964), pp. 119-122, 127-132.

17. Sovetskaiia iustitsiia, no. 8, (April 1967): 32. Categories dating from 1963 Council Ministries RSFSR resolution amended on October 19, 1965.

18. Pravda, August 16, 1972, p. 3.

19. Alekseev, op. cit., p. 16; Korneev and Kon'kov, op. cit., p. 16. p. 16.

20. Korneev and Kon'kov, op. cit., p. 16.

21. Ibid., p. 6.

22. Alekseev, op. cit., pp. 17-18; Sbornik zhilishchnogo zakonodatel'stvo, 1963, p. 210.

23. "Ob uporiadochenii l'got dlia lits, rabotaiushchikh v raionakh krainego severa i v mestnostiakh, priravnennykh k raionam krainego severa," Ukaz of the Presidium of the USSR Supreme Soviet, February 10, 1960, Vedomosti Verkhovnogo Soveta SSSR no. 7 (991), February 18, 1960; and Alekseev, op. cit., pp. 19-20.

24. Sosnovy, Housing Problem, op. cit., p. 119; Sosnovy, "The Soviet Housing Situation Today," Soviet Studies IX, no. 1 (July 1959): 9.

25. Viktor G. Vishniakov, Uchastie deputatov mestnykh sovetov v raspredelenii zhiloi ploshchadi (The Participation of the Deputies of Local Soviets in the Distribution of Living Space) (Moscow: Iuridicheskaia literatura, 1964), pp. 43-47.

26. Morton, op. cit., p. 209.

27. See Iu. K. Tolstoi, op. cit., pp. 10-11; M. F. Konovalov and V. M. Iezuitov, "Moskovskii sovet, ego zadachi i itogi deiatel'nosti" (The Moscow Soviet, Its Tasks and Activities) Sovestskoe gosudarstvo i pravo, no. 4, (April 1967): 16; M. S. Studenikina, Formy uchastiia obshchestvennosti v rabote mestnykh sovetov deputatov trudiashchikhsia (Forms of Public Participation in the Work of the Local Soviets of Workers' Deputies Moscow: Goziurizdat, 1963); p. 88; Vishniakov, op. cit., pp. 53-54; V. Tel'nov, "Novoe pazvitie v raspredelenii zhil'ia" (New Development in the Distribution of Housing,) Sovetskie profsoiuzy, no. 11 (June 1964): 44.

28. Vishniakov, op. cit., pp. 48-49.

29. Pravda, March 10, 1960.

30. G. Makarov, op. cit., p. 29.

31. Chubarov, "Kak my raspredeliaem zhil'e" ("How we Distribute Housing"), Sovetskoe profsoiuzy, no. 8, (April 1964), p. 21.

32. Ibid.

33. Brezhnev, "Report of CC CPSU to the Twenty-Third Congress of the CPSU," March 29, 1966, Pravda, March 30, 1966.

34. Izvestia, November 24, 1964.

35. Kommunist Tadzhikistana, April 21, 1962, and February 14, 1963.

36. Iu. K. Tolstoi, op. cit., p. 16.

37. Ibid., p. 19.

38. See Korneev and Kon'Kov, op. cit., pp. 10-11, and Iu. K. Tolstoi, op. cit.

39. Biulletin' Verkhovnogo suda SSSR, no. 2 (1962), p. 30.

40. Paragraph 13, "Pravila pol'zovaniia zhilym pomeschchenniem" (Rules for the Use of Living Quarters), Resolution of the RSFSR Council of Ministers, October 18, 1962, in Zhilishchno-bytovye voprosy (sbornik rukovodiashchikh materialov) (Moscow: Profizdat, 1964), p. 105.

41. Paragraph 7, "Pravila pol'zovaniia zhilym pomeshcheniem," Zhilishchno-bytovye voprosy, p. 104; Iu. K. Tolstoi, op. cit., pp. 100-101.

42. Article 321 of the Civil Code of the RSFSR, 1964; and Korneev and Kon'kov, op. cit., p. 29.

43. V. Tolstoi, "Poniatie sem'i v sovetskom prave," (The Understanding of "Family" in Soviet Law), Sovetskaiia iustitsiia, no. 19 (October 1969): 5-6.

44. D. Vatman, "Prava i obiazannosti chlenov sem'i nanimatelia" (Rights and Obligations of Members of the Tenant's Family) Sotsialisticheskaia zakonnost', no. 10 (October 1969): 52-54; Iu. K. Tolstoi, op. cit., p. 63; Article 301 of the RSFSR Civil Code, 1964.

45. Cited in H. Kent Geiger, The Family in Soviet Russia (Cambridge, Mass.: 1968, p. 209.

46. Korneev and Kon'kov, op. cit., p. 23; Iu. K. Tolstoi, op. cit., pp. 62-63; Sovetskaiia iustitsiia, no. 11 (1961): 28.

47. Korneev and Kon'kov, op. cit., p. 25.

48. Iu. K. Tolstoi, op. cit., p. 65.

49. Korneev and Kon'kov, op. cit., p. 26.

50. Ibid., pp. 27-28.

51. Korneev and Kon'kov, op. cit., pp. 31-32.

52. Part III, Paragraph 2, Article 306, Civil Code of the RSFSR.

53. Article 308, Civil Code of the RSFSR, 1964; "O bronirovanii zhiloi ploshchadi," Resolution of the CC CPSU and USSR Council of Ministers, April 1, 1958, Sobranie postanovlenii SSSR, 1958, no. 6, in Zhilishchnobytovye voprosy, op. cit., p. 123; "Ob uporiadochenii l'got dlia lits, rabotaiushchikh v raionakh krainego severa i v mestnostiakh, priravnennykh k raionam krainego severa," Ukaz of the Presidium of the USSR Supreme Soviet February 10, 1960, Vedomosti verkhovnogo soveta SSSR, no. 7 (991), February 18, 1960; D. Vatman, "Bronirovanie zhilykh pomeshchenii" (The Reservation of Housing Space), Sovetskaia iustitsiia, no. 9 (May 1969): 2. p. 2.

54. Part III, Paragraph 5, Article 306, Civil Code of the RSFSR (1964); and Korneev and Kon'kov, op. cit., p. 34.

55. Paragraph 5, "Instruktsiia o poriadke obmena zhilykh pomeshchenii," Prikaz of the Ministry of the Communal Economy RSFSR, January 9, 1967, no. 12, Sovetskaiia iustitsiia, no. 6 (March 1967): 31.

56. Paragraph 9 of the "Instructions on the Procedure for the Exchange of Living Quarters," January 9, 1967, Sovetskaiia iustitsiia, no. 6 (March 1967): 32; Article 326, Civil Code of the RSFSR, 1964.

57. Ibid., Paragraph 10.

58. "On the Work of the Bureau of Exchanges of Living Quarters under the Board on the Waiting List and Distribution of Living Space," Biulleten' ispolkoma Moskovskogo gorodskogo Soveta deputatov trudiashchikhsia, no. 22 (1956): 1-3; and Vishniakov, op. cit., pp. 14-15.

59. See, for example, A. I. Mal'ginova and D. P. Vatman, "Spornye voprosy obmena zhilymi pomeshcheniiami" (Controversial Problems in the Exchange of Apartments and Rooms), Sovetskoe gosudarstvo i pravo, no. 6 (June 1968); 111-115; E. Blazhenko, "Sporny o prave chlenov sem'i na obmen zhilogo pomeshcheniia" (Conflicts Concerning the Right of Members of the Family to Exchange Their Living Quarters), Sotsial' naia zakonnost', no. 6 (June 1968): 44-46.

60. Article 332, Civil Code of the RSFSR; "On the Court Practice in Civil Housing Matters," Biulleten' verkhovnogo suda SSSR, no. 3 (1964): 22; and V. P. Skripko, "Vyselenie iz vedomstvennykh zhilykh domov" ('Eviction from Departmental Housing'), Sovetskaiia gosudarstvo i pravo, no. 3 (March, 1969): 142.

61. Korneev and Kon'kov, op. cit., p. 48.

62. Biulleten' verkhovnogo suda SSSR, no. 1, (1963): 14-16.

63. Articles 331, 332, Civil Code of the RSFSR; and V. P. Skripko, "Vyselenie v sviazi so snosom doma" (Eviction Resulting from the Demolition of a House), Sovetskaiia iustitsiia, no. 10 (May 1968): 16.

64. "Sudebnaiia praktika po delam o vyselenii nanimatelei s predostavleniem zhiloi ploshchadi" (Court Practice in Cases of Evictions with the Assignment of Living Space), Sovetskaiia iustitsiia, no. 13 (July 1969): 5.

65. Vechernaia Moskva, March 19, 1964.

66. A. V. Ryabinin, Deputy Chairman of the Mosispolkom, Vechernaia Moskva, March 25, 1964.

67. Article 333, RSFSR Civil Code, 1964.

68. See, for example, Korneev and Kon'kov, op. cit., pp. 51-52.

69. K. Butuzova, Deputy Head of Construction Section of the CC CPSU, Pravda, July 22, 1962.

70. Ibid. It should be noted that in 1962 "exile" from the cities was seen as a convenient method for ridding urban areas of socially undesirable persons. This was the heyday of the Anti-Parasite laws with their sweeping exile provisions.

71. Iu. K. Tolstoi, op. cit., p. 167.

72. Biulleten' verkhovnogo suda RSFSR, no. 4 1963: 2

73. Biulleten' verkhovnogo suda RSFSR, no. 1 1965: 8-9; and Iu. K. Tolstoi, op. cit., 195.

74. Iu. K. Tolstoi, op. cit., p. 171; Biulleten' verkhovnogo suda SSSR, no. 4 1963: 31.

75. See Tomsen, op. cit., pp. 22-34, and "Blago Naroda—glavnaia tsel'" (The People's Well-Being Is the Main Aim), Pravda, February 8, 1971, p. 2.

76. V. P. Skripko, I. B. Martkovich, P. G. Solov'ev, Zhilishchnoe zakonodatet' stvo v SSSR i RSFSR (Moscow: Stroiizdat, 1965), p. 218.

77. "O kvartirnoi plate i merakh k uregulirovaniiu pol'zovaniia zhilishchami v gorodakh poselkakh," Resolution of the Central Executive Committee and Council of People's Commissars of the USSR, June 4, 1926 (On Apartment Rent and Measures for Regulating the Use of Housing in Urban Settlements), Zhilishcho-bytovye voprosy (sbornik), p. 140.

78. Ibid.; and Iu. K. Tolstoi, op. cit., p. 94. p. 94.

79. "Ob plate zhilykh pomeshchenii v gorodakh i rabochikh poselkakh" (On Paying for Living Quarters in Urban and Workers Settlements) Resolution of the Central Executive Committee and the RSFSR Council of People's Commissars, May 14, 1928, Zhilishchnobytovye voprosy, p. 143.

80. Ibid., p. 144.

81. "O zhilishchnoi politike," Paragraph 11, January 4, 1928, Zhilishchno-bytovye voprosy, p. 157.

82. Korneev and Kon'kov, op. cit., p. 20.

83. See pp. 219-227.

84. Skripko, Martkovich, and Solov'ev, op. cit., p. 245; Resolution of VTsIK and SNK of the RSFSR, May 14, 1928; Instructions of the NKVD and NKIU, June 28, 1928; Instructions of MKKh RSFSR, October 15, 1960.

85. "O poriadke oplaty pol'zovaniia tsentral'nym otopleniem" (Procedure for Paying for the Use of Central Heating), Postanovlenie SNK RSFSR, May 4, 1927, Zhilishchno-bytovye voprosy, p. 159.

86. B. Belolinetskii, "Okhrana zhilishchnykh prav grazhdan" (Protecting the Housing Rights of Citizens), Sovetskaia iustitsiia, no. 1 (January 1967): 8.

6

HOUSING MANAGEMENT AND
THE ORGANIZATION OF LIFE
IN THE APARTMENT BUILDING

In previous chapters we found that coordination between a multitude of organizations, agencies, and ministries and the local Soviet is a fundamental problem in almost all phases of the planning, financing, and constructing of Soviet urban housing. The major difficulty seems to be the result of overlapping authorities, a conflict over the right to control any stage of housing operations, and a reluctance on the part of the central leadership to give local governments the real power they need to fulfill their many responsibilities in city development. Only the distribution of living space appears to be basically under the administration of the local Soviet. What when is the situation in regard to the actual management of the housing fund? Does the battle between the city housing authorities and the industries intensify or weaken along the operational front? What effect, if any, did the 1957 economic-administrative reorganization have on this aspect of Soviet housing? Is there a trend toward greater departmentally operated houses or more control by the local Soviet? What is the role of the house management or the housing Operations Office (Zhek)?

At the November 1962 Central Committee Plenum, N. S. Khrushchev launched another drive to transform the Soviet state into the State of the Whole People. At the same time, an ukaz was issued calling for the broad enlistment of the masses in the administration of everyday affairs. Great stress was placed on the importance of the local Soviets and the development of the "Voluntary Principle." Out of this movement emerged the deputies' councils and a rejuvenated domkom (house committee of tenants). In addition to their role in the allocation of housing, what other functions do the deputies' councils perform and why did they appear? The post-Revolutionary years saw the development of house committees of tenants and then house leasing cooperatives to manage their state-owned apartment buildings. Why did these institutions disappear for almost twenty years, and then suddenly reappear in the new form of the domkom at the end of the 1950s? The modern domkom seems to be active in every aspect of life within the apartment. It is a significant institution for increased public participation in the administration of housing affairs. How is the domkom organized and who provides its leadership? More importantly, what does it mean to the average Soviet apartment dweller?

WHO MANAGES SOVIET PUBLIC HOUSING?

Dating from the years of the first Five Year Plan, public housing in the Soviet Union increasingly came under the control of the various departments and ministries. Viewing the provision of housing as an extra attraction for drawing needed manpower, each enterprise jealously guarded its right to operate housing for its workers. Suggestions that the local Soviets could do a better job and save the state money by unifying the city's housing into a single system were met by strong enterprise resistance. Such an important incentive as housing would not easily be taken out of the departments' hands, no matter how powerful the economic rationale, and no matter how much the retention of housing by the industries would decrease its value as a public service. We remember the great predictions made at the outset of the 1957 administrative-economic reforms that set up the regional economic councils. Decentralization was to strengthen the role of the local Soviet, lift from industry the burden of ministering to the everyday needs of the people, and insure city Soviet control over housing. Since housing was only a sideline of the enterprises, it was assumed that the removal of all housing operations from the enterprises would enable them to devote all their energies to production. By consolidating the city's housing economy in the hands of the local Soviet, it was theorized, both the Soviet and the population would benefit. In reality, the sovnarknoz took a major role in all communal services, and further entangled the already snarled communications between the local government, the ministries, and the enterprises. Industry was not about to hand its control of housing over to the Soviets. In the ensuing power struggle, the centralized industries had powerful spokesmen close to the important decision-making centers, while the local Soviets had only a few weak voices that were scattered and poorly organized. It is not difficult to see who won the initial battle. By 1962 the departments (sovnarkhoz, ministries, enterprises) still owned and operated 68 percent of the urban housing fund throughout the USSR, 67.6 percent in the RSFSR (see Table 8). This fragmented, departmental control is a primary cause for keeping the housing economy one of the most technologically backward branches of the urban economy. In some cases divided among hundreds of different

156

TABLE 8

Data on Owners of the State Urban
Housing Fund, 1962

| | Owners | |
	Sovnarkhozy, Ministries, Departments	Local Soviets
USSR	68.0%*	32.0%*
RSFSR	67.6%	32.4%
Moscow	42.8%	57.2%
Sverdlovsk	84.7%	15.3%
Magnitogorsk	98.5%	1.5%
Chirchik	92.4%	7.6%

*According to data of January 1, 1960, census.

Source: V. A. Semenenko, "K voprosy o vedemstvennom zhilishchnom fonde" (Concerning the Problem of the Departmental Housing Fund), Gorodskoe Khoziaistvo Moskvy, no. 3 (March 1964): 22; M. Postinikov, "Planirovanie razvitiia gorodskogo khoziaistva" (Planning the Development of the City Economy), Planovoe Khoziaistvo, no. 4 (April 1965): 22.

operators, a city's housing fund severely suffers from neglected repairs and a very low level of technical operations. The departmental approach to housing management also hinders a single, city-wide technical and economic policy of repair. What is more, as a rule the level of technical upkeep of the departmental housing fund is lower than that of the local Soviets', even though the departmental fund is frequently newer. For example, on January 1, 1963, in the housing fund of Moscow's raion Soviets, around 37.4 percent of all space was located in buildings built before the Revolution, but in the departmental fund only 5.8 percent.[1] Departmental housing is not only in poorer repair, but it is also usually run less efficiently and economically, and has a much shorter life expectancy when compared to housing of the local Soviets.[2] The dispersal of the housing fund among the departments only increases the number of administrative personnel. According to the data of the Central Statistical Administration, in 1964 the departmental housing fund in the RSFSR belonged to 19,800 owners. Each of them had an average of about 9,000 square meters of living space. At the same time, the housing fund of the local

157

Soviets in the RSFSR was pooled into 2,846 housing administrations, with each one servicing an average of 31,000 square meters. This greater concentration of housing in the local Soviets enables the housing administrations to employ a greater number of engineering-technical specialists and permanent, better qualified workers, while sharply curtailing administrative expenses.[3]

	Housing Fund of Raion Soviets			Departmental Housing Fund		
------	Total Expenditure	Total Income	Deficit	Total Expenditure	Total Income	Deficit
1959	3r 30k	3r 10k	20k	4r 68k	2r 18k	2r 50k
1960	3r 29k	3r 02k	27k	4r 47k	2r 12k	2r 35k
1961	3r 22k	3r 05k	17k	4r 71k	2r 28k	2r 43k
1962	3r 20k	3r 08k	12k	4r 75k	2r 26k	2r 49k

In 1964 departmental buildings were spending, on the average, nine kopecks more for the maintenance of administrative personnel than buildings of the local Soviets. These "nine kopecks" extra for administration add up to 16 million rubles a year.[4] Between 1957 and Khrushchev's outser in October 1964, there was some slow progress in transferring housing from departmental to local Soviet control. During these same years, the local Soviets were urged to consolidate their scattered housing operations into unified housing offices. For example, in Moscow in 1964 about 55 percent of the city's housing fund—26.2 million square meters out of 47.6 million square meters— was operated by the Moscow Housing Administration (Moszhiluprav-lenie). The remaining part belonged to more than three hundred departments, including different branches of the Mossoviet, the city sovnarkhoz, the Ministry of Communications, and other agencies. Clearly, the situation in urban house management was extremely complicated.[5]

Soon after Khrushchev's forced retirement, the Soviet press once again was filled with proposals to transfer all department housing to the local Soviets. It should be noted that this was the stated policy during the Khrushchev years. But the re-emphasis on the proposals after the new leadership took over was part of the campaign to discredit Khrushchev's 1957 and 1962 reforms. The November 1962 reorganization of Soviet organs according to the production principle, in particular, was blamed for humbling the local Soviets. A lead editorial in Izvestia pointed to the reoranization's negative effects on the housing fund. For all the talk of transferring the entire state housing fund to the Soviets, noted the editorial, up until the time in a number of cities the housing fund was still in the hands of dozens of departments. The newspaper strongly implied that the 1962 reforms were at fault.[6] In

any case, the post-Khrushchev leadership has continued the process
of transferring all state housing to the local Soviets. The process,
however, still remains a slow one. By 1969, for example, the percentage of Moscow's housing operated by the raiispolkoms had risen
from the 1962 level of 57.2 percent to 60.2 percent.[7] In 1969 throughout the Soviet Union the great proportion of housing and communal
enterprises was still under many separate authorities, and a great
number of state organs were invested with powers to control housing
and communal work programs.[8] In the largest Soviet republic, the
RSFSR, 43.9 percent of the state housing fund belonged to the ministries and departments. Spokesmen for the local Soviets and the ministry of the Communal Economy continued to complain that the pace
of concentrating the administration of the housing economy in a unitary
system under the local Soviets was extremely slow.[9] In the course
of 1970, there were promising reports that the tempo of consolidation
had picked up slightly. Some communities indicated a parallel success
in cutting back many departments of housing and the communal economy,
while centralizing their cities' housing operations. At the same time,
on the whole, the local Soviets have maintained their record of spending
more on housing and its proper upkeep and getting more for their
rubles than the departments.[10] Yet, other communities express their
continued frustration in developing a strong, centralized housing
authority. If fact, the 1971 decrees on strengthening the raion and
city Soviets reported that in many cities two-thirds of state housing
was in the hands of the various ministries and departments.[11] Two
years after the passage of those decrees, various cities indicated that
the enterprises and department heads are not transferring the housing
under their jurisdiction to the local Soviets in good condition, as required
by the resolutions.[12] Saratov, for instance, echoes a problem familiar
to most city Soviets, namely, that the city housing administrations lack
sufficient rights in deciding many questions. The Saratov Director
of the City Housing Administration argued that the city government
should have the right to dismiss surplus workers in the communal
economy and to increase the economic incentives of the remaining
employees, in other words, to employ fewer people to do a greater
volume of work within the existing wage fund. In short, he was seeking
to introduce into the communal economy the system for which the
Shchekino Chemical Combine has become famous, in order to develop
a strong, well-equipped repair center. Unfortunately, the province
department of the Communal Economy of the RSFSR Ministry of the
Communal Economy put an end to Saratov's proposal. As a result
of Saratov City's weak housing authority, the transfer of departmental
apartment houses to the local Soviets has been hindered. Thus, the
total housing supply under the departments in Saratov is twice as much
as that under the city, and Saratov is not an isolated case. It seems,

however, that the plants and enterprises are more than willing to turn over their neglected housing to the local Soviets.[13] What the case of Saratov illustrates is the local government's continuing lack of sufficient rights to carry out the efficient running of the communal economy.

POST-REVOLUTIONARY EXPERIENCE IN
HOUSE MANAGEMENT AND THE DEVELOPMENT
OF THE HOUSING OFFICE (ZhEK)

In the years immediately following the October Revolution, the young, inexperienced Soviet state had neither the skill nor inclination to take on the maintenance of the municipalized housing fund that it had suddenly acquired. For the most part, this job was left to the inhabitants of the buildings. Improvisation and local initiative were the demands of the times. Soon the residents in the larger cities were meeting those demands by spontaneously forming house committees (domkoms) to act as a collective housing management. By 1921 the domkom was legally recognized as the local Soviet's agent in housing administration. It had the responsibility of managing the building and keeping the tenants in contact with the city government. Out of these house committees developed the House Leasing Cooperative Societies (Zhilishchno-arendnye kooperativnye tovarishchestvy—ZhAKTy), which were officially authorized by a 1924 law "On Cooperative Housing" to manage the municipalized housing fund. The ZhAKTy rented the housing from the local Soviets on a long term basis, collected rents, conducted voluntary repairs, and distributed living space among their members. Eventually these cooperatives became the principal form of management within the municipalized housing fund. At the time the ZhAKTy were proclaimed the best form of management of the municipalized fund. To this day Soviet urban economists point out that the ZhAKTy played a positive role in the preservation of the housing fund, at least in the first period of the development of the socialist economy.[14] In view of the ZhAKTy's sudden demise in October 1937, the praise for their earlier work is always qualified by underlining the charge that even at the beginning of the 1930s the ZhAKTy were not realizing their full economic potential and were doing an inadequate job in running their buildings. As the Soviet political climate became more severe under Stalin, the cooperative leasing society, along with the house building cooperative, came under increasing criticism. With the changed social conditions, the ZhAKTy were no longer meeting the functions that had been assigned to them. In other words, the cooperative form no longer answered the political requirements of direct control that characterized Stalin's style of government. Local initiative and improvisation had outlived their usefulness and were even proving antiprogressive. The October

17, 1937, Party and state decree "On the Preservation of the Housing Fund and the Improvement of Housing in Cities" put an end to the house ZhAKTy and effectively ended the house building cooperatives. Both a declaration of the state's confidence in its ability to directly control expanded areas of life once left to less formal organizations and a major statement of policy, the October 1937 decree charged the cooperatives with a series of serious shortcomings and announced the state's intention of directly administering the entire urban housing fund through the local Soviets, the central ministries, and industrial enterprises. The decree's preamble justified the changes:

> The existing method of management . . .does not guarantee the preservation of the public housing fund as state property, and its exemplary maintenance, but quite to the contrary, it hinders the further improvement of the housing economy. The house-management system and the laws regulating the construction of houses, the distribution and the use of dwellings preserve harmful survivals from that period . . . when the local Soviets, because of their organizational and economic weakness, were forced to transfer the administration of housing and the right to distribute living space to individual collectives of tenants—the house leasing cooperative. As a result, instead of the state distribution and use of houses, achieved through the local Soviets, a significant portion of state housing actually wound up in hands primarily uncontrolled by and independent of the local Soviets. . . . The local Soviets themselves and even the commissariats of the communal economy have not only been unable to do away with this totally unacceptable practice, but, on the contrary, they have readily turned over to the house leasing cooperatives their rights to administer housing.
> The fund of 53 million square meters operated by the ZhAKTy is in a completely unsatisfactory condition. The great majority of the ZhAKTy do not in fact manage the houses, do not take care of repairs, and do not keep the houses in a civilized condition. In some cases, the neglect of management frequently reduces the buildings to ramshackles. . . . Elementary rules of sanitation are not observed. . . . Furthermore, not a few ZhAKTy are abetting speculation in housing space.

The preamble went on to accuse the cooperative leasing associations of spending a great deal of money to maintain their administrative apparatus, without achieving the proper management of the housing fund. Curiously, the preamble also stated that the "buildings under the direct management of the local Soviets, governmental institutions and industries are also in an unsatisfactory condition."[15] It is not surprising that the ZhAKTy were liquidated during the Great Purges. From Stalin's point of view, the house leasing cooperative, like other cooperative societies, could not be trusted to administer its sphere of activity without strong, close central control. At least in theory, personal responsibility in a single head took over from collective responsibility. In contrast to the cooperative house management that had been elected by its members, the post-1937 house managers were directly appointed by the local Soviets. As agents of the state, the house managers were expected to strengthen their contact with state, police, and party organs. The new house managements were an example of the regime's desire and readiness to invade every aspect of its citizens' lives. At the same time, the decision was made to gradually replace all non-Party house managers with trusted Party members.

The state housing fund was then operated by the local Soviets' or enterprises' housing boards or administrations and subordinate house managements (domoupravleniia). These small house managements had neither the necessary technical specialists nor a sufficient production base to tackle the job of raising the technical operational level of the housing fund. They were staffed by personnel who were poorly educated and poorly paid. Lack of timely repairs was the domoupravleniia's major weakness. With the unveiling of the dynamic house construction program in 1957, it became evident that some new form of house management would have to be created, particularly in the larger urban centers. To meet the new requirements, the Housing Operations Office or Housing Office subordinate to the city or raion housing board was created in 1959-1960. In Moscow, for example, 350 Housing Operations Offices (ZhEK) were organized in place of the smaller 1,500 house managements. By 1968 the number of Moscow ZhEK expanded to 453, handling an average of seventy-five thousand square meters of living space each.[16] In large cities, such as Moscow and Leningrad, the head of the Housing Operations Office or Housing Office is appointed by the raion housing boards, with the approval and confirmation of the All-City Housing Board (zhilishchnoe upravlenie) and the raiispolkom respectively. In other cities the housing offices are subject to the city or raion housing boards or to the raiispolkoms' sections on the communal economy.[17] The Housing Communal Offices (zhilishchno-kommunal'nye kontory—ZhKO), subordinated to the directors of the enterprises of institutions, are the organizations responsible for operating the departmental housing fund.[18]

According to the laws and the house manager's handbook, the housing office is responsible for the proper technical and sanitary operation of the buildings and their equipment, the timely repair of the houses and prompt notice to the city or raion housing board of the need for any capital repair, the fulfillment of the economic-financial plan for the profitable management of the houses and for the economic accountability of its own activities, the assignment of personnel, the proper distribution of work and the observation of labor discipline, and for the hiring and firing of laborers. In addition, the housing office must assume the responsibility for fire prevention in the building, for concluding rent agreements, and for enlisting the help of the social and voluntary organizations in carrying out all its management functions.[19]

The Housing Operations Offices (ZhEK) have provided important means for bringing unity to a city's housing management. At the same time, while able to attract more qualified workers through an upgrading of the wage scale, the housing offices still face major difficulties in their work because of a lack of sufficiently qualified personnel. As a result, lengthy delays or nonfulfillment of tenants' requests for repair and bad repair jobs are frequent. The tekhnik somtritel', the technical inspector, of the Housing Office is considered a central pillar of the urban housing economy. Unfortunately, because of their low level of technical training, many such inspectors cannot insure the quality of even small repair jobs. In 1964, for example, of the two thousand tekhnik smotritel' in Moscow's ZhEK's, only four hundred fifty or 23 percent had a higher or secondary education and 1,200 or 60 percent had less than five years' work experience.[20] The problem of insufficiently trained and low-caliber personnel continues to hamper the operations of the housing offices, as well as the affairs of all branches of the local government. It is part of the larger problem of the low status of local government in the Soviet Union and of the question of "home rule."

Naturally, the housing offices, like all other Soviet administrative institutions, must carry out their work under a myriad of controls. In addition to all the checks from the local government and the republic ministries concerned with housing, the deputies' councils, public inspection groups, and even the domkoms, the housing office, and the house manager are under the careful eye of the Party. Every ZhEK, house manager's office, and individual building has its primary Party organization. Tension between the housing workers and the Party units at times reaches an intolerable level. In 1967, for example, the Party journals, Partiinaii zhizn' (Party Life), took up the problem in answering the question, "Are party organizations of the house managers' offices taking advantage of their rights to control the work of the administration?" The Party journal's editors replied that according to the rules of the CPSU, the primary Party organizations of the housing administrations are not provided with the right to control the work of the administration. However, they then went on to emphasize that "it doesn't mean that the Party organization limits its role to the dissemination of propagandistic, mass-political and cultural-educational work, and that it should not investigate the situation of the housing economy." No, indeed! One of the main missions of the Party organizations of the housing administrations, conclude the editors, consists of

> leading the struggle for the preservation of the housing fund, fulfillment of the plan and improvement in the quality of the buildings' repairs, upkeep of the streets and courtyards, directing the work of the housing committees (domkom), women's councils, comrades' courts, concerning themselves with the organization of work with children, and the maintenance of social order.[21]

The party organization and every communist must take it his job to see that the apartments are warm in the winter, that all essential services are functioning smoothly, and "that the roof doesn't leak." As one handbook puts it, "it is well known that everyday disorders give rise to complaints, spoil the mood of the people, and lower the quality and tempo of their labor." Consequently, it is very important for party organizations to keep these daily problems at the center of their attention.[22] Furthermore, Party organizations must show special concern that "politically mature, experienced comrades" are selected to the housing administrations, "men capable of conducting an active control, so that the decrees of the Party and state in the field of the housing economy and culture-service will be fulfilled." Finally, Party Life exhorted Party organizations to uncover all shortcomings in the work of the housing administrations, bureaucratism, dishonesty, and indifference.[23] Where the line is drawn between "the right to control" the activities of the housing administration and the "important Party missions" is almost impossible to see.

TOWARD THE STATE OF THE WHOLE PEOPLE: THE DEPUTIES' COUNCILS AND HOUSE COMMITTEES

> Every Soviet man must become an active participant in the administration of the affairs of society!—That is our slogan, our task.—N. S. Khrushchev, Twenty-Second Party Congress, 1961

At the end of the 1950s, Khrushchev advanced the concept of
the State of the Whole People, with its emphasis on increased public
participation in the administration of public affairs. Stress on the
"voluntary principle" led to the development during the 1960s of the
deputies' councils or deputies'groups located at the housing offices.
As in other spheres of activity, Soviet leaders seemed to be looking
back to their early post-Revolutionary experiences in order to advance
into the communism of tomorrow, for the deputies' council had its
model in the 1920s. The idea was that if the deputies began to work
collectively in the microraions, their effectiveness and activity would
grow. In the previous chapter we discussed the role of the deputies'
councils in the distribution of living space. One of their main functions
is to attract volunteers for the job of daily inspecting communal problems and managing public affairs. The principle task of the deputies'
council is to direct the organizational work at local levels, put into
practice the resolutions of the Soviet government and the decisions of
the raion and city Soviets, and to funnel information up to regular
governmental channels. Among their rights, the deputies' councils
have the right to exercise some control over the means allotted for
current and capital repairs of the housing fund, to check up on the
quality of construction and repair work, to inspect the condition of
the streets, squares and public order in their microraions. The
deputies' council also has the job of looking over the work of the
housing office.24 Every deputies' council conducts educational work
among the population of its microraion. For example, with the Party
organization, the council might organize a circle for the study of
materials from the latest Party congress, or circles on current
policies. Thus, the council is one more way for the state to inform
its citizens of their obligations and to develop the proper communist
point of view. A large part of the council's functions seems to be
serving as a safety valve by providing a channel for the receipt of
citizens' complaints. In this role, the deputies' council is a significant
factor in the development of consultative bureaucratic government in
the Soviet Union. The councils also have a close connection with
another revival from the Soviet past, the domkom. Before the creation of the deputies' councils, the house committees (domkom) had to
turn for help to the leaders of the Housing Operations Office (ZhEK),
who more often than not sent them to the housing administration,
which sent them back to the ZhEK's, effectively frustrating any real
initiative. Apparently, the domkom was having a difficult time getting
to the ispolkom. With the appearnace of the deputies' councils, the
domkom at least found a channel for its initiative. The year 1962
seemed to be a good one for the appearance of other institutions of
mass participation in addition to the deputies' councils. In that year,
the repair druzhiny (remontnye druzhiny) made their debut in Moscow.

The Street (Block) Committees [ulichnye (kvartal'nye) komitety] were billed as an important and active organizational form of uniting activists in helping the executive organs of the raion Soviets in the work of city planning and improvement. During the 1930s these committees had received a great deal of publicity, then faded from the public spotlight, only a regain official attention with the re-emphasis on the voluntary principle. The Street Committee is one more quasi-voluntary public organization in a field full of public, governmental, Party, and trade-union committees. Its functions include: helping the raiispolkom in the work of improving the streets, sectors, and buildings; organizing public control over the building manager's beautification and improvement work; conducting cultural-educational work among tenants and working with children; exercising control over the observance of the rules of the socialist way of life and taking measures for insuring social order.[25] The proliferation during the 1960s of voluntary organizations carrying out the same or similar functions is indeed dizzying. For all this increased control, a reading of the Soviet press makes it difficult to believe that economic accountability and operations of the housing fund were greatly improved.

The House Committee (Domkom)

Soviet political theory places the highest importance on organizing urban life for optimal communal activity. It is assumed that the more intense the communal life, the greater the individual's pleasure and social development. In the late 1950s the house committee of tenants (domovyikomitet) or domkom was rescued from the dustbin of history where it had lain for many years. Soon the domkom's many subcommittees, task forces, and special groups would be striving to achieve the active participation of every inhabitant in the apartment building. Here, then, was an organization that might provide the institutional framework for an expanded public participation in the administration of housing and daily affairs, and thereby constructively aid the development of a more intense and gratifying communal experience—or so it was hoped. Unlike its post-Revolutionary predecessor, the modern domkom is not a spontaneously formed committee of tenants with the primary responsibility for managing the building. It is an assistant to and a control over the house management. Official statutes and supplementary commentaries point out that the domkom has the very important function of waging a struggle against the uneconomical expenditure of resources and materials in the housing economy, and against squandering and wastefulness. The domkom, therefore, performs an audit function. But no less important is its assignment to train tenants in the spirit of the careful treatment of the housing fund,

166

to raise the resident's responsibility for the maintenance of his apartment and building, and to organize the leisure time of the resident,
especially of the children.[26] Though the domkom's participation in
solving the practical tasks of improving the operation and maintenance
of the housing fund is seen as the most important measure of its value,
its work in organizing the social life of its building's inhabitants should
not be neglected.

Located in the apartment buildings, the house committee works
in close contact with primary Party organizations, with Soviet, trade-
union, and komsomol organizations, with standing committees of the
local Soviet, with the town and district housing administrations, the
ZhEK's the departments of housing and municipal services, and with
the house managements. Those domkoms whose membership is made
up of people "who take the initiative" have been called the most successful in solving the tasks assigned to them. And it is is the primary
Party organization in the house managements, the ZhEK's and ZhK's,
that must play a large role in the selection of the domkom's staff, to
insure the recruitment of the most reliable and active tenants.
Communists who are registered in the Party organization at their
place of residency are told to consider their work in the domkoms as
a most important Party mission.[27] The domkoms in the local Soviet's
housing fund are directly subordinate to the raiispolkoms, and those
in departmental houses to the trade union committees.[28] Consequently,
the ispolkoms and trade union committees are to provide the leadership
for the house committee's activity. Legislation of 1968 underlines the
responsibility of the Housing Operations Office for taking part in the
house committee's work. The domkom is selected by open vote at
a general meeting of tenants for a two-year term. The committee
must have no fewer than seven persons, and usually has between seven
and twenty-five members. Once the committee is formed, it selects
its own chairman, vice-chairman, and secretary, and divides responsibility among the remaining members of the committee. At least once
a year the domkom is required by law to report on its work to a
tenants' meeting. If representatives of the Comrades' Courts and
Parents' Committee and those responsible for fire prevention are not
elected to the domkom, they are enlisted to participate in the committee's work. The domkom's real work is carried out through its
councils of volunteers, commissions, subcommittees, task forces
and special groups. These various subgroups may include a council
of volunteers for work with children and adolescents, a council of
physical culture and health, the commission or subcommittee on
economics and finances (or management and finances), beautification.
sanitation, culture and education, and fire prevention. As for meetings
the house committee conducts them when ever it feels it is necessary.[29]
Besides the subcommittees, a Parents' Committee (roditel'skii

komitet) is created under the domkom. This Parents' Committee is especially concerned with helping the family and school to rear the children. It is selected at a general meeting of parents, composed of from five to seven persons and, like the domkom, has a two-year term.30 We should note that the domkom's highly structured form was solidified only in 1968, and is a result of almost a decade of domkom experience. In 1968 it appears that the Soviet leadership undertook to rationalize, more carefully define, and give clearer direction to the many quasi-public organizations that sprang up during the Khrushchev era. It was also in 1968 that new legislation appeared on the People's Control Commission.

SubCommittees of the Domkom

Since most of the domkom's work is conducted in subgroups, it is enlightening to examine the operations of these organizations. Every commission or subcommittee, composed of from three to eight persons, must work according to a monthly, quarterly, semi-annual, or annual plan. These plans define what has to be done in the given period and who is expressly responsible for fulfillment of the work. It is the task of the subcommittee chairman to maintain a list of all work carried out by the subcommittee, as well as by each one of its members and activist associates. On the basis of the subcommittee's work plans, the larger domkom works out its own work plan, which includes general measures being carried out by the house management, the ZhEK, and the housing office in addition to those of the subcommittees. For example, the domkom's work plan may include the conducting of general meetings of tenants; public examinations (or raids) of the technical and sanitary state of the apartments, entrances, and buildings; checking on the observance of the rules for the use of the apartments and conditions of the lease for living quarters; arranging lectures; and creating various study circles.31

Economic-Financial Subcommittee

The economic-financial subcommittee (khoziaistvenno-finansovaiia komissiia—khoz-finkom) is one of the most important of the domkom organizations. Its main concern is, as its name implies, the organizational, technical, and management-financial operation of the building according to the khoz-fin plan (the economic-financial plan). The khoz-fin plan includes the management's income and expenditures, special collections—including payments for municipal services to the tenants—and the organization of labor and wages. In addition to general estimates for operational expenses, the khoz fin plan encompasses a schedule for current repairs and technical inspection. The khoz-finkom tries to enlist engineers, technicans, economists, planners, accountants, clerical workers, and any skilled workers who may be living in the building. If it is successful in achieving such a specialized composition, the subcommittee creates several special task forces for the solution of specific problems. One such group of activists will check on the state of the building's technical documentation. For the legal operation of a building every house management must have complete technical documentation that certifies receipt of the building from the construction organization and includes the house management's general plan and plans for each floor, diagrams of the outside and inside network of water pipes, sewerage, and so on, elevator permits, and documents on the building's repair. A second group of specialists takes part in the public inspection of the building. A third group checks out the boiler, pipes, heating system, sewerage, and electrical system. The struggle against escaping water is one of the khoz-finkom's most important practical jobs. Control over the tempo and quality of repairs and the proper use of finances for repairs is handled by yet another subgroup of volunteers. Concern for the building's winterizing is also part of the khoz-finkom's responsibility. Still one more group follows up on the state of rent payments and the correct payments for heating and other municipal services. Finally, a large group, including those persons elected as "authorized" (upolnomochennye) or "responsible" (otvestvennye) for the building, the entrances, and apartments, participate in an inspection of the use and maintenance of living quarters.

Subcommittee on Sanitation

The subcommittees on sanitation are "active conductors of health culture," "active fighters for the carrying out of measures for greater sanitation in daily life."[32] Naturally, these sanitation committees seek those residents who are medical workers, members of the first-aid units of the Red Cross, and a wide group of activists in the health-sanitation field. This committee has the job of establishing sanitary or health posts (first-aid posts) in every building and in every section of large buildings. One of the health committee's most important tasks is the broad dissemination of the rules or personal hygiene and sanitation. Inspections of apartments and courtyards and lectures are conducted by the committee's members. An important event in the life of the committee is the Medical Worker's Day, which takes place annually on the third Sunday of June. The Medical Worker's Day is a relatively recent special day, its first observance being in

1966. For the subcommittee, the day means a public inspection of its achievements in the health field and a chance for another raid on individual living quarters.

SubCommittee on Beautification

Those with a green thumb and a yen for nature will feel right at home in this subcommittee, which does "invaluable" work in planting and greenification of courtyards, grounds, and city streets in conjunction with the All-Russian Society for the Preservation of Nature. Play ground planning and educational work about nature form part of the committee's assignment. The beautification committee also plans for its big event—"Garden Week," the Day of the Birds (Den' ptits), and Forest Month (mesiachnika lesa).

SubCommittee on Cultural and Educational Life

A major domkom subcommittee is the subcommittee on cultural and educational life, which works under the leadership of the primary Party organization. It is this committee that has the serious mission of educating the workers in the spirit of high idealism and communist morality. This cultural and educational subcommittee has been criticized for lack of creativity in capturing the imagination of the residents. It has been exhorted to use as many different forms of communications as possible in its work, such as lectures, individual discussions, special reports, meetings with teachers, doctors, poets, artists, advanced workers, question and answer sessions, and the collective viewing of films, plays, and exhibits. Organizing recreation for children and adolescents also comes under the committee's responsibilities. The "Red Corners" have a prominent place in the committee's work, as well as organizing libraries and reading rooms. The subcommittee on cultural and educational life is important enough to receive up to 2 percent of the housing organ's yearly operational expenses.[33]

The wall newspapers (stengazety) of the domkoms, published jointly with the Party, trade union, and komsomol organizations, provide another means to educate the tenants in the proper treatment of housing. They also help bring pressure to bear on any deviants, for "in the pages of a building's wall newspaper, it is not rare to find criticism of violators of the rules of socialist communal living, trouble-makers, squabblers, and brawlers."[34]

After this brief examination of the domkom and its subgroups, it becomes clear that the house committee is not only a part of a

control function to improve the housing fund and to check violation,
it is also part of a larger political and social system that strives to
accomplish the total active involvement of every Soviet citizen in all
spheres of life. Perhaps because of the rent policy that maintains very
low rent levels, the inhabitants must be mobilized to do a great deal of
the checking and controlling for the building's upkeep. But with all the
controllers, both public and official, with overlapping functions, many
areas of the housing economy still manage to escape effective control.
The 1968 resolutions on the domkom indicate that many housing committees, especially those in the departmental housing fund, are not
succeeding in mobilizing the population in the struggle for the preservation of residential buildings. A major criticism of the domkom's
activities was that they were not showing any real initiative. One reason
for this condition is the fact that the domkom has very little power.
The ispolkoms, trade union committees, and especially the leaders of
the housing organizations pay the domkom little mind and violate the
domkom's few rights.[35] It was this "benign neglect" that was so
strongly criticized in 1968, when the Russian government expressed
its determination to strengthen the domkom's rights to participate
in house management, particularly the right to have control over the
activity of the housing organizations (ZhEK). It was proposed to repeat Moscow's experience in setting up raion public councils of house
committees to assist the raiispolkoms and trade union committees in
working and carrying out measures concerning the housing fund.
Strengthening the domkom through these councils might have been an
attempt to provide another check on the housing offices, which were
already being overseen by the deputies' councils and Party organizations. Press reports and People's Control Sheets indicate that the
housing offices are not doing a good enough job in operating state
housing. The loudest complaint seems to be that the 1962 resolution
urging all raiispolkoms to "develop and disseminate, on the voluntary
principle, public forms of apartment house maintenance services . . .
with an eye to reducing the number of service personnel under the
apartment house administrations" was being grossly distorted in
certain housing administrations. In Krasnodar, for example, tenants
in some buildings were forced to hire their own janitors to clean the
stairways and halls and provide usual services, because the housing
administration decided to "save money" by extending the "voluntary
principle" to those activities. However, there seemed to be not indication of what the housing administration did with its savings. As the
control sheet entitled "What Should Be Done?" concluded, "the public
principle in voluntary forms of apartment building maintenance
services is a necessary thing. But it must not be applied through
complusion."[36] In addition to its control-audit functions, a significant
part of the domkom's work is to convince residents that voluntary

participation is a source of personal and communal satisfaction and is not forced participation.

As the Soviet society moves closer to its national goal of a separate, well-built apartment for every family, its leaders may becoming more aware of the need for new institutions to insure that Soviet home life remains centered in the communal life. If the individual's apartment becomes more spacious, comfortable, and private, will he still be as concerned about and as anxious to engage in an intense collective experience, or will he begin to see his apartment as his protection against the intensity of the community? In the past the "housing closeness" has driven the individual seeking to enjoy his leisure out of his room into collective forms of recreation. Since life inside the crowded apartment was not very restful or private, the tenant had to rely on public forms of entertainment or walk the streets for privacy. It was rare for the average Soviet urban dweller to "live" in his apartment or room; he simply slept there or used the kitchen. Now that all this changing, can Soviet social theorists be so sure that the more intense one's communal life, the greater will be one's pleasure and social development? The house committees of tenants, along with a myriad of other social and political organizations, may be one attempt to encourage the citizen's fullest participation in the affairs of the community. The domkom's revival at the end of the 1950s and its further institutionalization during the 1960s may very well be an indication of the regime's acute awareness of the changing social aspects brought about by improved housing conditions. It is likely that the house committee's social functions will become even more important in the future, and that the tenant will be called upon more and more frequently to participate in its activities.

NOTES

1. A. Semenenko, "K voprosy o vedomstvennom zhilishchnom fonde" (Concerning the Problems of the Department Housing fund), Gorodskoe khoziaistvo Moskvy, no. 3 (March 1964): 22.

2. Ibid., p. 23.

3. A. Balaianta, "Housing Should Have One Master," Izvestia, November 15, 1964.

4. Ibid.

5. G. M. Klysh, "Sovershenstvovat' upravlenie zhilishchnym khoziaistvom" (Perfect the Administration of the Housing Economy), Gorodskoe khoziaistvo Moskvy, no. 8, (August 1964): 29.

6. Izvestia, December 19, 1964; See also Izvestia, November 14 and November 24, 1964.

7. T. A. Selivanov and M. A. Gel'perin, Planirovanie gorodskogo khoziaistva (na primere Moskvy) (Planning the Urban Economy: the Moscow Example) Moscow: Ekonomika, 1970, p. 120.

8. V. P. Semin, "A Union Republic Ministry and the Local Soviets," Sovetskoe gosudarstvo i pravo, no. 9 (September 1969): 91.

9. See, for example, ibid., p. 92.

10. M. Naimushin, "The Soviet Is Master of the City," Izvestia, February 14, 1970, (CDSP, XXII, 7, p. 19): Semin, Sovetskoe gosudarstvo i pravo, no. 9 (September 1969), p. 91.

11. Pravda, March 14, 1971, and March 20, 1971.

12. See, for example, Izvestia, April 7, 1973, p. 5.

13. I. Bochkarov, "Yes, That's Advantageous," Izvestia, February 21, 1970.

14. See: Selivanov and Gel'perin, op. cit., p. 119.

15. Preamble to "O sokhranenii zhilishchnogo fonda i uluchshenii zhilishchnogo khoziaistva v gorodakh" (On the Preservation of the Housing Fund and the Improvement of Housing in Cities), October 17, 1937, Sobranie zakonov SSSR (Collection of Laws, USSR), 1937, I, 69, Art. 314.

16. Selivanov and Gel'perin, op. cit., p. 120.

17. "Iz pravil i norm tekhnicheskoi ekspluatatsii zhilishchnogo fonda" (From the Rules and Norms of the Technical Operations of the Housing Fund), Chapter II, Paragraph 13, Prikaz of the RSFSR Ministry of the Communal Economy, November 21, 1960, Zhilishchno-bytovye voprosy, p. 81.

18. Ibid., Paragraph 14.

19. T. Alekseev, Spravochnik po zhilishchnomu zakonodatel'stvu, Chapter VIII, pp. 226-280; "Rules and Norms for the Technical Operations of the Housing Fund," RSFSR Ministry of the Communal Economy," November 21, 1960, in Zhilishchno-bytovye voprosy, pp. 81ff. Max E. Mote, "Leningrad Municipal Administration," Doctoral Thesis University of Washington, 1966, p. 226.

20. G. Klysh, op. cit., p. 29.

21. "Pol'zuintsia li partorganizatsii domoupravlenii pravom kontrolia deiatel'nosti administratsii?" (Are Party Organizations of the House Managers' Offices Taking Advantage of their Rights to Control the Work of the Adminsitration?), Partiinaiia zhizn', no. 10, (May 1967): 50-51.

22. S. N. Rozantsev, Spravochnik po zhilishchnym voprosam (Moscow: Moskovskii Rabochii, 1967), p. 173.

23. Partiiniia zhizn', no. 10 (May 1967): 50-51.

24. P. S. Tsidilin, Chudesnoe sredstvo (Splendid Means) (Moscow: Moskovskii rabochii, 1962), pp. 10-11.

25. M. Studenikina, Formy uchastiia obshchestvennosti v rabote mestnykh sovetov deputatov trudiashchikhsia (Moscow: gosiurizdat, 1963), pp. 91-92.

26. Rozantsev, op. cit., pp. 159-160; "Ob usilenii roli domovykh komitetov v upravelenii gosudarstvennym zhilishchnym fondom" (On Strengthening the Role of the House Committees in the Administration of the State Housing Fund), Resolution of the RSFSR Council of Ministers and All-Union Central Council of Trade-Union Councils August 9, 1968, in Spravochnik profsoiuznogo rabotnika 1969 (Moscow: Profizdat, 1969), p. 441.

27. Rozantsev, op. cit., p. 160.

28. "On Strengthening the Role of the House Committees in the State Housing Fund," p. 443.

29. Ibid., p. 444.

30. V. N. Tel'nov, Obshchestvennyi domovyi komitet (Moscow: Profizdat), 1962, p. 9.

31. Rozantsev, op. cit., pp. 162-163.

32. Ibid., p. 167.

33. Materials on the domkom and its subcommittees from: "On Strengthening the Role of the House Committees in the Administration of the State Housing Fund," Resolution of the RSFSR Council of Ministers and the All-Union Central Committee of Trade Union Councils, August 9, 1968, in Spravochnik profsoiuznogo rabotnika 1969, pp. 441-446; and Rozantsev, Spravochnik po zhilishchnym voprosam, pp. 159-169.

34. Telnov, op. cit., p. 79.

35. "On Strengthening the Role of the House Committees," p. 442.

36. People's Control Sheet No. 128: "What Should be Done?" Izvestia, July 9, 1968 (CDSP XX, no. 28: 31).

7

THE COOPERATIVE
HOUSING MOVEMENT

After twenty years of virtual extinction, the house construction cooperative (zhilishchno-stroitel'nyi kooperativ or ZhSK) was suddenly given a second chance at the end of the 1950s. It has since been increasingly favored and defended as a respectable socialist means for solving the Soviet housing problem. The present chapter will take a brief look at the cooperative's early history and reasons for its abrupt purge in 1937 from the ranks of the acceptable. Why did the house construction cooperative come out of limbo in 1958, and what is its role and importance in the larger picture of Soviet housing? Like all other forms of housing, cooperative housing has had its share of difficulties and serious shortcomings. We will try to point out these shortcomings and examine the steps taken to overcome them.

The ZhSK's organization will be a significant part of this study. What are the house construction cooperative's rights, privileges, and obligations, and what obligations and rights do the local Soviets possess in the cooperative field? How is the cooperative managed? Who are its members and what are their rights? And finally, what role do the Soviets, housing agencies, and Party organizations play in the cooperative's operations?

EARLY SOVIET EXPERIENCE
IN COOPERATIVE HOUSING

In its attempts to come to grips with an intensifying housing shortage in the 1920s, the Soviet government turned to its citizens for help. The important August 19, 1924, Decree "On Cooperative Housing" set a two-fold policy to combat the housing crisis by encouraging house building and house management "on the principles of self-help of the toiling masses" through voluntary cooperative housing societies. Two kinds of house construction cooperative associations (ZhSKT) were allowed, in addition to the house leasing

175

cooperative (ZhAKT). The housing cooperative associations of both types were part of a hierarchical system of controls through single city-wide unions of housing cooperatives. The city unions then formed the next units of the krai or oblast unions, and finally the krai or oblast unions of housing cooperatives joined into the republic unions (Centrzhilsoiuz). Sitting at the top of the cooperative pyramid was the All-Union Council of Housing Cooperatives, which directed the republic unions. The Workers' House Construction Cooperative Associations (Rabochie zhilishchno-stroitel'nye kooperativnye tovarishchestva or RZhSKT) could only accept members who were designated as workers or employees of state, cooperative, and social organizations, or more officially "those persons not deprived of electoral rights." Members of the Workers Cooperative (RZhSKT) could not subscribe for more housing space than provided by the legal norms. A member of one of the General House Construction Cooperative Associations (Obshche-grazhdanskie zhilishchno-stroitel'nye kooperativnye tovarishchestva or OZhSKT) could be any citizen. Allowing its member to subscribe for as much housing space as he desired and could afford, the OZhSKT was designed to attract bourgeois, nepmen, and other private capital into the housing fund.[1] From the outset, however, the General Coopera-tive was treated with reservation, and in the long run it would play a very minor role in the development of Soviet housing. Naturally, the Workers' House Construction Cooperative held the favored position, and was entitled to long-term (fifteen years and then extended to a maximum period of sixty years) state loans for up to 80 to 90 percent of the building's costs, that is, the minimum down payment was set at between 10 and 20 percent. In 1927 the RSFSR set the figure at 13 per-cent for the ZhSKT.[2] The individual who became a member of the General Cooperative (OZhSKT) was required to present a down payment of 30 percent of the cost of the building.[3] In addition to cash payments, members of the house cooperative associations could pay for their shares with construction materials and personal labor. Furthermore, members of the RZhSKT, like all Soviet citizens, always ran the risk of losing their right to vote in Soviet elections, and simultaneously of losing their right to housing space in the cooperative.[4] By the time of its drastic "reorganization" in 1937, the cooperative construction of housing accounted for less than 10 percent of the total amount of new housing construction, and probably less than 7 percent of that built by the public sector.[5]

There are good reasons for the relatively poor showing of co-operative house construction in the 1920s and 1930s. One of the most important causes, perhaps, is the basic pocketbook issue of the cost to a potential cooperative member. The individual worker who was in search of housing, and who either did not desire or saw no chance of obtaining state housing, was presented with the choice of building a private house, which required a 30 percent down payment, or entering a cooperative house building association with a down payment as low as 10 percent of the building cost. At first glance, it appears the man would surely choose the cooperative route to shelter. A closer examination, however, would reveal that 30 percent of the cost of a small wooden structure would be far less than 10 percent of the construction costs of a modern, multi-unit apartment building. What is more, the cooperative house member would have to pay a much higher monthly figure to the cooperative for the building's amortization and operational expenses than the tenant in a municipalized building would have to pay for rent. Uncertainty about the cooperative's status and future was another obstacle to the public's interest in joining house construction cooperatives. By the early 1930s it was becoming increasingly clear that official fervor for the cooperative form was quickly cooling. Even the semblance of independence was no longer acceptable. As was openly admitted in 1931,

> a socialist cooperative cannot even be imagined as existing outside of state control since it is a part of the overall economy which has been entrusted to the management of the officers elected by the occupants of the (cooperative) dwelling. During the reconstruction period, housing is directly drawn into the service of production, that is, it becomes inevitable and wholly subject to state control which decides all disputes, within Soviet cooperatives, between socialist and individualist tendencies in the interests of the state.[6]

Yet another cause for the failure of cooperative house construction was the ease with which members' rights were abused or ignored. According to the Model RZhSKT Charter of 1928, for example, cooperative construction loans were permitted from the ispolkoms, state enterprises, and cooperative organizations, so that the lenders might exercise the right of telling the cooperative who should be settled into 50 percent of the living quarters built with the loans. And the persons so designated did not have to be standing members of the cooperative. The same Model Charter allowed the setting up of a system of turns for satisfying the cooperative members' demands for living quarters. What this provision meant for many cooperative members was years of "malicious litigation."[7] It facilitated the use of favoritism and patronage, and ended up in an unhealthy situation where some members were not provided with housing. Those with the right "know who" usually had little trouble in quickly obtaining cooperative housing, whereas the less fortunate cooperative member might have to sit it out for several years.

In any event, late in 1937 the entire cooperative movement was to fall into official disgrace. The management of the basic state housing fund was taken away from the house leasing cooperative associations (ZhAKT) and placed in the local Soviets, state institutions, and industrial enterprises. The ZhAKTy were abolished. At the same time, the October 17, 1937, law "On the Preservation of the Housing Fund and the Improvement of Housing in Cities" effectively stifled the house construction cooperatives. The house construction cooperatives were charged with using long-term state loans to become "privileged property owners of living space." According to the decree's indictment, the "housing built by the construction cooperatives which cost the state one and one-half billion rubles [that is, old rubles] has in fact become the personal property of the members of the ZhSKT." Because of the 1924 and 1927 laws that extended long-term (up to sixty years) loans of from 80 to 90 percent of the cost of housing construction to the cooperatives, the 1937 decree points out, "the cooperative members received at government expense apartments for their permanent use, not subject to withdrawal, and in fact these members became the privileged property owners of the space, having paid only a negligible portion with their own funds." Consequently, instead of tapping private sources of capital to increase the amount of residential construction, "the housing cooperative built almost entirely at state expense, while at the same time the organs of the communal economy did not secure the right to use and manage." Furthermore, the preamble states, though the number of paid-up cooperative members increased from year to year, the house construction cooperatives did not satisfy them with dwelling space.

Part I (Section 3) of the actual Party-state decree struck down the construction cooperatives by declaring that all buildings built or in the process of being built by the ZhSKT mainly with the help of government funds shall be transferred

(a) To the administration of the local Soviets, if the buildings in question have been financed by direct credits from the Central Bank of the Communal Economy (Tsekombank) or from local municipal banks from their special capital funds;
or (b) To the administration of the appropriate organizations, or enterprises if the construction financing came from their funds.

By way of exception, the house construction cooperatives could retain control of their buildings if they could completely repay the state loans within six months. In the future, however, the cooperatives could build houses and dachas only with their own funds, without any credit.

State institutions and enterprises were expressly forbidden to invest "in any form whatever" their financial or material resources in construction by the cooperatives (Part 1, Section 4).[8] Since the state loans were paid off within six months in only a very few cases, in effect the house construction cooperatives were laid to rest with the house leasing cooperatives. In most cases the former cooperative members were allowed to remain in their dewllings. Control of the buildings, however, was turned over to regular state agencies.

It was clear from the outset of this early Soviet venture in cooperative housing that the cooperative form would be sailing on troubled waters. First of all, the great expectations that private capital would come flowing into cooperative house construction were contradicted by the regime's reluctance to trust the private investor. To a large extent, cooperative housing never really had a chance to become effective in solving the housing crisis. While it was still in its infancy, the changed political climate insured its early death. In 1929, for example, the General Housing Construction Cooperative Associations (OZhSKT) were subject to a series of sweeping confiscations, which signaled the end of an old era and the beginning of the new era that would increasingly bear the Stalinist stamp. As we have noted, in many instances the name "cooperative" was just a thin cover, too easily penetrated by "outside" influences. If a person with the right Party connections, or even favored groups of noncooperative members could move in and take over housing space designated to members of long standing, then the cooperative surely had dim prospects for success. Though it offered shelter to some Soviet citizens during the 1920s and 1930s, the house construction cooperative's real value may lie in the fact that it would provide the post-Stalinist leadership with concrete, legitimate models from their own country's past that they could apply in the present.

HOUSE CONSTRUCTION COOPERATIVISM REDISCOVERED

During the first few years of the Post-Stalin period, particularly after the Twentieth Party Congress in 1956, there was a great deal of attention paid to finding solutions to long neglected problems. As the Soviet Union was moving to an acceptance of the idea of many roads to socialism, so too it was realizing that there were many ways of eliminating its lingering housing shortage. Fresh consideration was given to early experiments in cooperative house construction. Concern grew for developing every aspect of residential building. By the end of 1956, the call for reviving the cooperative housing organizations grew in volume. Letters to the editors of the central

newspapers stressed the necessity of urgently restoring the cooperative's rights by changing the October 17, 1937, decree that prohibited
the granting of loans to housing construction cooperatives.[9] Seven
months later, in July 1957, the next step was taken. As part of its
sweeping program to expand housing construction, the 1957 decree
"On Developing Housing Construction in the USSR" permitted the
USSR Ministry of Finance to grant loans to "citizens jointly erecting
multiple-apartment houses on the same terms that it grants loans to
private builders." It spoke of "organizing individual builders into
housing cooperatives." Furthermore, the decree directed the republic
governments to amend the then existing regulations concerning private
building and the organization of housing collectives.[10] In other words,
the Party and state were announcing their intention to overhaul the
Stalinist housing policy embodied in the October 17, 1937, law. Let
us recall that while exhorting the Party, government, and trade unions
to develop all aspects of housing, including individual building, the
1957 decree is searching for new socialist solutions to the housing
problem. Its latent anti-private housing attitude was to become manifest in 1961-1962 in a wave of confiscations of privately owned housing,
and in an earnest turning to cooperative forms of housing construction
and ownership. Always on the lookout for new means to increase the
pace of socialist house construction, Khrushchev in a pre-election
speech on March 14, 1958, asked for innovative thoughts about ways
to draw into the housing construction program "the means of those
strata of the population who have savings and at the same time who
are in need of better living conditions." Khrushchev then went on to
suggest the "fresh idea" of organizing housing construction cooperatives.[11] On March 20, 1958, less than a week after Khrushchev's
speech, the USSR Council of Ministers issued its decree "On the House
and Ducha Construction Cooperative," which breathed new, though
weak, life into cooperative house construction. The 1958 decree and
subsequent model charters (1958) of House Construction Cooperatives
did little else but announce that the cooperative form was no longer
in disfavor, and that it should be more widely developed. They did
not extend state credits for the construction of cooperative housing.[12]
In an attempt to upgrade the construction of such cooperatives, the
1958 model ZhSK charters stipulated that the cooperative's buildings
could be built only by skilled contractors, that is, state contract construction organizations. In other words, they placed cooperative
house construction within the limits of the state plan for construction.
Furthermore, all construction cooperatives were limited to organization on the production principle, or formation at the enterprises,
institutions, and organizations. Citizens from different labor organizations could not come together to create a house construction cooperative.[13] It is not surprising to learn that there was no sudden

upsurge of cooperative house construction. In fact, the individual who
sought to improve his housing conditions with some of his own means
found it more favorable to construct a home as an individual builder
than as a cooperative member. Individual home builders were given
state credit for seven to ten years, whereas ZhSK members were
denied any government loans. Unable to obtain building materials at
wholesale prices, the ZhSK found that the cost of building a cooperative
apartment house was considerably higher than the cost of state housing
construction. The additional burden of having to deposit in the bank
the full cost of constructing the cooperative building even before the
start of construction slowed down any rush to cooperative house construction.[14] Only the wealthiest could afford to solve their housing
needs through the cooperative construction form.

Yet, with the official proclamation of Soviet society's entering
the transition period to communism, the continued investment of considerable private resources for individual house construction with the
aid of state loans seemed a less and less tolerable survival from the
past. At the 1960 All-Union Conference on City Planning and Construction, the need for radical measures to regulate the private construction of housing was emphasized. Conference participants advocated a more resolute shift to cooperative forms fo building multi-
unit apartment houses.[15] A little later, in July 1961, the Director of
the Institute of the Theory and History of Architecture and Construction Technology, K. Ivanov, made it absolutely clear that individual
housing construction promotes the stubborn persistence of small-
property survivals in the consciousness of the people. He admitted
that the Soviet Union could not abandon individual construction for
the time being. It was necessary, however, "to direct such construction through cooperative channels of large, multi-story houses."[16]
Change was in the wind. One small, but important step was taken in
1960 to encourage cooperative building. Before 1960 the ZhSK had to
pay a land rent for the use of the land plot, as well as a tax for its
structures. An April 23, 1960, RSFSR resolution freed the ZhSK from
the tax for structures and from land rent.[17] The idea of granting
long-term state credits to cooperatives began to catch on in Soviet
legal literature.[18] With the 1961 New Party Program's hope of a
foreseeable end to the housing shortage and the promise of a well-
built, separate apartment for each family within the near future,
housing cooperatives would be singled out for an imporatnt role in
solving the Soviet housing problem. The big breakthrough came in
June 1962 when the Central Committee of the CPSU and the USSR
Council of Ministers issued a joint resolution "On Individual and
Cooperative Housing Construction." Henceforth, the housing construction cooperative could receive state credits for up to 60 percent of
the estimated cost of construction for a period of from ten to fifteen

years. Cooperative house construction was to be assured a place in the state plan for contract construction-assembly work, and the stress was to be on standard designs. In contrast to previous experience, the cooperative building's construction costs and time were to be brought into conformity with costs and schedules for the construction of state housing. Materials and fixtures could be purchased at wholesale prices. The ZhSK was granted the perpetual (bessrochnoe) use of land tracts in districts, with roads, water mains, sewerage, and electricity. The 1962 resolution amended the 1958 requirement that limited the creation of cooperatives to single organizations, denying membership to any persons who were not employed by the organization. Cooperatives could now be created under the local Soviets by persons employed in different organizations. All branches of government were called upon to give assistance to the ZhSK's organization. While the housing construction cooperative suddenly gained in stature, the 1962 resolution struck a decisive blow at the individual home builder. In the first paragraph, the Party and government stated their aim of realizing in future years the gradual shift from individual single-unit home construction in urban areas to multi-unit, large cooperative house construction. A later section of the resolution indicated the necessity of ceasing the granting of land and credit in the union republic capitals for individual house construction. It gave the union republic councils of ministers the right to stop land allotments and credits to individual builders in other cities and urban settlements.[19] As the campaign for cooperative housing picked up momentum, a series of decrees and resolutions put the cooperative on a firmer basis and further weakened the support for individual building. As of January 1, 1964, for example, private housing construction was banned in all large cities (of more than 100,000 persons) as well as in resort cities, while credits for cooperative construction were increased (Izvestia, September 20, 1963). Finally, a November 19, 1964, resolution "On Further Development of Cooperative Housing Construction" gave the cooperative the right to have the municipal housing agencies service cooperative buildings at the same rates established for servicing buildings in the state housing fund. The same law greatly widened the possibilities of cooperative house construction by allowing the ispolkoms in settlements of the Kazakh Republic and in a number of krais, oblasts, and the autonomous republics of the RSFSR to lower the required down payment of construction costs before construction could be started from 40 to 30 percent, and by extending the terms of state credit up to twenty years. At the same time, cooperatives were permitted to be organized not only in cities and urban areas, but also in sovkhozes and rural settlements. The cooperatives were also legally freed from the heavy burden of reimbursing the costs of razed structures and the cost of fruit and berry plantings located on personal property, as

well as from having to allocate housing to persons displaced from
their private housing. These responsibilities were now placed on the
ispolkoms. Furthermore, the ispolkoms were authorized to act as
clients in the construction of cooperative housing.[20] At the Twenty-
Third Party Congress in 1966, both Brezhnez and Kosygin urged the
expansion of cooperative housing "in every possible way." "Every
encouragement must be given to cooperative construction," stated
Kosygin, "whose volume is to increase by 200 percent to 300 percent.
. . ."[21] The post-Khrushchev leaders, however, showed less of a
bias against private builders, who were also encouraged.

In the same year, the suggestion was made that the down payment
for cooperative housing be not 40 percent but 5 percent, and that there
be serious consideration given to the proposal for shifting from public
housing to cooperative housing. Writing in Novyi mir, A. Birman urged
that urban housing construction be basically cooperative. He argued
that housing shareholders treat housing much more attentively and
economically, and their participation in housing administration serves
to train them in social responsibility. Birman went so far as to pro-
pose that the cooperative principle be extended to movie theaters,
circuses, laundries, photo studios, even repair and rental shops.[22]
While there has been little movement in that direction, there has been
further discussion about lowering the down payment for house cooperative members, in order to broaden the social base of the cooperative.

Most Soviet authors discussing cooperative housing turn to Lenin
to legitimize the cooperative device, pointing out that the first leader
of the Soviet state indicated the necessity of full support and development of the cooperative movement, and that this all-round support
should consist of a number of economic and financial privileges.[23]
They also feel the necessity of justifying the use of the cooperative
form as socialist, and of explaining the difference between cooperative
housing in capitalist countries and socialist ones. Shala Chikvashvili,
Soviet legal specialist on cooperative housing, for example, emphasizes
that behind the surface goal of cooperative "is hidden the fact that
house construction cooperatives in capitalist countries in reality are
capitalist enterprises, yielding, like any capitalist productive enterprise, a profit." He goes on to stress that in capitalist countries
membership in housing cooperatives requires large monetary fees,
beyond the means of the wide strata of toilers. "Hence, it is clear
that in the majority of cases the shareholders are the petty bourgeoisie, the bureaucratic strata and the most highly paid top of the
working class."[24] By contrast, it is argued that in the Soviet Union
the property of the house construction cooperative is by its socio-
economic nature socialist property. However, though a socialist form
of property, the cooperative property has peculiarities that distinguish
it from the state form of socialist property. Cooperative socialist

property has a group rather than a public character. This simply means that it does not belong to all the people like state property, but to the ZhSK, the collective of its members as a whole.25

The ideological correctness of the cooperative device seems to be of considerable concern to Soviet urbanists. Of equal concern is the distributing "class" appearance in some Soviet house cooperatives. In 1965, in a Kommunist article, B. Svetlichny criticized the prevailing view that individual house construction must gradually be curtailed in favor of expanded cooperative house construction. Why was Svetlichny fighting against the seeming trend? He was arguing that cooperative housing construction cannot take the place of individual construction, or individual construction of the cooperative form, because of economic differences between the persons involved in the two forms. Since those who join the cooperatives are "mostly well-to-do city dwellers, specialists and highly skilled workers," their housing requirements and desires are different from those of the individual builder, not to mention their ability to pay for housing. In order to make cooperative housing more accessible, "not only to higher-paid workers and employees, but to all strata of the population," Svetlichny suggested that the down payment could be reduced from 40 percent to 20 percent of the apartment's cost, so that a one-room apartment could be obtained at an initial cost of only five hundred rubles, and a two-room apartment for about eight hundred and fifty rubles. He also felt it desirable to extend the terms of the loans and to consider the family's material resources and composition. According to Svetlichny (see Chapter 2), the current cooperative member, usually in somewhat better circumstances than his average follow citizen, frequently wishes to improve his living conditions, lives separately from grown children, and moves from an overcrowded communal apartment into a separate, comfortable apartment in a modern building. Since cooperatives are called upon to help expedite the elimination of the housing shortage, it is logical, Svetlichny emphasizes, to grant privileges first to those families living in overcrowded and substandard quarters. He concludes that "it would be wrong if cooperative housing, for which the state provides credit and material resources and services of the construction organizations, were erected for citizens already living in good conditions, simply because they have money. Such a practice may even hinder the solution of the housing problem."26

The Soviet leadership's concern for a more intensive development of cooperative housing appears to be part of its desire to satisfy the demands of various high-paid, influential elite groups. Increased automobile production resulting from the Soviet agreement with the Italian Fiat Company provides another example of the regime's efforts to meet elites' demands for a better material life. Although most of the legislation and rules concerning cooperatives stipulate that the

buildings should be built according to standard models, exceptions
are allowed, particularly in cases involving certain elite groups.
The Georgian Council of Ministers, for example, allowed the Union
of Artists and the Board of Directors of the Georgian Republic to work
out an individual plan for a sixty-unit apartment house. In another
case, the USSR Gosstroi permitted a cooperative of the Academy of
Sciences to build a residential building on an individual design.[27]
While they offer these important groups a chance for improved housing,
the house construction cooperatives also serve to absorb a large
amount of private money that otherwise would surely strain the consumer sector. Money going into cooperative housing is money that
reduces the individual's consumer purchasing power. This fact is
clearly illustrated in a 1964 Sovetskaia Rossiia article urging citizens
to invest their savings in cooperative apartments. One chairman of
a housing cooperative frankly admitted that "for fifteen years my wife
and I put part of our pay in a savings bank. We figured on accumulating
money to buy a Moskvich automobile. But what is more important: a
luxury item or a necessity?" The chairman then went on to suggest
that "the time has come to look differently at those who stubbornly
strive to get an apartment from the state, while themselves buying
dachas and cars and squandering money. . . ."[28]

ADVANCES AND SETBACKS IN
COOPERATIVE HOUSE CONSTRUCTION

After the 1958 resolution reinstating cooperative house construction to a respectable, socialist position, the pace of actual cooperative
construction was very slow. By 1965 only 6 to 7 percent of all housing
construction in the Soviet Union was of the cooperative type, compared
with 30 to 50 percent in Hungary, Bulgaria, and East Germany, and
by 1968 the volume of cooperative housing in the USSR still remained
below 10 percent of the total volume of new housing construction.[29]
The development of cooperative housing lagged woefully behind planned
targets. For the RSFSR as a whole, for example, in the first half of
1963 the plan for opening up cooperative housing was only fulfilled by
about 37 percent.[30] Though the 1964 plan was once again underfulfilled
(only 89 percent fulfilled), there was 160 percent more cooperative
housing built than in 1963.[31] But in the same year, Azerbaidzhan
managed to meet only 42 percent of its cooperative construction plan,
Tadzhikistan 57 percent, and the Kirgiz Republic 87 percent.[32] In
other terms, of the 4,019 housing cooperatives registered in the USSR
in 1964, only four were located in Turkmenistan and two in Tadzhikistan. Of the 1,710 apartment houses built in that year by cooperatives,
only five were built in Azerbaidzhan and only one each in Tadzhikistan

and Turkmenistan.[33] Clearly, those cooperative buildings erected
were concentrated in the larger cities closer to the center of national
power. In all, from 1962 through 1969, 17.3 million square meters of
living space were built and 700,000 families received apartments as
a result of cooperative construction in the Russian Republic. However,
even during 1969 cooperative construction plans were not fulfilled,
and the Russian Republic's cooperative housing construction of 2,498,000
square meters of living space for the year was lower than its 1967
total of 2,791,300 (see Table 9).[34] According to the 1971 National
Economic Plan, 7 million square meters of housing were expected to
be built in the USSR through house construction cooperatives, or the
same amount of cooperative housing that was opened up in 1966.[35]
This figure represented a little less than 6 percent of the total new
expected housing space (of 117.8 million square meters) to be built
through all sources of finances, or 9.8 percent of new housing to be
built through state resources.[36] Although there has been noticeable
growth of cooperative housing since 1963, its annual share of the total
new housing is actually slightly lower than the 1963 figure of between
6 and 7 percent. Reportedly, the volume of cooperative apartment
house construction is to increase by 240 percent over the 1971-1975
period, thus increasing its importance in solving the housing problem.[37]

There are many reasons for the relatively slow development of
cooperatives in the Soviet Union. One fact has become vary clear
over the years. Many local Soviets and their agencies have treated
the housing construction cooperatives as second-class citizens and
have hindered their advance by intolerable delays and unjustified
costs. Cooperatives were often allotted lands only after months of
delay. These lands more often than not were remote from the center
of the city and required expensive site preparation. Regardless of
legal prohibitions, cooperatives too frequently were required to build
roads, lay underground communications and pipes, and even raze
existing structures at their own expense.[38] In the early days of the
cooperative revival, ispolkoms even requested that the cooperative
pay for the building of everyday service enterprises.[39] The November
19, 1964, decree did set a one-month time limit on the allocation of
land plots for cooperative construction and instructed ispolkoms to
assign territories that have been earmarked for mass housing construction and that are located near the work sites of the shareholders.
As we have seen, the cooperative was also freed from paying for the
demolition of structures on the site. But the local Soviets were too
busy with meeting more important sectors of the plan to spend much
energy helping the house cooperative. One example is the local
Sovict's unsatisfactory checking up on the work of the contract construction organizations, who also looked on the cooperative as less

TABLE 9

Housing Built by
Housing Construction Cooperatives in the RSFSR

	Number of Co-operatives (at end of the year)	Number of Share-holders (at end of the year in thousands of persons)	Housing Built [in thousands of square meters of total (Useful) floor Space]
1963	1,331	102.1	1,277
1964	2,658	225.6	3,493
1965	3,020	272.5	4,487
1966	3,199	289.0	4,505
1967	2,996	274.7	4,222
1968	2,709	259.5	4,196
1969	2,573	251.0	3,945

Note: The figures represent total floor space and not living space, which is a smaller figure. For example, in 1967 while the total floor space built was 4,222,000 square meters, the total amount of living space was 2,791,300 square meters.

Source: Central Statistical Administration of the RSFSR Council of Ministers, Narodnoe khoziaistvo RSFSR v 1969 9. (The National Economy of the RSFSR for 1969) (Moscow: Statistika, 1970), p. 301.

than worthy of their full efforts.[40] The length of time needed just to review all the required documents was at least six months, and often longer, before any construction work could actually begin. City agencies were also exceedingly remiss and tardy in drawing up plans and estimates for cooperative housing, and often the plans they did provide had little to do with the real needs of the shareholders.[41] To make matters worse, before 1964 the house construction cooperatives had to make arrangement with various contract building organizations on their own. As of January 1, 1964, the ispolkoms have acted as clients for the cooperatives by contracting the builders. The results of this change may be seen in the 1964 total of 4.8 million square meters, an obvious advance over the 1963 figure of 1.8 million square meters.[42]

The problem of standard designs has set up one more obstacle blocking a more enthusiastic leap to cooperative forms of house construction. Some cities' Architectural and Planning Commissions have given prospective cooperative members little choice in building designs and size of apartments. Moreover, designers have tried to lower the cost of construction at the expense of quality and comfort, particularly the size of the apartment. The number of rooms will determine the overall cost to the individual member. In Moscow's Biryulevo Borough, for example, as well as in other boroughs and other cities, housing cooperatives had been presented standard designs with very few one-and two-room apartments. As a recent Izvestia article noted, as a rule almost half the apartments have three rooms, but of the 60,000 families in Biryuleva Borough wishing to join a cooperative apartment house, only three thousand need three-room apartments.[43]

Many of the difficulties facing the cooperatives are the same ones involved in the construction of any Soviet housing, only intensified. For example, according to the Assistant Director of the USSR Construction Bank's Cooperative and Individual Housing Construction Department, P. D. Vasilyev, almost everywhere in the Soviet Union the actual time needed to build cooperative apartment houses greatly exceeds the technical norms. To illustrate the point, he relates that in the RSFSR the construction of a five-story brick cooperative apartment house requires on the average 467 days, instead of the stipulated 265 days. As for large-panel construction of the same size buildings, 295 days instead of 207 days are required. And, as usual, the situation is even worse in Azerbaidzhan, "where construction time from start to finish drags on to 900 days and more."[44]

> Not least among the numerous reasons for construction
> delays is the extra trouble involved in authorizing a
> cooperative, obtaining a site and having this construction
> included in the work programs of the contractors.[45]

It is no wonder that Soviet citizens become frustrated with the cooperative device for relieving their housing needs.

Perhaps the lion's share of the blame for the setbacks to cooperative house construction belongs to the construction organizations themselves. Why are cooperative construction plans so regularly underfulfilled? Because the construction organization's primary concern is fulfillment of the plan for state-financed housing construction. If need be, builders have few qualms about using resources allotted for cooperative construction to fulfill or overfulfill the state-financed housing construction plans. For example, Trust No. Three of the Russian Republic Ministry of Rural Construction met only 55 percent of its cooperative housing plan in 1968, while managing to overfulfill its own construction plan by 100 percent![46] The construction organizations have been slow to accept seriously cooperative construction assignments. They still consider them secondary jobs, somewhat beyond the law of the plan. Then, too, the lack of material incentives plays a significant role in the contractors' attitude. While construction organizations receive 10 percent of the state housing they build, they do not receive 10 percent of the cooperative housing space they build. Furthermore, failure to fulfill their plan for cooperative construction has absolutely no effect on the bonuses they receive.[47] It appears likely that this situation might soon be corrected. To remedy the situation, a Stroibank official recently has suggested that Gosplan make an equivalent allotment of funds (10 percent) to construction organizations for erecting cooperative apartment houses. Presumably, there would also be adjustments in the bonus-incentive system.[48]

In an attempt to stabilize their populations, certain union republics and individual cities have added extra restrictions to those who would like to join housing cooperatives. The Uzbek Model ZhSK Charter for the city of Tashkent, for instance, stipulates that the prospective cooperative member must have resided in Tashkent for at least three years. In some other cities, the ispolkoms have limited cooperative housing only to those citizens who are in front-rank positions on the waiting list for housing. Some cities, such as Moscow, have even imposed a ten-year residency requirement. Still other cities have set various limits on the maximum amount of space per person. In the opinion of some legal authors, these "local" restrictions are contrary to the basic aim of cooperative construction, which is to attract the greatest amount of private funds to a socialist way for solving the housing shortage.[49]

One very crucial factor in the slow growth of cooperative house construction is the cost, the same factor that restrained the earlier cooperative movement of the 1920s and 1930s. If the average two-room cooperative apartment (with kitchen and bathroom) costs approximately 4,250 to 4,500 rubles, a 40 percent down payment would require a sum of 1,700 to 1,800 rubles, a considerable figure for the average worker. If the cooperative received a ten-year loan for the remaining 60 percent of the cost, in this case the member would have to pay 21.5 rubles to 22.5 rubles a month, in addition to monthly operating expenses and payments for communal services. Even with the maximum credit period of fifteen years (with a small interest charge of 0.5 percent per annum), the monthly cost for a two-room apartment in a cooperative building would be substantially higher than monthly rents in the state housing fund, and enough to tarnish the alluring shine of cooperative housing for the majority of Soviet wage earners. Once again, these economic facts encourage cooperative house construction for the Soviet elites, while discouraging the device for most other citizens.

ORGANIZATION AND OPERATION
OF THE ZhSK

Housing construction cooperatives may be organized under
either an agency of the ispolkom of the local Soviet or an enterprise
organization or institution. In contrast to earlier legislation, the present laws and model ZhSK charters permit workers from several
different small enterprises and organizations, as well as pensioners,
to unite into the same cooperative.[50] In the nation's two principal
cities, Moscow and Leningrad, at least sixty persons are needed to
form a housing construction cooperative. Forty-eight persons are
required in Russian cities with a population of over 100,000, as well
as in the capitals of the autonomous republics and in krai and oblast
centers. In all other towns and urban settlements of the Russian
Republic, twenty-four persons form the minimum for organizing a
ZhSK, and in sovkhozy and rural settlements, only twelve need come
together to constitute a housing cooperative (Paragraph 2, RSFSR
Model ZhSK Charter, 1965). The model ZhSK charters of other union
republics set different minimum requirements. In the Ukraine, for
example, the republic's eight largest cities, including Kiev, Khar'kov,
and Odessa, must have no less than forty persons to form a cooperative, other oblast centers only twenty-four, and in the remaining towns
just sixteen persons. Estonia, Moldavia, and Turkmen republics call
for no fewer than eight persons.[51] If the cooperative is being formed
at an enterprise, then the enterprise applies to the ispolkom of the
raion or city Soviet with its petition for organizing a ZhSK. Individuals
or other groups wishing to set up cooperatives apply directly to the
ispolkom. According to the current rules, at least three general
meetings must be held before the cooperative can even begin to function, thereby making the cooperative housing venture a very long,
drawn-out procedure. When the sharcholders have no other common
bond except the waiting list for entry into the ZhSK, the process is
further complicated and slowed down, and the frustration level greatly
increased. The appropriate city housing agencies or enterprise
organization calls the first general meeting of those citizens wishing
to become members of the cooperative. It is at this meeting that a
general agreement is made on organizing a ZhSK. The next stage
involves obtaining the city or raion ispolkom's approval of the meeting's
decision, list of prospective cooperative members, and the names of
those members of their families who will share the cooperative housing. The ispolkom then has the responsibility of verifying housing
conditions of prospective members, and checking out through its
various planning, financial, and architectural departments all the legal
and technical questions involved in organizing the cooperative. Decisions of land allotment and inclusion of the cooperative in the state

plan for construction-assembly work are also made at this time.[52]
Once the approval is given to organize the cooperative, a second
general meeting is held to write up a charter. The charter, based on
the republic's model charter, defines the cooperative's legal position,
its internal structure, and the members' rights and obligations. The
adopted charter is then registered with the appropriate housing board,
where it is checked to see that it conforms to the Model ZhSK Charter
and current legislation (Paragraph 3, RSFSR Model ZhSK Charter,
1965). One defect in the law is the absence of any time limit on the
ispolkom's decision to register the charter. The overworked city
housing agencies have usually not given the housing cooperatives any
top priority, and this attitude prolongs the wait. Certain large cities,
however, have set up special divisions within their housing agencies
to expedite cooperative house construction and to provide a more uniform city control over cooperative construction activity. Once the
city officially registers the charter, a third general meeting must be
held to select the cooperative's board of directors and audit or inspection commission (Paragraph 4, RSFSR Model Charter). It is at this
third meeting that the question of initial down payments is settled.
Actual construction of the cooperative apartment house can only begin
after no less than 40 percent of the cost of construction is deposited
in the bank and state credits are secured. Before the union resolution
of November 19, 1964, "On the Further Development of Cooperative
Housing Construction," many housing construction cooperatives were
forced to carry out contract negotiations with construction agencies
on their own. The result was confusion and discouragement for ZhSK
members. After the decree the ZhSK was allowed to place its functions as clients for construction on the ispolkom's boards of capital
construction. This law relieved a significant burden from the cooperative, which was usually in no position to handle the complex
problems of trying to get a building erected. It also insures greater
local Soviet control over cooperative construction.

After the building has been completed, the cooperative member
has the right to receive a separate apartment, the size of which depends upon the amount of his shares and the number of persons in his
family, but which can be no more than sixty square meters of living
space (Paragraph 16, Model ZhSK Charter). According to Paragraph
17 of the Model Charter, the amount of each member's share should
correspond to the cost of the particular apartment assigned to him in
the cooperative building. The construction cost of the apartment is
determined by procedures outlined by the State Committee on Civil
Construction and Architecture of Gosstroi, dated May 20, 1965, that
define the construction cost by the amount of useful space, in contrast
to earlier practices that determined the cost of a cooperative apartment by the amount of living space.[53] We should recall that useful

space includes the floor space in bathrooms and kitchens, whereas living space does not include these two rooms. Since cooperative apartments are individual apartments sheltering one family, the inclusion of kitchens and bathrooms in the cost to each shareholder is a logical requirement.

The cooperative member also has the right, with the consent of the general meeting of shareholders, to transfer his share to any adult member of his family who lives with him, or to carry out an exchange of living quarters, with the ispolkom's approval (Paragraph 19, Model Charter). He exercises most of the same rights and takes on most of the obligations that a tenant in state housing does. Whereas in the state housing sector, however, the building's management is not selected by the inhabitants, in cooperative buildings, all members have an equal right to participate in the management of the cooperative's affairs and to elect the management. The cooperative is run on the principles of internal "self-management," and only its shareholders in the general meeting have the right to distribute its property. The use of cooperative property by state organs and public organizations may be allowed, but only on agreed upon principles and for payment.[54]

THE COOPERATIVE'S ORGANS
OF ADMINISTRATION AND CONTROL

According to the Model ZhSK Charter, the general meeting (obshchee sobranie) of cooperative members is the highest organ of the cooperative. The general meeting: (a) accepts or rejects members into the cooperative; (b) approves the plan for the building's construction; (c) approves the service-management structures of the cooperative and the annual management-financial plan and reports on its fulfillment; (d) receives state credit for construction; (e) distributes living space among cooperative members and approves transfers of shares; (f) establishes the amount of the entry fee and initial down payment, as well as dues for the building's upkeep and operation; (g) forms special funds; (h) selects the board of directors and audit (inspection) committee; and (i) reorganizes and liquidates the cooperative. In addition, the general meeting examines complaints about the directors and audit commission (Paragraph 29, RSFSR Model ZhSK Charter, 1965). The general meeting is convened by the cooperative's board of directors no less than twice a year. If necessary, extraordinary general meetings may be held within six days by a request of one-third of the cooperative members, as well as by a request of the audit commission or ispolkom (Paragraph 30). To ensure control, the ispolkom receives all minutes of the general meetings.

To carry out its general decisions, and to provide daily management of cooperative affairs, the general meeting elects for a two-year term its executive organ, the board of directors of the cooperative (pravlenie kooperativa), composed of at least three cooperative members. The board then selects its chairman and vice-chairman (or chairmen) (Paragraph 32, RSFSR Model ZhSK Charter, 1965), treasurer, and secretary. Although it is a collegial organ, as Chikvashvili points out, its decisions are not necessarily unanimous. A majority vote of those present at a board session is sufficient for a decision to be binding. The Chairman of the Board of Directors has the right to sign agreements and payment vouchers, call sessions of the board, and act as power of attorney for the cooperative in its transactions, including court cases. Usually the board divides responsibilities among its members. However, with the approval of the general meeting, it may hire full-time workers, paid from ZhSK accounts, when it has a great volume of work.[55] In the large housing cooperatives, the boards of directors rely on permanent standing social committees (housing and daily services committee, repair-construction committee, committee on cultural and educational work, sanitation, fire-prevention, and so on). These committees fulfill the functions of a domkom.

The list of responsibilities outlined by the Model ZhSK Charter for the cooperative's board of directors is quite extensive, and includes the following: the board of directors (a) receives all dues established by the general meeting; (b) draws up plans, estimates, and reports; (c) manages the building's finances and upkeep; (d) hires and fires workers, clerical help, bookkeepers, engineers, and so on; (e) concludes agreements, pays off loans and debts; (f) carries out the technical supervision over the building's construction and participates through the chairman in the state commission for the acceptance of buildings for use; (g) as already noted, represents the cooperative in all legal dealings; and (h) examines all questions of membership (Paragraph 33).

The other administrative organ selected by the general meeting for a two-year term is the audit or inspection commission (revizionnaia komissiia), whose main task is to control and review the activities of the cooperative's board of directors (Paragraph 35). The Model Charter is explicit in stipulating that no relatives of any kind may sit on both the board of directors and the audit commission, and that no one may be a member of both the audit commission and board of directors at the same time (Paragraph 36). The audit commission is independent of the board of directors, and only answerable to the general meeting. At least twice a year the audit commission must conduct a review of the board of directors' business and financial activity.

The long procedure for organizing the housing construction cooperative and the work placed on the shoulders of the directors, as well as the time-consuming general meetings of shareholders, have been cited as reasons for discouraging the growth of cooperative housing. Since the members of the board of directors are volunteers, they have outside jobs. The great amount of time required to manage the cooperative often means that regular jobs are being neglected. "This is why it is so difficult to select a good board chairman," wrote one raiispolkom member; "this is why various rogues sometimes land in this position."[56] Being able to afford permanent workers and management personnel, cooperatives made up of wealthier members are in a better position to escape the time-consuming burden of management. Usually, however, every time a new shareholder is to be admitted to the cooperative, another general meeting must be called. Admittedly, the mandatory participation of shareholders in general meetings on many occasions is tiring for cooperative members, who realize that their participation is simply of a formal nature.[57]

To take the heavy burden from the cooperative's directors and members, and to provide more efficient and economical servicing of cooperative buildings, there have been suggestions for the creation of a city Housing Cooperative Affairs Administration which, in effect, would serve as a placement bureau for those who wish to live in a cooperative apartment building and would take the place of the board of directors. The aim of the proposal is to reduce the cooperative member's concerns to paying his money and receiving an apartment.[58] Indeed, if the cooperative form of housing is to grow and attract larger amounts of private capital, the complexities of organizing the construction and servicing of buildings have to be greatly simplified.

We noted that the Model Charter speaks of the cooperative's operating on the principles of "self-management." Later sections of the charter, however, make it very clear that the ZhSK must be under the close supervision and leadership of the government. The cooperative's self-management "does not mean its isolation from the socialist government, and its standing aloof in the general system of the national economy."[59] Self-management is limited to the distribution of cooperative property. Like all Soviet organizations, the housing cooperatives are restricted to a very narrow field of "self-management." The organization and successful operation of the housing construction cooperative "are unthinkable without state leadership." Although guidance by state organs "should not include administering," but only recommending and advising the ZhSK's, "however, . . . the method of direct instructions to the ZhSK's from competent state organs" is not excluded.[60] Direct leadership and daily control over the cooperative's practical activity is placed on the city housing administration and boards of the communal economy of the ispolkom. And the ispolkom always "has the right to change the decision of the general meeting of cooperative members, if it contradicts current legislation and the present charter" (Paragraph 37, RSFSR Model ZhSK Charter, 1965). The Party also plays a significant role in cooperative buildings, similar to its role in other forms of state housing. In those cases when there is a primary Party organization in the cooperative, consisting of workers in the house management and communists who live in the building, the cooperative's board of directors must conduct all its work in close contact with the Party organization and under its leadership.[61] The various controls on the cooperative's self-management also open up the cooperative system of distribution of apartments to abuses and pressures for accepting certain persons for membership out of turn and speeding up apartment assignments to others.

SUMMARY

From its weak revival in the late 1950s, the housing construction cooperative has slowly but steadily grown in importance. Perhaps the cooperative's most significant, and to some most disturbing, role is its offering the Soviet elites a better and quicker way to satisfy their housing desires. From the regime's point of view, the housing cooperative is an excellent device for absorbing private funds from those influential groups or persons who would be seeking to purchase more consumer goods, for relieving the pressure on the state housing fund, and for fulfilling elite demands for better living conditions. From the idealist's point of view, however, the present cooperative form just segregates persons by economic class and status and emphasizes the society's inequalities. The suggestions for a lowering of down payments are attempts to broaden the cooperative base for an inclusion of many more citizens. Even for the better-off of the society, the cooperative has not always meant instant satisfaction. Almost all house construction cooperatives have experienced months, sometimes years, of frustrating delays. In the past the local housing boards have not offered the ZhSK much help, and even now some local agencies still manifest open hostility to the cooperative. As the cooperative form has developed, new legislation has attempted to overcome its planning, financial, and construction shortcomings, and considerable progress has been made. With the enthusiastic support of the Soviet leadership, the housing construction cooperative should prosper and grow, but it will probably never rival the state housing sector's dominance in Soviet housing. However, cooperative housing may eventually be the long-sought solution to elimination of a stubborn survival from the past—the private house builder.

NOTES

1. Sobranie zakonovirasporiazhenii SSSR, 1924, No. 5, Art. 60; and SZ SSSR, 1937, I, No. 69, Art. 314.
2. SU RSFSR, 1927, No. 101, Art. 683.
3. Ibid.
4. Biulleten' NKVD, no. 39 (1928), with amendments of October 8, 1932 Biulleten' Narkomzhoza, no. 3 (1932), cited in Ivan P. Prokop-chenko, Zhilishchno-stroitel'nye kooperativy v SSSR (Moscow: Stroiizdat, 1965), p. 16.
5. Sosnovy, op. cit., pp. 64 and 91.
6. Larin, "Zhilishchnyi vopros v rekonstruktivnyi period" (The Housing Question in the Reconstruction Period), Sovetskoe stroitel'stvo, nos. 5-6 (1931): 156; also quoted in Sosnovy, op. cit., p. 27.
7. Prokopchenko, op. cit., p. 18.
8. "On the Preservation of the Housing Fund and the Improvement of Housing in Cities, October 17, 1937," Sobranie zakonov i rasporiazhenii, SSSR (Collection of Laws), 1937, I, No. 69, Art. 314.
9. See, for example, A. Ladinsky, "Develop Every Aspect of Housing Construction," Izvestia, December 12, 1956, and A. Shulpin, "Develop Work of Housing Construction Cooperatives on a Broad Scale," Pravda, December 17, 1956.
10. Pravda and Izvestia, August 2, 1957.
11. Izvestia, March 15, 1958.
12. "O zhilishchno-stroitel'noi i dachno-stroitel'noi kooperatsii, March 20, 1958" (On the House and Dacha Construction Cooperative) Resolution of the USSR Council of Ministers, Sobranie postanovlenii SSSR (SP SSSR), 1958, No. 5, Art. 47.
13. See, for example, model ZhSK and DSK charters for the RSFSR, SP RSFSR, 1958, No. 13; and Prokopchenko, op. cit., p. 19.
14. Sh. A. Chikvashvili, Zhilishchno-stroitel naia kooperatsiia v SSSR (Moscow: Iuridicheskaia literatura, 1965), p. 7.
15. V. A. Kucherenko, Chairman of the USSR State Committee on Construction, "The State of Urban Construction in the USSR, and Measures for Its Improvement," Pravda, June 8, 1960.
16. K. Ivanov, "Are Such Houses Necessary?" Izvestia, July 6, 1961 (CDSP XVII, no. 27: 33-34).
17. Sobranie Postanovlenii RSFSR, 1960, No. 18, Art. 79.
18. See: V. A. Tadevosian, "Several Problems of Housing Law," Sovetskoe gosudarstvo i pravo, no. 6 (1958); 45; T. N. Lisnichenko, "What is Holding Back Cooperative Housing Construction?" Sovety deputatov trudiashchikhsia, no. 10 (1960): 70-71; Ia. F. Mikolenko, The Right of Cooperative Ownership in the USSR (Moscow: Akademiia Nauk SSR, 1961), p. 84.

19. "Ob individual'nom i kooperativnom zhiliohohnom stroitel' stve" (On Individual and Cooperative Housing Construction), Resolution of the CC of the CPSU and the USSR Council of Ministers, June 1, 1962, No. 561, Sobranie Postanovlenii SSSR, 1962, No. 12, Art. 93.

20. "On the Further Development of Cooperative Housing Construction," Resolution of the USSR Council of Ministers, November 19, 1964, No. 943, SP SSSR, 1964, No. 25, Art. 147.

21. A. Kosygin, Pravda, April 6, 1966.

22. A. Birman, "Prodolzhenie razgovora," Novyi mir, no. 5 (May 1966): 199-200.

23. See V. I. Lenin, "O Kooperatsii," January 4, 1923, in Polnoe sobranie sochenenii, Fifth Ed., Vol. 45 (Moscow: Politicheskaia literatura, 1970), p. 373.

24. Chikvashvili, op. cit., pp. 11-12.

25. Ibid., pp. 16-17.

26. Svetlichny, "Improved Housing for Soviet People," Kommunist, no. 6 (April 1965): 41-51 (CDSP XVII, no. 22: 11-12). See also A. I. Mal'ginova and D. P. Vatman, op. cit., p. 114.

27. Chikvashvili, op. cit., p. 52.

28. Sovetskaia Rossiia, May 24, 1964.

29. Svetlichny, "Improved Housing," op. cit., p. 11; Svetlichny, "Is It not Better Without the Mystique?" Literaturnaia Gazeta, no. 30 (July 24, 1968) (CDSP XX, no. 31: 20).

30. A. S. Boldyrev, "New Scope to the Construction Cooperative," Izvestia, September 20, 1903, p. 1.

31. Svetlechny, "Improved Housing," op. cit., p. 11.

32. D. Pudikov, "To Increase the Number of New Cooperative Residents: Develop More Quickly the Housing Construction Cooperative," Pravda, November 20, 1964, p. 2.

33. Svetlichny, "Improved Housing," op. cit., p. 11.

34. B. Robotov, Manager of the Russian Republic Office of the USSR Stroibank, "Problems of the Housing Cooperative," Sovetskaia Rossiia, February 4, 1970, p. 1.

35. N. K. Baibakov, Chairman of the USSR Gosplan, "On the State Plan for the Development of the USSR National Economy in 1971," Pravda and Izvestia, December 9, 1970, (CDSP XXII, no. 49: 14).

36. Ibid.

37. Izvestia, October 29, 1970, p. 5.

38. Svetlichny, "Improved Housing," op. cit., p. 11; Pudikov, op. cit.

39. Pravda, May 8, 1959.

40. Pudikov, op. cit.

41. See, for example, Kazakhstanskaia Pravda, November 14, 1964.

42. Pravda, January 30, 1965.

43. "The Stories of a Cooperative Apartment House," Izvestia, October 29, 1970, p. 5.

44. Izvestia, October 29, 1970.

45. Ibid.

46. Robotov, op. cit., p. 1.

47. Izvestia, October 29, 1970; Robotov, op. cit. Rossiia, February 4, 1970.

48. Robotov, op. cit.

49. See, for example, Chikvashvili, op. cit., pp. 123-129.

50. "Primernyi ustav zhilishchno-stroitel'nogo kooperativa" (Model House Construction Cooperative Charter) Resolution of the RSFSR Council of Ministers, October 2, 1965, in Spravochnik profsoiuzhnogo rabotnika 1969, pp. 431-441. The Charter will henceforth be cited as the RSFSR Model ZhSK Charter, 1965.

51. Chikvashvili, op. cit., pp. 35-36.

52. Ibid., p. 41.

53. "O proektirovanii, stroitel'stve i opredelenii stoimosti kooperativnykh zhilykh domov i kvartir," May 20, 1965 ("On the Planning, Constructing and Determining the Cost of Cooperative Houses and Apartments").

54. Chikvashvili, op. cit., p. 17.

55. Ibid., p. 71.

56. A. Romanov, "Pending the Housewarming," Pravda, September 24, 1968, p. 3 (CDSP XX, no. 39: 31).

57. Ibid.

58. See, for example, Romanov, op. cit.

59. Chikvashvili, op. cit., p. 15.

60. Ibid., p. 60.

61. Prokopchenko, op. cit., pp. 79-80.

That the Soviet housing system is very much a system in the process of becoming is one of the outstanding conclusions of this study on Soviet housing problems and policies. Until the launching of the monumental 1957 program on the development of housing, it was difficult even to discern the existence of a housing system in the Soviet Union. The year 1957, however, truly marks the beginning of a "New Day" in Soviet housing, for it was only in 1957 that the Soviet regime raised the position of housing on its list of priorities. In the years following the 1957 decisions, significant changes took place in the housing field. The Soviet government and the Communist Party pledged to end the housing shortage and to provide separate, well-appointed apartments to every family by the end of the 1970's.

To achieve these goals, concrete reforms were undertaken. In the house construction industry, for example, the new industrialized construction techniques and prefabrication—which grew out of the post-World War II emergency situation—required a basic reorganization and reform of the industry. Characterized by a vast number of small, poorly trained and equipped construction organizations, subordinated to many different, unrelated departments, ministries, and agencies, the construction industry underwent a process of concentration and amalgamation during the late 1950s and 1960s, a process which continues today. Many of the scattered, small construction units were combined into large construction organizations with stronger technical production bases. Attention to improving the level of skills of construction workers and the bonus-incentive system has begun to pay off in an increased tempo and volume of housing construction. However, the old criterion of "val" or volume still has a powerful grip on the construction industry, and recent reforms have only just begun to tackle the problem of quality as part of plan success indicators. Unfortunately, improvements in quality have been slow, victim of the drive to plan fulfillment in terms of square meters.

The acceptance of faulty buildings, consequently, is not rare even today. Closely suited to the requirements of the new techniques of prefabrication and conveyor-belt methods of assembling a building, the house construction combine (DSK), which made its first appearance in Leningrad in 1959, has proven a major step forward in the reorganization of the Soviet house construction industry. While the house construction combine has helped to lower construction time and to raise labor productivity, it has not always improved the city-wide coordination of construction plans; for the DSK, like the smaller construction organizations, find themselves subject to many different organizations.

Our conclusion on the Soviet house construction industry is very tentative. Given the recent impetus of the reforms and reorganizations, the possibility of realizing an improved Soviet house construction system seems more likely today than even ten years ago. Much will depend on the fate of the national economic reforms, with their accent on economic accountability, and the profit-bonus system.

Throughout all phases of Soviet housing, coordination emerges as the most serious problem. In theory, the local Soviet should have overall control of house planning and construction and city development on the local level. In practice, however, the local Soviet is far from being the "Master of the City." It must struggle against powerful, well-entrenched ministerial and enterprise interests, which not infrequently are in direct conflict with general city plans. The local Soviet's relatively weak position means that it must go begging for financial resources to meet its heavy responsibilities in house construction and municipal services. Since the city budget is part of the republic's budget, the city must engage in prolonged negotiations with the republic and central ministries, which often have little knowledge of local needs but all too frequently have the deciding voice. During the period of the sovnarkhozy (regional economic councils, 1957-1965), the local Soviet found itself in a still weaker position to control city plans. Even its traditional function of allocating housing space was being complicated by sovnarkhoz interference. Since the abolition of the sovharkhoz system in 1965, at least the local Soviet's allocation role has been restored. It appears to be the one area in the housing process where the local Soviet has managed to achieve a considerable degree of city-wide coordination and control.

While the stated Soviet policies indicate a serious concern for ending the urban housing shortage by providing substantial and growing state investments, the shortage seems to continue. Its final solution is still far off in the future. As we have seen, the reasons for the housing problem are complicated and tied to many different interests and power considerations. To a great extent the problem is prolonged by the reluctance of the central authorities to give local government the power it needs to accomplish its tasks in city development. In this

regard, Soviet claims that their centrally planned economic system
will enable the Soviet Union to achieve successful and well-coordinated
city planning and to solve the basic problem of housing all its people
are not justified. It is true that the abolition of private ownership of
land and of the means of production has made it easier for the central
government to formulate a union-wide housing policy. It has not, however, always made it easier for the city planner to overcome departmental interests. The dominating drive at all levels of society is to
produce as much as possible, and fulfillment of the national economic
plan has frequently meant neglect of local city problems and flagrant
disregard of city housing plans. Soviet experience with restrictions
on industrial expansion and development in large cities and on population migration has proved only partially successful, and even then
at the price of severe labor shortages in urban areas. Despite all
legal restrictions and official exhortations, industries keep on building
in the cities and attracting more and more people, hampering all
efforts to solve the urban housing shortage once and for all.

Soviet planners have shown a great deal of flexibility in their
city planning. Obviously the restrictions on population in the big
cities and set definitions of the "optimal sized city" have not been
successful. By 1958 there was a shift from an emphasis on the
artificial restriction of urban migration to an emphasis on the concentrated development of small and medium-sized towns. At the same
time, the satellite city concept was put into practice as a means for
decentralizing the urban center and for developing a more rational
distribution of the urban population. While the satellite city concept
has not been abandoned, it has not hardened into a rigid city-planning
creed. Once again economic pressures for industrial expansion have
greatly modified neatly drawn plans for a system of satellite cities
in the major metropolitan areas. There now seems to be less concern
about mechanical ways to redistribute the urban population and greater
recognition of the benefits to labor productivity and to culture in the
large and superlarge cities. Presently policy-makers and planners
seem to be concentrating more on solving the basic problems of the
urban agglomerations and less on stopping urban growth, which the
centrally planned economic system tends to accelerate.

The microraion idea has been one major Soviet contribution to
the organization of life within a city. It is a concept that focuses on
the community rather than the individual apartment as the center of
urban life. The full realization of the microraion concept, with its
integrated system of housing and public services, has also been
hindered by the problems of coordination and ineffective controls,
and especially by departmental interests. While the microraion has
emerged as the basic city-planning unit, the completion of its public
services schemes has lagged sorrowfully behind its housing successes.

While the public service aspect of the microraion has been less than successful, concern for community development has grown in importance. Since in Soviet political theory, the more intense one's communal involvement, the more satisfying one's personal life, the Soviet citizen is constantly called upon to participate actively in the collective life. When in the late 1950s the Soviet Union was proclaimed to be entering the transition phase to full communism, the concept of the State of the Whole People was launched. Khrushchev became its most ardent proponent. In practical terms, the State of the Whole People meant a host of new quasi-voluntary citizen groups active in control and inspection of daily affairs. This great outburst of "public participation" created an even greater degree of confusion and diffusion of administrative authority. Since Khrushchev's ouster, the concept of the State of the Whole People has been toned down, and the many public organizations then created have been rationalized and disciplined. The deputies' councils and the house committees of tenants (domkom) stem from the activities of the Khrushchev era. With their position in the housing operations offices, the deputies' councils have strengthened the local Soviet's control over the allocation and management of state housing, improved the communication of Party and government policies to the populace, and provided a safety valve for citizens' complaints and a channel for gathering important information. In conjunction with the activities of other local committees, the deputies' councils are a significant factor in the development of consultative bureaucratic government in the Soviet Union. The house committee, or domkom, works closely with the deputies' council, housing agencies, and Party organizations. Since its revival in the late 1950s, the domkom has formed part of the Soviet political and social system, which strives to realize the total active involvement of every Soviet citizen in all spheres of life—in this case, the involvement of every tenant in the affairs of his apartment building. While the domkom's assignment of waging a resolute struggle against the uneconomical expenditure of resources in the housing economy by controlling the work of the house management is important, its assignment to raise the tenant's sense of responsibility for the careful treatment of his apartment and building and, especially, to organize the leisure time of residents is no less important. Under the watchful eye of the primary Party organization, the domkom has the crucial task of organizing the social life of the inhabitants. It also has the responsibility of convincing residents that their voluntary participation in the collective's life is truly a source of great personal gratification.

We have seen that housing conditions are very slowly but steadily improving in the Soviet city, and have indicated that the Soviet leaders are becoming aware of the need for new institutions to insure that Soviet home life remains centered in the communal life as society moves closer to its goal of a separate, well built apartment for every family. In the past the home afforded little chance for privacy or relaxation. With the improved housing conditions, however, the individual may be more reluctant to turn to collective forms of entertainment and participation. We conclude that the house committee is one more organization, under the supervision of the Party and government, to encourage the citizen's continued participation in communal affairs, and that this socio-political aspect of the domkom will grow in importance as Soviet housing improves.

At the beginning of this study we mentioned the dual nature of Soviet housing policy—housing as an incentive and housing as a public service. These two aspects of housing have remained in competitive coexistence since the earliest days of the Soviet state. Decent housing for every Soviet citizen became a right and a national goal. At the same time, the national goal of industrialization, requiring a high rate of labor productivity, usually overshadowed the public service aspect of housing, particularly during the Stalin era. Even today, however, the two goals come into conflict. From a purely rational view, the local Soviets operate the housing fund more economically and efficiently than do the industrial enterprises. But the complete transfer of state housing operations to the local Soviets has been exceedingly slow and stubbornly resisted by the ministries and their enterprises. The main cause for this resistance is the fact that housing helps the enterprise attract and keep laborers. It is an important factor in stabilizing labor turnover and population mobility and is closely tied to the rewards system. The various enterprise funds provide for the construction of housing. Presumably, the greater the enterprise's labor productivity, the more money can be invested in housing. Let us recall that construction organizations receive the added incentive of 10 percent of all the state housing they build. The allocation system of living space provides another example of housing an as incentive, with special privileges for the society's most productive or influential. Even cooperative housing offers an incentive for Soviet society's more affluent citizens. It provides a means for satisfying the housing demands of the Soviet elites and, hopefully, for insuring their political reliability. On the other hand, Soviet rent policy reflects the policy of providing housing as a public service to all Soviet citizens, regardless of their ability to pay. In fact, the declared national policy envisions rent-free housing for all by the end of the decade.

In a sense, Soviet society is striving to combine both the public service and incentive aspects of its housing policy. While it is managing to improve the housing conditions of the lot of its citizens, it has decided to improve the housing of certain select groups or individuals faster than others. Indeed, the overall improvement of housing has become a major concern in recent years. Reportedly the public unveiling of the 1971-1975 Five Year Plan was delayed two years to allow state planners time to find "additional resources to create still greater material benefits for the population, in particular, to increase the amount of housing constructed."[1] It does appear that the public service and incentive sides of Soviet housing will continue for some time. Only when and if the Soviet Union passes from the preliminary stages of communism, where the socialist principle "to each according to his labor" still predominates, to the full communism of "to each according to his needs," will decent housing emerge above all as a public service and guaranteed right of all citizens.

NOTES

1. According to an interview with Alexsei A. Goreglyad, a first deputy chairman of Gosplan, published in Moskovskaia Pravda, quoted in the The New York Times, February 22, 1971.

SOVIET SOURCES

Alekseev, Tikhon D. Spravochnik po zhilishchnomu zakonodatel'stvu (Handbook on Housing Legislation). Moscow: Profizdat, 1963 and 1966.

_____. Zhilishchnye l'goty grazhdan SSSR (Housing Privileges of Citizens of the USSR). Moscow: Gosiurizdat, 1962.

Alexandrov, A., and M. Garin. "Bureaucratic Fetters," Izvestia, June 28, 1956, p. 2 (Current Digest of the Soviet Press [hereafter cited as CDSP] VIII, no. 26: 14).

Arutiunian, N. Kh. "Both All-Union and Republic," Izvestia, December 29, 1966, p. 5.

Baibakov, N. K. "On the State Plan for the Development of the USSR National Economy in 1971," Pravda and Izvestia, December 9, 1970.

Balaiants, A. "Housing Should Have One Master," Izvestia, November 15, 1964, p. 2.

Baranov, N. V. "On the State and Problems of Urban Planning and the Introduction of Advanced Methods of Community Planning," Pravda, June 8, 1960 (Soviet Review I, no. 2 (September, 1960): 38-40).

Belolinetskii, V. "Okhrana zhilishchnykh prav grazhdan" (Protecting the Housing Rights of Citizens), Sovetskaia iustitsiia, no. 1 (January 1967), pp. 8-9.

Belopolsky, Ya. "Build Economically, Rapidly, Durably: Concerning Building in the Southwest Part of the Capital," Izvestia, November 12, 1955, p. 2 (CDSP VII, no. 45: 10).

Berezin, V. "Beauty and Expediency," Pravda vostoka, April 7, 1960, p. 3.

Biely, M., and I. Orlov. "La cite des sciences de novossibirsk," Arkhitektura SSSR, no. 6 (1960), pp. 4-8, (Recherches internationales à la lumiére du Marxisme (VII-X [1960]: 230-236).

Birman, A. "Prodolzhenie razgovora" (Continuation of the Conversation), Novy mir, no. 5 (May 1960): 187-200.

Blazhenko. "Spory o prave chlenov sem'i na obmen zhilogo pomeshcheniia," (Conflicts Concerning the Right of Members of the Family to Exchange Their Living Quarters), Sotsialisticheskaia zakonnost', no. 6 (June 1968): 44-46.

Bocharov, Iu. P. "Sotsial'nye problemy zarubezhnogo gradostroitel' stva," (Social Problems of Town Building Abroad), Voprosy filosofii, no. 1 (1964): 90-101.

_____, and V. I. Rabinovich. "Stroitel'stvo kommunizma i problemy razvitiia nashikh gorodov" (The Construction of Communism and the Problem of the Development of Our Cities), Voprosy filosofii, no. 2 (1962): 25-36.

Bochkarev, I. "Yes, That's Advantageous," Izvestia, February 21, 1970, p. 5.

Boldyrev, A. S. "New Scope to the Construction Cooperative," Izvestia, September 20, 1963, p. 1.

Boldyrev, A. S. "Rewarding with Differentiated Bonuses—Why Has Construction Time on Buildings and Installations Been Increasing?" Izvestia, July 9, 1970, p. 5 (CDSP XXII, no. 27: 28-29).

Boldyrev, V. "Why a Man Quits," Pravda, January 20, 1971, p. 3 (CDSP XXIII, no. 3: 14, 17).

Bol'shaia sovetskaia entsiklopediia (Great Soviet Encyclopedia) (1930 edition), Vol. XVIII.

Brezhnev, Leonid I. "Report of the CPSU's Central Committee to the Twenty-Third Congress of the CPSU," Pravda, March 30, 1966 (CDSP XVIII, no. 12: 21).

_____. "The Report of the CPSU Central Committee to the Twenty-Fourth Congress of the CPSU," Pravda, Izvestia, March 31, 1971 (CDSP XXIII, no. 13: 1-15).

Brig, B., and Ye Koppel. "Big Cities and the Ministries," Pravda, May 21, 1969 (CDSP XXI, no. 21: 27).

Broner, David L. Sovremennye problemy zhilishchnogo khoziaistva (Contemporary Problems of the Housing Economy). Moscow: Gosizdat, "Vysshaia shkola," 1961.

_____. "Zhilishchnaia problema v trudakh i gosudarstvennoi deiatel'nosti V. I. Lenina" (The Housing Problem in the Labors and State Activities of V. I. Lenin), Vestnik statistiki, no. 3 (1970): 3-12.

_____. Zhilishchnyi vopros i statistika (The Housing Problem and Statistics). Moscow: Statistika, 1966.

Broons, D. "The Architect's Authority," Izvestia, October 7, 1970, p. 3 (CDSP XXII, no. 40: 22).

Bruk, S. I. "Etnodemograficheskie protsessy v SSSR (po materialam perepisi 1970 goda)" (Ethnodemographic Processes in the USSR [on materials from the 1970 census]), Sovetskaia etnografiia, no. 4 (1971): 8-30.

"Builders' Labor Exploits," editorial, Pravda, February 4, 1957, p. 1 (CDSP IX, no. 5: 28).

"Build for the Ages: All-Union Architects' Congress," Pravda, October 22, 1970.

"The Building in which We Live," lead editorial, Sovetskaia Rossiia, August 28, 1962.

"But the Heat Is Escaping," Pravda, September 24, 1969, p. 3.

Butuzova, K. "Apartment Houses Are Our Wealth," Pravda, July 22, 1962.

Bzhilianskii, Iu. "Metodologicheskie predposylki prognozirovaniia narodnonaseleniia" (Methodological Prerequisites for Population Forecasting), Planovoe Khoziaistvo, no. 1 (1972): 76-80.

_____. "The Political and Economic Problems of Population under Socialism," Voprosy ekonomiki, no. 10 (October 1972): 66-76 (CDSP XXV, no. 10: 21).

"The Capital Prepares for the Lenin Jubilee: Session of the Moscow City Soviet," Izvestia, December 4, 1968, (CDSP XX, no. 49: 26).

"Celebration by Moscow Builders," Pravda, February 5, 1957, p. 1 (CDSP IX, no. 5: 27-28).

Central Committee CPSU and the USSR Council of Ministers. "The General Plan for the Development of Moscow," Pravda, June 10, 1971, pp. 1-2.

Central Research and Design Institute of Town Planning, State Committee of Civil Engineering and Architecture under Gosstroi USSR. Osnovy sovetskogo gradostroitel'stva, 3 volumes (Principles of Town Planning in the Soviet Union). Moscow: Stroiizdat, 1966-1967.

Central Statistical Administration (Board) of the RSFSR Council of Ministers. Narodnoe khoziaistvo RSFSR v 1969 godu: statisticheskii ezhegodnik (The RSFSR National Economy in 1969: Statistical Yearbook). Moscow: Statistika, 1970.

_____. RSFSR v tsifrakh v 1968 g, (The RSFSR in Figures for 1968). Moscow: Statistika, 1969.

_____. RSFSR v tsifrakh v 1971 g: kratkii statisticheskii sbornik (The RSFSR in Figures for 1971). Moscow: Statistika, 1972.

Central Statistical Administration of the USSR. Narodnoe khoziaistvo v 1968 g: statisticheskii ezhegodnik (The National Economy in 1968: Statistical Yearbook). Moscow: Statistika, 1969.

_____. Narodnoe khoziaistvo SSSR v 1970 g: statisticheskii ezhegodnik (The National Economy in 1970: Statistical Yearbook). Moscow: Statistika, 1971.

_____. Narodnoe khoziaistvo SSSR v 1922-1972 g: (The National Economy of the USSR, 1922-1972). Moscow: Statistika, 1972.

_____. SSSR v tsifrakh v 1971 godu (The USSR in Figures for 1971). Moscow: Statistika, 1972.

_____. Soviet Union 50 Years: Statistical Returns. Moscow: Progress Publishers, 1969.

_____. USSR in Figures for 1959: Brief Statistical Returns. Moscow: Foreign Languages Publishing House, 1960.

Chikvashvili, Shala D. Zhilishchno-stroitel'naia kooperatsiia v SSSR (The House Construction Cooperative in the USSR). Moscow: Iuridicheskaia literatura, 1965.

Chubarov, G. "Kak my raspredeliaem zhil'e," (How we Distribute Housing), Sovetskie profsoiuzy, no. 8 (April 1964): 20-22.

The Civil Code and the Code of Civil Procedure of the RSFSR 1964, trans. A. K. R. Kiralfy, in Law in Eastern Europe, no. 11. Leyden: Sijthoff, 1966.

Danilov, V. "Why Is the New Tenant Unhappy?" Pravda, November 21, 1972, p. 3.

Danin, D. "Material and Style," Novy mir, no. 1 (January 1961) (CDSP XIII, no. 3: 10-15).

Davidovich, V. G. "Satellite Cities and Towns of the USSR," in Goroda-Sputniki, pp. 5-39. Moscow: Geographical Publishing, 1961. (Soviet Geography, III, no. 3 [March 1962]: 3-35).

Davydchenkov, V. "Office Shuffers," Izvestia, January 9, 1963 (CDSP XV, no. 2: 24-25).

"Defense Against Heat Loss," Pravda, November 24, 1969, p. 3.

Demichev, P. "New Stage in the Development of the Soviet Capital," Izvestia, August 19, 1960, p. 1 (CDSP XII, no. 33: 20-21).

"Directives of the Twenty-Fourth CPSU Congress for the Development of the USSR National Economy in 1971-1975," Pravda, April 11, 1971, pp. 1-7.

Direktivy KPSS i sovetskogo pravitel'stva po khoziaistnym voprosam 1917-1957, Volume I. Moscow: Gospolitizdat, 1957-1958.

"The Discipline of Urban Construction," editorial, Pravda, February 24, 1970, p. 1 (CDSP XXII, no. 8: 23-24).

"Draft of the Central Committee CPSU: The Directives of the Twenty-Fourth CPSU Congress for the Five-Year Plan for the Development of the USSR National Economy in 1971-1975," Pravda, Izvestia, February 14, 1971, pp. 1-5 (CDSP XXIII, no. 7: 6-16).

Dukelski, G. "Les premiers microrayons de la première ville satellite," Stroitet'stvo i arkhitektura Moskvy, no. 4 (1960), pp. 13-15 (Les recherches internationales à la lumière du Marxisme, VII-X (1960): 237-245.

Dryagoz, M. "Crisis of Flat Cities and the Three-Dimensional City of the Future," Nauka i zhizn', no. 7 (July 1968): 97-101 (Current Abstracts of the Soviet Press [hereafter cited as CASP] I, no. 6: 7-10).

Feofanov, Iu. Feuilleton: "Husband for Housing," Izvestia, December 20, 1970, p. 6.

"First in the World: Experimental Apartment House on Olminsky Avenue," Pravda, April 19, 1964.

Fomin, G. "The Architect's Responsibility," Pravda, October 21, 1970.

_____. "Our Home and City," Pravda, July 2, 1969.

Gaiduk, A. K. "Increasing Labor Productivity in Construction," Biulleten' stroitel'noi tekhniki, no. 12 (1968): 28-30 (JPRS: USSR Trade and Services, no. 12 [April 28, 1969]: 1-7).

Galich, B., and M. Yorovoi, "Satellite Towns," Izvestia, August 13, 1958.

Ganenko, I. "Esthetics and the Present Day: Against Alien Influences," Oktiabr, no. 4 (April 1960) (CDSP XII, no. 22: 27-29).

"General Plan for the Development of Moscow," Izvestia, September 18, 1966, p. 2.

Gerashchenko, M., and V. Tsingalenok. "People's Control Sheet No. 155: No Exceptions—Stricter Quality Control in Housing Construction," Pravda, December 16, 1971, p. 3 (CDSP XXII, no. 50: 38-39).

Gerasimov, K. M. "On the State Plan for the Development of the USSR National Economy in 1971, the USSR State Budget for 1971 and the Fulfillment of the USSR State Budget for 1969," Izvestia, December 10, 1970, p. 2 (CDSP XXII, no. 50: 16-18).

Girshberg, B. I. "Zhilishchnomy khoziaistvy-pooshchritel'nyi fond" (An Incentive Fund for the Housing Economy), Gorodskoe khoziaistvo Moskvy, no. 8 (August 1965): 21-22.

Gorshtein, Ia., and A. Kaliaev. "Ne pravil'naiia praktika zhilishchnykh organov" (Wrong Policy of Housing Agencies), Sovetskaia iustitsiia, no. 22 (November, 1963): 18-19.

Grishmanovskii, A. Letter to Pravda: "Like Supplicants," Pravda, April 13, 1973, p. 3.

"Honorable and Noble Labor of Builders," editorial, Pravda, August 10, 1958.

"The Housing Construction Cooperative," Izvestia, October 9, 1965.

"Housing Construction Is a Matter of Prime Importance," editorial, Pravda, October 8, 1958.

"Housing Construction Should Be at a High Tempo," lead editorial, Kazakhstanskaia Pravda, June 18, 1960.

Iagina, Z. N. Gorod budushchego (City of the Future). Moscow: Znanie, 1968.

Iamenfel'd, G. "Poriadok obmena zhilymi pomeshcheniiami" (Procedure in the Exchange of Rooms and Apartments), Sotsialisticheskaia zakonnost', no. 6, (June 1967): 84-85.

Iankoit', G. Obshchestvennyi kontrol' za zhilishchnobytovym stroitel'-stvom (Public Control Over Housing and Service Construction). Moscow: Profizdat, 1964.

Illarionov, A. "From Nothing to the Key in the Door," Pravda, December 7, 1969, p. 3 (CDSP XXI, no. 49: 35-36).

'Implementing Decisions of the Twenty-Fourth CPSU Congress: Put Reserves at the Service of the National Economy," on A. N. Kosygin's Speech at the September 30, 1972 Gosplan meeting, Planovoe khoziaistvo, no. 11 (November 1972): 3-8, (CDSP, XXV, no. 3: 5-9, 15).

"Important Stimulus," Official Department, Izvestia, November 13, 1966, p. 2.

"Initiative and Efficiency," lead editorial, Izvestia, December 19, 1964.

"Instruktsiia o poriadke obmena zhilykh pomeshchenii" (Instructions on the Procedure for the Exchange of Living Quarters), Order of the RSFSR Ministry of the Communal Economy, January 9, 1967, no. 12, Sovetskaia iustitsiia, no. 6 (March 1967): 31-32.

Isarov, G. Z. Spravochnik nanimatelia zhilogo pomeshcheniia v voprosakh i otvetakh (Handbook for Tenants of Apartment Dwellings in Questions and Answers). Moscow: Stroiizdat, 1966.

Isayev, V. "Make Good Preparations for the Economic Reform in Construction and Carry It out Successfully," Ekonomicheskaia gazeta, no. 26. (June, 1969): 3-4 (CDSP XXI, no. 25: 15-16, 21).

Ivanov, K. "Are Such Houses Necessary?" Izvestia, July 6, 1961 (CDSP XVIII, no. 27: 33-34).

Ivanov, V. "Urbanizatsiia: nastoiashchee i budushchee" (Urbanization: Present and Future), Voprosy ekonomiki, no. 11 (December 1969): 153-156.

Kachalovsky, Ye. "Deputy and Life: Harmonious Development for the City," Izvestia, August 27, 1969, p. 3 (CDSP XXI, no. 35: 29-30).

_____. "Dnepropetrovsk Grows Up," Pravda Ukrainy, June 6, 1969, p. 3.

"Kakie prava i preimshchestva v obespechenii zhiloi ploshchad'iu imeiut mnogodetnye sem'i?" (What Rights and Privileges Does a Family with Many Children Have to Living Space?), Sovetskaia iustitsiia, no. 8 (April 1967): 32.

Kharitonova, A. E. "Osnovy etapy zhilishchnogo stroitel'stva v SSSR" (The Basic [Main] Stages of Housing Construction in the USSR), Voprosy istorii, no. 5 (1965): 50-64.

Khodiaev, D., and N. Selivanov. "Un Quartier residentiel experimental a Moscou" (An Experimental Residential District in Moscow), Stroitel'stvo i arkhitektura Moskvy, no. 12 (1960) (Recherches internationales a la lumiere du Marxisme, VII-X, cahiers 20-21 (1960): 196-207).

Khorev, B. "How Should the Problems of the Small City Be Solved?— Problems of the New Five-Year Plan," Pravda, March 2, 1971, p. 3.

_____. "Satellite Cities and Towns of Gorky," in Goroda-Sputniki. Moscow: Geographical Publishing House, 1961 (Soviet Geography III, no. 3 [March 1962]: 51-68).

_____. "What Kind of City Is Needed?" Literaturnaia gazeta, no. 14 (April 2, 1962): 12 (CDSP XXI, no. 14: 12 and 27).

Khrushchev, N. S. "Control Figures for the Development of the USSR National Economy in 1959-1965," Report to the Twenty-First Party Congress, Pravda and Izvestia, November 14, 1959, pp. 1-9 (CDSP X, no. 48: 3-7).

_____. O merakh po vypolneniiu programmy KPSS v oblasti povysheniia blagosostoianiia naroda (Concerning the Measures for the Fulfillment of the CPSU Program in the Area of Raising the Well-Being of the People), Report and Closing Word at the July 13 and 15, 1964 Session of the USSR Supreme Soviet. Moscow: Politizdat, 1964.

_____. "On the Control Figures for the Development of the USSR National Economy in 1959-1965," Report to the Twenty-First Party Congress, Pravda, January 28, 1959, pp. 2-10 (CDSP XI, no. 3: 3-10).

_____. "On the Program of the CPSU," Report to the Twenty-Second Congress of the CPSU, October 18, 1961, Pravda and Izvestia, October 19, 1961 (CDSP XIII, no. 44: 3-20, 28).

_____. Sorok let Velikoi Oktiabr'skoi sotsialisticheskoi revoliutsii (Forty Years of the Great October Socialist Revolution). Moscow: Pravda Publishing House, 1957.

Kiseleva, G. "Scientific Life: Population Growth and Its Regional Features," Voprosy ekonomiki, no. 8 (August, 1968): 153-155 (CASP I, no. 5 [October 1968]: 20).

Klysh, G. M. "Sovershenstvovat' upralenie zhilishchnym khoziaistvom," (Perfect the Administration of the Housing Economy), Gorodskoe khoziaistvo Moskvy, no. 8 (August 1964): 29-30.

Klyushnichenko, Ye. Ye. "Determining the Effectiveness of the Renovation of Buildings with Consideration of Major Repairs of Housing," Stroitel'stvo i arkhitektura, no. 1 (1969): 10-11 (JPRS, USSR Trade and Services series, no. 11 [April 22, 1969]: 20-26).

Kondratyev, N. "Toward One Goal," Izvestia, April 3, 1962, p. 3 (CDSP, XIV, no. 14: 20-21).

Kononenko, Yelena. "Concerning a Letter: Natalya and Others," Pravda, May 16, 1969, p. 3 (CDSP XXI, no. 20: 20).

Konovalov, M. F. "Formy uchastiia obshchestvennosti v upravlenii zhilishchnym khoziaistvom," (Forms of Public Participation in the Administration of the Housing Economy), Gorodskoe khoziaistvo Moskvy, no. 8 (August 1964): 38-40.

_____. "Uluchshit' organizatsionno-massovuiu rabotu sovetov," (Improve the Organization-Mass Contact Work of the Soviets), Gorodskoe khoziaistvo Moskvy, no. 2 (February 1967): 7-9.

_____, and V. M. Iezuitov. "Moskovskii sovet:ego zadachi i itogi deiatel'nosti," (The Moscow Soviet, Its Tasks and Activities), Sovetskoe gosudarstvo i pravo, no. 4 (April 1967): 13-20.

Konstantinov, O. A. "Some Conclusions on the Geography of Cities and the Urban Population of the USSR from the 1959 Census," Izvestiia akademii nauk SSSR, Seriia geograficheskaia, no. 6 (1959) (Soviet Geography I, no. 7 [September 1960]: 59-75).

Kordo, N., and M. Fradin. "Housing: Comfort of an Apartment and Placement," Izvestia, July 15, 1966, p. 3 (CDSP XVIII, no. 28: 22-23).

Korneev, S. M., and Iu. M. Kon'kov. Pravo na zhiluiu ploshchad' v SSSR. (Right to Living Quarters in the USSR). Moscow: Znanie, 1968.

Koryakov, V. "People's Control Sheet No. 128: What Should Be Done?" Izvestia, July 9, 1968, p. 4 (CDSP XX, no. 28: 31).

Kosygin, Alexsei. "Directives of the Twenty-Third CPSU Congress for the Five Year Plan of the Development of the USSR National Economy in 1966-1970," April 5, 1966, Pravda, Izvestia, April 6, 1966 (CDSP XVIII, no. 14: 1-21, 28).

_____. Report on "The Directives of the Twenty-Fourth CPSU Congress for the Five-Year Plan for the Development of the USSR National Economy in 1971-1975," Pravda, Izvestia, April 7, 1971 (CDSP XXIII, no. 15: 1-10).

Krasnikov, S. "Build Excellently," Trud, February 15, 1969, p. 2.

Krugliak, V., and R. Dal. "What Should the Microborough Be Like?" Pravda, July 23, 1972, p. 3.

Krylov, N., and N. Putintsev. "Who Is the Master of Housing: Direct Affair of the Soviets," Izvestia, November 24, 1964, p. 3.

Kucherenko, V. A. "The Future of Our Cities," Pravda, October 25, 1959 (CDSP XI, no 43: 22-24).

_____. "On the State of Urban Development in USSR and Measures for Improving It," Pravda, Izvestia, June 8, 1960 (CDSP XII, no. 23: 13-18, and Soviet Review I, no. 2 [September 1960]: 29-38).

_____. "Several Questions of Soviet Urban Planning," Pravda, June 1, 1960 (CDSP, no. 32: 23-27).

Kuleshov, N. "Harmony of a City? Capital's Architects Meet in Moscow City Soviet Executive Committee," Izvestia, March 30, 1963.

Kurashov, S. V. "Providing Public Services, Landscaping and Improving the Sanitary Condition of Cities," Pravda, June 8, 1960 (CDSP XII, no. 23: 19-20).

Kuzmenko, N. "From the Courtroom: Cash on the Barrelhead," Izvestia, August 15, 1970, p. 6, (CDSP XXII, no. 33: 11-12).

"Labor Step of the Five-Year Plan: Report of the USSR Central Statistical Administration on Results of the Fulfillment of the State Plan for the Development of the USSR National Economy in 1969," Pravda, Izvestia, January 25, 1970, pp. 1-2 (CDSP XXII, no. 4: 3-6, 10).

Ladikov, P. Kontrol' profsoiuzov za zhilishchno-bytovym stroitel'stvom, (Trade Union Control over Housing and Service Construction). Moscow: Profizdat, 1963.

Ladinsky, A. "Develop Every Aspect of Housing Construction," Izvestia, December 12, 1956.

Larin. "Zhilishchnyi vopros v rekonstruktivnyi period," (The Housing Question in the Reconstruction Period), Sovetskoe stroitel'stvo, nos. 5-6 (1931): 156.

Lenin, V. I. "O kooperatsii," January 4, 1923 (On the Cooperative), in <u>Polnoe sobranie sochenenii</u>, Vol. 45, 5th Ed. Moscow: Politicheskaia literatura, 1970.

"Letters to Izvestia: The New Home," <u>Izvestia</u>, October 14, 1969, p. 4.

Levina, E., and Ye. Syrkina. "Reflections on the Microdistrict," <u>Zvezda</u>, no. 10 (October, 1966): 150-156 (<u>CDSP</u> XIX, no. 3: 35).

Lisnichenko, T. N. "Chto sderzhivaet kooperativnoe zhilishchnoe stroitel'stvo" (What is Holding Back Cooperative Housing Construction?), <u>Sovety deputatov trudiashchikhsia</u>, no. 10 (1960): 70-71.

Litovkin, V. N. "Osnovaniia i poriadok predostavleniia grazhdan gosudarstvennoi zhiloi ploshchadi" (Grounds for and Procedure in Assigning Government Housing to Citizens), <u>Sovetskoe gosudarstvo i pravo</u>, no. 10 (October 1968): 143-146.

Lopatina, Ye. B. "The Formation of Leningrad's Satellite Places," in <u>Goroda-Sputniki</u>, pp. 50-59. Moscow: Geographical Publishing House, 1961 (Soviet Geography III, no. 3 [March 1962]: 43-50).

Loveiko, I. I. "Moscow Redevelopment Plan Underway," <u>Izvestia</u>, August 7, 1958.

Lyashchenko, S. "Land and Cities: Spread of Industry, Not Cities Will Crowd Land," <u>Literaturnaia gazeta</u>, no. 31 (August 2, 1967): 10-11 (<u>CDSP</u> XIX, no. 31: 13).

Makarov, G. "Komu byt' novo-selom?" (Who Should Get a New Apartment?), <u>Sovetskie profsoiuzy</u>, no. 16 (August 1966): 28-28.

Mal'ginova, A. I., and D. P. Vatman. "Spornye voprosy obmena zhilymi pomeshcheniiami," (Controversial Problems in the Exchange of Apartments and Rooms), <u>Sovetskoe gosudarstvo i pravo</u>, no. 6 (June 1968): 111-115.

Manko, E., and N. Utkin. "Keys to Reserves—The Meaning of the Decisions of the Twenty-Fourth Party Congress," <u>Pravda</u>, April 7, 1973, p. 3.

Markov, G. "For Moscow Builders," <u>Sovetskaia Rossiia</u>, May 16, 1957.

Maslennikov, G. "House out of Order," Pravda, July 31, 1969.

Milolenko, Ia. F. Pravo kooperativnoi sobstvennosti v SSSR (The Right of Cooperative Ownership in the USSR). Moscow: Academiia Nauk, 1961.

Mishchenko, G. Ye. "Satellite Cities and Towns of Moscow," in Goroda-Sputniki, pp. 40-49. Moscow: Geographical Publishing House, 1961 (Soviet Geography III, no. 3 [March 1962]: 35-43).

Naimushin, M. "Deputy's Rostrum: The Soviet Is Master of the City," Izvestia, February 14, 1970, p. 1 (CDSP, XXII, no. 7: 19).

Narodnoe khoziaistvo SSSR (The National Economy of the USSR, statistical annual). Moscow: Statistika.

Nazarov, Iu. A. Opyt raboty domovykh komitetov (Work Practice of House Committees). Moscow: Stroiizdat, 1966.

Nekrasov, Viktor. "About Past, Present and a Little Bit of the Future," Literaturnaia gazeta, February 20, 1960 (CDSP XII, no. 11: 3-8).

"New Regulations Governing the Exchange of Living Quarters," Trud, March 4, 1967, p. 4.

Nezhny, A. "Goroda, Kotorye my stroim" (Cities that We are Building), Novy mir, no. 10 (October, 1969): 188-206 (CASP II, no. 3 [March 1970]: 25-26).

Nezhny, A. "Goroda, kotorye my stroim," (Cities that We are Building), Novy mir, No. 10 (October, 1969), pp. 188-206.

Novoplianskii, D. "The Road to New Housing," Pravda, February 16, 1973, p. 3.

"Novye kvartaly iugo-zapadnogo raiona," (The New Blocks of the Southwest District), Stroitel'stvo i arkhitektura Moskvy, no. 2 (1961): 2-31.

"Ob individual'nom i kooperativnom zhilishchnom stroitel'stve," (On Individual and Cooperative Housing Construction), Resolution of the Central Committee of the CPSU and the USSR Council of Ministers, June 1, 1962, No. 561, Sobranie postanovlenii SSSR, 1962, No. 12, Art. 93.

Obraztsov, A. Novaia sistema obsluzhivaniia nashikh gorodov (The New Service System of our Cities). Moscow: Znanie, 1968.

_____. "What Will Our Future Cities Look Like?" Nedelia, December 25, 1960 (Soviet Review II, no. 4 (April 1961): 34-37).

"Observe State Discipline in Urban Construction and Housing Official Department, Izvestia, February 25, 1970, p. 3.

"Ob uporiadochenii l'got dlia lits, rabotaiuschikh v raionakh krainego severa i v mestnostiakh, priravennykh k raionam krainego severa" (On the Regulations of Privileges for Persons Working in the Regions of the Far North or in Localities Similar to the Regions of the Far North), ukaz of the Presidium of the USSR Supreme Soviet, February 10, 1960, Vedomosti verkhovnogo soveta SSSR, no. 7 (991), February 18, 1960.

"Ob usilenii roli domovykh komitetov v upravlenii gosudarstvennym zhilishchnym fondom" (On Strengthening the Role of the House Committees in the Administration of the State Housing Fund), Spravochnik profsoiuznogo rabotnika 1969 (The Trade Union Worker's Handbook), pp. 441-446. Moscow: Profizdat, 1969.

"Once More about New Way of Life Housing Complexes," Literaturnaia gazeta, no. 35 (August 30, 1972): 10.

"On Developing Housing Construction in the USSR," Decree of the CC CPSU and the USSR Council of Ministers," July 31, 1957, Pravda and Izvestia, August 2, 1957, pp. 1-2 (CDSP IX, no. 31: 3-6, 32).

"On Eliminating Waste in Design and Construction," Decree of the CC CPSU and the USSR Council of Ministers, Pravda and Izvestia, November 10, 1955 (CDSP VII, no. 43: 14-16, 20).

"On Improving Design and Estimate Work," CC CPSU and the USSR Council of Ministers, Izvestia, June 21, 1969, Pravda, June 22, 1969 (CDSP XXI, no. 25: 13-15).

"On Improving the Planning of Capital Construction and Increasing Economic Incentives in Construction Work," CC CPSU and the USSR Council of Ministers, Pravda and Izvestia, June 20, 1969 (CDSP XXI, no. 25: 8-11).

"On Intensifying the Struggle Against Persons Who Avoid Socially
Useful Work and Lead an Antisocial, Parasitic Way of Life,"
Decree of the Presidium of the Russian Supreme Soviet, May 4,
1961, Sovetskaia Rossiia, May 5, 1961, p. 3 (CDSP XIII, no. 17:
8-9).

"On Measures for Improving the Quality of Housing and Civil Construction," CC CPSU and the USSR Council of Ministers, Izvestia,
June 20, 1969, Pravda, June 21, 1969 (CDSP XXI, no. 25: 11-13).

"On Measures for the Further Improvement of the Work of the District and City Soviets," Resolution of the CC CPSU, Pravda
and Izvestia, March 14, 1971 (CDSP XXIII, no. 11: 1-4).

"On Putting in Order Expenditures of Funds and Materials for the
Construction of Administrative, Sports, and Other Public Buildings and Structures," CC CPSU and the USSR Council of Ministers, Pravda and Izvestia, October 5, 1958 (CDSP X, no. 40:
10-11).

"On Results of the Fulfillment of the State Plan for the Development
of the USSR National Economy in 1972," Pravda and Izvestia,
January 30, 1973, pp. 1-3 (CDSP XXV, no. 5: 7-14, 24).

"On the Basic Rights and Duties of the City and Borough Soviets,"
Decree of the Presidium of the USSR Supreme Soviet, Izvestia,
March 20, 1971, p. 4 (CDSP XXIII, no. 13: 27-30, 38).

"On the Procedure of Examining Proposals, Applications and Complaints of Workers," Ukaz of the Presidium of the Supreme
Soviet of the USSR, (April 12, 1968), Vedomosti verkhovnogo
soveta SSSR, no. 17: 144.

"On the State Plan for the Development of the USSR National Economy
in 1973—Report by Deputy N. K. Baibakov," Pravda and Izvestia,
December 19, 1972, pp. 2-3.

Orlovsky, P. Ye. "On the Right of the Personal Ownership of Housing,"
Sovetskoe gosudarstvo i pravo, no. 7 (July 1961) (CDSP XIII,
no. 39: 3-6).

Osipov, G. V., ed. Studies in Soviet Society, Vol. II: Town, Country
and People. London: Tavistock Publication (prepared for
publication by Novosti Press Agency), 1969.

"O sokhranenii zhilishchnogo fonda i uluchshenii zhilishchnogo khoziaistva v gorodakh" (On the Preservation of the Housing Fund and
the Improvement of Housing in Cities), Resolution of the Central
Committee and USSR Council of People's Commissars, October
17, 1937, Sobranie zakonov SSSR, 1937, I, 69, Art. 314.

Pavlov, P. "Intensifikatsiia proizvodstva i trudovye resursy" (Labor
Resources and the Intensification of Production), Voprosy
ekonomiki, no. 3 (March 1972): 15-21.

Pchelintsev, O. S. "Problems of the Development of Large Cities,"
Sotsiologiia v SSSR II (1965): 270-285 (Soviet Review VII, no.
4 [Winter 1966-1967]: 15-22).

Perchik, L. Bol'shevistskii plan rekonstruktsii Moskvy (Bolshevik
Plan for the Reconstruction of Moscow). Moscow: Partizdat,
1935.

_____. The Reconstruction of Moscow. Moscow: Partizdat, 1936.

Perevedentsev, V. "Cities and Years," Literaturnaia gazeta, no. 9
(February 26, 1969): 12, (CDSP XXI, no. 9: 8-9).

_____. "Concerning Demographic Ignorance and the Problem of
Birth Rate," Literaturnaia gazeta (August 13, 1966), p. 2.

_____. "Continuation of a Controversy," Literaturnaia gazeta,
no. 12 (March 20, 1968): 11.

_____. "Population Migration and the Utilization of Labor Re-
sources," Voprosy ekonomiki, no. 9 (September 1970): pp. 34-
43 (CDSP XXIII, no. 2: 1-6).

Pergament, A. I. "Pravovoi statut ZhSK" (Legal Status of the House-
Construction Cooperative), Sovetskoe gosudarstvo i pravo, no.
4 (April 1966): 146-148.

Petrov, V. "The Welfare of the People Is the Main Aim," Pravda,
February 8, 1971, p. 2.

"Place Allocation of Housing Under Public Supervision," editorial,
Izvestia, June 11, 1958.

Polukhin, Iurii. "Not Dream, but Reality," Literaturnaia gazeta,
no. 45 (November 6, 1968): 10 (CDSP XXI, no. 3: 16-18).

"Pol'zuiutisa li partorganizatsii domoupravlenii pravom kontrolia deiatel'nosti administratsii?" (Are Party Organizations of Residential Managers' Offices Taking Advantage of Their Rights to Control the Work of the Administration?), Partiinaiia zhizn', no. 10 (May 1967): 50-51.

Posokhin, M. "The City of the Future Is Being Built Today," Pravda, July 26, 28, August 2, 7, 1964 (CDSP, XVI no. 32: 18-23).

_____. "Moscow Today and Tomorrow," New Times (Moscow), no. 41 (October 16, 1968): 29.

_____. "Moscow Today and Tomorrow," Pravda, July 8, 12, 18, 1962 (CDSP XIV, no. 28: 11-14).

Postinikov, M. "Planirovanie razvitiia gorodskogo khoziaistvo" (Planning the Development of the City Economy), Planovoe khoziaistvo, no. 4 (April 1965): 21-26.

Pravila i normy planirovki i zastroiki gorodov (Rules and Norms for Urban Planning and Construction). Moscow: Gosstroiizdat, 1959.

"Primernyi ustav zhilischno-stroitel'nogo kooperativa," (Model House Construction Cooperative Charter), Resolution of the RSFSR Council of Ministers, October 2, 1965, in Spravochnik profsoiuznogo rabotnika 1969, pp. 431-441. Moscow: Profizdat, 1969.

Prokopchenko, Ivan P. Obshchestvennye organizatsii v zhilishchnom khoziaistve (Volunteer Organization in the Housing Economy). Moscow: Stroiizdat, 1966.

_____. Zhilishchno-stroitel'nye kooperativy v SSSR (Housing Construction Cooperative in the USSR). Moscow: Stroiizdat, 1965.

Promyslov, V. F. "Moscow is Marching Forward," Ogonek, no. 52 (December 21, 1968): 1-3.

_____. "Principles of the General Plan for the Capital," Izvestia, October 5, 1966.

_____. "Speech at the Twenty-Third Party Congress," Pravda, April 8, 1966.

Pudikov, D. "A Great and Perspective Affair: To Develop Cooperative Housing Construction," Pravda, May 19, 1963, p. 3.

_____. "Housing: The Stepchild," Izvestia, January 17, 1965, p. 2.

_____. "To Increase the Number of New Cooperative Residents: Develop More Quickly the Housing Construction Cooperative," Pravda, November 20, 1964, p. 2.

Repenko, A. Ekonomika stroitel'stva, no. 2 (1969): 3-8 (JPRS, USSR Trade and Services series, no. 13 [May 5, 1969]: 54-63).

Riabinin, A. V. "Uluchshit' ekspluatatsiiu zhilishchnogo fonda," (Improve the Operation of the Housing Fund), Gorodskoe khoziaistvo Moskvy, no. 8 (August 1965): 15-18.

Robotov, B. "Problems of the Housing Cooperative," Sovetskaia Rossiia, February 4, 1970, p. 1.

Romanov, A. "Problems and Judgments: Pending the Housewarming," Pravda, September 24, 1968, p. 3 (CDSP XX, no. 39: 31).

Rostislavskii, N. "Pretenzii k proektirovshchikam," (Pretentions of the Planners), Sovetskaia Latviia, February 4, 1969.

Rozantsev, S. N. Spravochnik po zhilishchnym voprosam (Handbook on Housing Questions). Moscow: Moskovskii rabochii, 1967.

_____. Sto otvetov na voprosy po zhilishchnomu zakonodatel'stvu, (One Hundred Questions and Answers on Housing Legislation). Moscow: Profizdat, 1965.

Rubinshtein, M. "The City's Municipal Services," Izvestia, April 7, 1973, p. 5.

Ruzavina, E. "Economic Aspects in the Urbanization Process," Ekonomicheskie nauki, no. 2 (1969) (Problems of Economics XII, no. 4 [August 1969]: 68-79).

Rybina, Ye. "A Malicious Charge of 'Parasitism': Slanderer's Helpers," Izvestia, February 21, 1962 (CDSP XIV, no. 9: 15-16).

Ryaboshapko, Yu. "Builders Pool Their Experience," Zhilishchnoe stroitel'stvo, no. 1 (1969): 30-31 (JPRS, USSR Trade and Services series, no. 2: 5-6).

Sbornik zhilishchnogo zakonodatel'stva, (Collection of Housing Legislation). Moscow: Iuridicheskaia literatura, 1963.

"The Second All-Union Congress of Soviet Architects," CDSP current VII, no. 48: 13-20.

Selivanov, T. A., and M. A. Gel'perin. Planirovanie gorodskogo khoziaistvo: na primere Moskvy (Planning the Urban Economy: The Moscow Example). Moscow: Ekonomika, 1970.

Semenenko, V. A. "K voprosy o vedomstvennom zhilishchnom fonde" (Concerning the Problems of the Departmental Housing Fund), Gorodskoe khoziaistvo Moskvy, no. 3 (March 1964): 21-23.

Semin, V. P. "Ministerstvo soiuznoi respubliki i mestnye sovety deputatov trudiashchikhsia" (A Union Republic Ministry and the Local Soviets), Sovetskoe gosudarstvo i pravo, no. 9, (September 1969): 87-92.

Shapkov, Iu. "Why the New Tenant Is Unhappy," Pravda, September 18, 1969, p. 2.

Sharov, A. "Problems of Developing the Municipal Economy," Izvestia, June 16, 1957 (CDSP VIII, no. 24: 29-30).

Shavrikov, V., and A. Galaklionov. "Progressivnye osnovy planirovke zastroiki zhilykh raionov i mikroraionov" (Progressive Principles of Planning the Development of Residential Districts and Microraions), Arkhitektura SSSR, no. 1 (1961): 1-9.

Sheremet, K. F. Kompetentsiia mestnykh sovetov. Moscow: Moscow University, 1968.

_____. "New Rights and New Opportunities," Sovety deputatov trudiashchikhsia, no. 5 (1971) (The Soviet Review XIII, no. 2 (Summer 1972): 174-188).

Shestak, N. "The Soviets and the Urban Economy: Where There Is Agreement Among Comrades," Izvestia, October 4, 1968, p. 3 (CDSP XX, no. 40: 19).

Shneerson, Avraam I. Chto takoe zhilishchnyi vopros (What Is the Housing Question). Moscow: Higher Party School Under the Central Committee of the CPSU, 1959.

Shpakov, Yu. "Why the New Tenant Is Unhappy," Pravda, September 8, 1969, p. 2 (CDSP XXI, no. 36: 26-27).

Shulpin, A. "Develop Work of Housing Construction Cooperatives on a Broad Scale," Pravda, December 17, 1956.

Skripko, V. P. "Novyi poriadok ucheta grazhdan nuzhdaiushchikhsia v zhil'e, i raspredeleniiu zhiloi ploshchadi" (New Procedure for Waiting Lists of Persons Needing Housing and for the Distribution of Living Space), Sotsialisticheskaia zakonnost', no. 8 (August 1964): 83-86.

_____. "Vyselenie iz vedomstvennykh zhilykh domov" (Eviction from Departmental Housing), Sovetskoe gosudarstvo i pravo, no. 3 (March 1969): 142-146.

_____. "Vyselenie v sviazi so snosom doma" (Eviction Resulting from Demolition of a House), Sovetskaia iustitsiia, no. 10 (May 1968): 16-17.

_____, I. B. Martkovich, and P. G. Solov'ev. Zhilishchnoe zakonodatel'stvo v SSSR i RSFSR (Housing Legislation in the USSR and the RSFSR). Moscow: Stroiizdat, 1965.

_____, and I. B. Martkovich. Pravo na kooperativnuiu kvartiru v SSSR (The Right to a Cooperative Apartment in the USSR). Moscow: Znanie, 1970.

Sobranie postanovlenii i rasporiazhenii pravitel'stva RSFSR (SP RSFSR) (Collection of Decrees and Regulations of the Government of the RSFSR).

Sobranie postanovlenii i rasporiazhenii soveta ministrov RSFSR (SP RSFSR) (Collection of Decrees and Regulations of the Council of Ministers of the RSFSR). Moscow: Gosiurizdat.

Sobranie postanovlenii i rasporiazhenii pravitel'stva SSSR (SP SSSR) (Collection of Decrees and Regulations of the Government of the USSR).

Sobranie postanovlenii i rasporiazhenii Soveta Ministrov SSSR (SP SSSR) (Collection of Decrees and Regulations of the Council of Ministers of the USSR).

Sobranie uzakonenii i rasporiazhenii raboche-krest'ianskogo pravitel'
stva RSFSR (SU RSFSR) (Collection of Legislation and Regulations
of the Worker-Peasants' Governments of the RSFSR).

Sobranie zakonov i rasporiazhenii raboche-krest'ianskogo pravitel'stva
SSSR (SZ SSSR) (Collection of Laws and Regulations of the Worker-
Peasants' Government of the USSR).

Sokolov, A. "Soviets and the Economy: The Autonomy of the City,"
Izvestia, November 3, 1968, p. 12 (CDSP XX, no. 43: 25-26).

Sokolov, T. I. "Dlia blaga naroda" (For the Good of the People),
Ekonomicheskaia gazeta, no. 1 (January 1971): 3.

Sonin, M. "The Place of the 'Beautiful Half,'" Literaturnaia gazeta,
no. 16 (April 16, 1969): 11 (CDSP XXI, no. 16: 24).

"Sovershenstvovat' organizatorskuiu rabotu sovetov" (Perfect the
Organizational Work of the Soviets), lead editorial, Gorodskoe
khoziaiztvo Moskvy, no. 6 (June 1968): 1-2.

"The Soviets and Everyday Services: A House Undergoes Repairs,"
Izvestia, September 14, 1969, p. 3.

Spravochnik profsoiuznogo rabotnika 1969 (Trade Union Worker's
Handbook). Moscow: Profizdat, 1969.

"The Stories of a Cooperative Apartment House," Izvestia, October
29, 1970, p. 5.

"Stricter Control over the Distribution of Living Space, in the Presidium of the All-Union Central Council of Trade-Union Councils,"
Pravda, March 10, 1960, p. 2.

Studenikina, M. S. Formy uchastiia obshchestvennosti v rabote
mestnykh sovetov deputatov trudiashchikhsia (Forms of Public
Participation in the Work of the Local Soviets of Workers'
Deputies). Moscow: Gosiurizdat, 1963.

Strumilin, S. G. "Family and Community in the Society of the Future,"
Novy mir, no. 7 (1960) (Soviet Review XI, no. 2 [February 1961]:
3-29).

_____. Nash mir cherez 20 let (Our World in 20 Years). Moscow:
Sovetskaia Rossiia, 1964.

_____. "What Communism Is: Thoughts about the Future," Oktiabr, no. 3 (March 1960): 140-146 (CDSP XII, no. 15: 11-15).

"Submitted for Occupancy: Resolution 'On the Procedure for Commissioning Completed Housing Construction Projects,'" Official Department, Izvestia, August 11, 1970, p. 3.

"Sudebnaiia praktika po delam o vyselenii nanimatelei s predostavleniem zhiloi ploshchadi" (Court Practice in the Evictions of Tenants with the Assignment of Living Space), Sovetskaia iustitsiia, no. 13 (July 1969): 4-6.

Sukholutsky, M. "Cities and Transportation Facilities on the Negative Side of Virtues," Literaturnaia gazeta, no. 38 (September 8, 1968): 11 (CASP I, no. 5 [October 1968]: 21).

Svetlichny, B. "The City Awaits a Reply," Oktiabr, no. 10 (1966): 157-169 (CDSP XVIII, no. 48: 11-18).

_____. "Designing Beautiful Cities," Nauka i zhizn', no. 9 (1960) (Soviet Review II, no. 4 [April 1961]: 28-33).

_____. "Is It Not Better Without the Mystique?" Literaturnaia gazeta, no. 30 (July 24, 1968) (CDSP, XX, no. 32: 20).

_____. "Krupnyi istochnik ekonomii sredstv v stroitel'stve" (A Major Source of Economics in Construction), Voprosy ekonomiki, no. 6 (June 1959): 40-49.

_____. "Sovetskim liudiam blagoustroennye zhilishcha" (Improved Housing for Soviet People), Kommunist, no. 6 (April 1965): 41-51. Also translated in CDSP, XVII, no. 22: 10-14.

_____. "Some Problems of the Long-Range Development of Cities," Voprosy ekonomiki, no. 3 (1962) (Soviet Sociology I, no. 1: 58-66).

_____. "Soviet Town Planning Today," Voprosy ekonomiki, no. 7 (1960) (Problems of Economics III, no. 8 [December 1960]: 29-36).

_____. "Les villes de l'avenir" (Cities of the Future), V pomoshch politicheskomu samoobrazovaniiu, no. 10 (1959): 60-72 (Recherches internationales à la lumière du Marxisme VII-X [1960]: 208-229).

Tadevosian, V. S. "Nekotorye voprosy zhilishchnogo prava" (Several Problems of Housing Law), Sovetskoe gosudarstvo i pravo, no. 6 (1958): 45.

Taff, A. "From Plans to Construction Site," Pravda, August 19, 1969.

"Take Care of the People's Property," lead editorial, Pravda, March 19, 1960.

Tel'nov, V. "Novoe pazvitie v raspredelenii zhil'ia" (New Development in the Distribution of Housing), Sovetskie profsoiuzy, no. 11 (June 1964): 44-46.

_____. Obshchestvennyi domovyi komitet (Voluntary House Committee). Moscow: Profizdat, 1962.

_____. Obshchestvennyi domovyi komitet (Volunteer House Committee). Moscow: Profizdat, 1966.

Tolstoi, Iurii K. Sovetskoe zhilishchnoe pravo (Soviet Housing Law). Leningrad: Leningrad University, 1967.

Tolstoi, V. "Poniatie sem'i v sovetskom prave" (Understanding of "Family" in Soviet Law), Sovetskaia iustitsiia, no. 19 (October 1969): 5-6.

Tomsen, A. "Zhilishchnyi vopros: vazhnaia sotsial'naia problema sovremennosti" (An Important Social Problem of Our Time: Housing), Voprosy filosofii, no. 12 (1959): 22-34 ("Un grand probleme social de notre epoque," Recherches internationales à la lumière du Marxisme VII-X, cahiers 20-21 [1960]: 5-20).

Tsidilin, Pavel S. Chudesnoe sredstvo (Splendid Means). Moscow: Moskovskii rabochii, 1962.

Tutuchenko, Seymon. Housing in the USSR: Notes of an Architect. Moscow: Foreign Languages Publishing House, 1960.

Twenty-Third Congress of the Communist Party of the Soviet Union. Moscow: Novosti, 1966.

Upravlenie zhilishchnym khoziaistvom; kratkii spravochnik (Housing Management's Concise Handbook). Moscow: Stroiizdat, 1965.

Vaingort, L. "The Appearance of Our Cities: Economy, Utility and Beauty," Pravda, September 9, 1970, p. 3 (CDSP XXII, no. 37: 4).

Valentei, D. "Current Population Problems in the USSR," Ekonomicheskie nauki, no. 1 (1969) (Problems of Economics XII, no. 7 [November 1969]: 49-60).

_____. "On Demographic Behavior," Pravda, August 16, 1972, p. 3.

_____. "On the Construction of Cities During the Transition to Communism," Voprosy ekonomiki, no. 4 (1960) (Problems of Economics III, no. 5 [September 1960]: 48-54).

Vartanian, S. "The Housing Fund Is a National Resource," Kommunist (Erevan), August 21, 1962, p. 2.

Vatman, D. "Bronirovanie zhilykh pomeshchenii" (Reservation of Living Quarters), Sovetskaia iustitsiia, no. 9 (May 1969): 21-22.

_____. "Prava i obiazannosti chlenov sem'i nanimatelia" (Rights and Obligations of Members of the Tenant's Family), Sotsialisticheskaia zakonnost', no. 10 (October 1969): 52-57.

Velichkin, I. "Why Construction Projects Are Costly," Izvestia, September 2, 1970, p. 3 (CDSP XXII, no. 35: 28).

Vershinin, M. "The Soviets and the City Economy: The Fate of a Residential Building," Izvestia, April 1, 1970.

Veselovskii, B. B. Kurs ekonomiki i organizatsii gorodskogo khoziaistvo (Course on the Economics and Organization of the Municipal Economy). Moscow: Gosplanizdat, 1951.

Vinogradov, S. "For a Bribe," Pravda, August 13, 1969, p. 6.

Vishniakov, Viktor G. Uchastie deputatov mestnykh sovetov v raspredelenii zhiloi ploshchadi (The Participation of Deputies of the Local Soviets in the Distribution of Living Space). Moscow: Iuridicheskaia literatura, 1964.

Vlasov, V. A. "City Construction in Conditions of the Further Industrialization of the Construction Industry," Pravda, June 8, 1960 (CDSP, XII, no. 23: 18-19).

_____. "Report to the Third All-Union Congress of Soviet Architects," Pravda, May 19, 1961 (CDSP XIII, no. 20: 13-15).

Volodin, P. "Planned Flaws," Izvestia, June 2, 1960 (CDSP XII, no. 22: 26-27).

Voroninsky, S. "Normatives and Limits," Izvestia, September 16, 1970, p. 3 (CDSP XXII, no. 37: 4).

Vsesoiuznoe soveshchanie po gradostroitel'stvy, 7-10 iiunia 1960 g: sokrashchennyi stenograficheskii otchet (All-Union Conference on City Planning, 7-10 June, 1960: Abridged Stenographic Report). Moscow: Gosstroiizdat, 1960.

Vyatkin, A. "Esthetics of a City," Izvestia, April 5, 1963, p. 3.

"What Hampers Cooperative Housing Construction," Pravda, May 8, 1959.

"What's Happening to the New Way of Life Building?" Literaturnaia gazeta, no. 50 (December 9, 1970) (CDSP XXII, no. 52: 28, 44).

"Will the New Way of Life Remain?" Literaturnaia gazeta, no. 10 (March 4, 1969): 11, (CASP II, no. 5 [May 1970]: 14-15).

Yagodzinsky, A. "The Right of Master of the City," Izvestia, October 18, 1968 (CDSP XX, no. 42: 21).

Yegorychev, N. "All in the Name of Man" (Urban Renewal in Moscow), Izvestia, June 6, 1963, pp. 1, 3 (CDSP XV, no. 23 [July 3, 1963]: 15-17).

Yeremeyev, T. "For the Further Lifting of Housing Construction," Trud, September 13, 1958.

Yermolovich, N. "When a City Is Born," Izvestia, July 17, 1958, p. 2 (CDSP X, no. 29: 23).

"Yesterday in the Kremlin Conference on City Planning and Construction," Pravda, June 8, 1960 (CDSP XII, no. 23: 13-20).

Zakhlebina, L. "Concern of Soviet State for the Improving of Working People's Housing," Izvestia, November 18, 1955, p. 2 (CDSP VII, no. 45: 10-11).

Zakov, I. "Eksperimentalnye mikroraiony v gorodakh Moskovskoi oblasti" (Experimental Microraions in the Towns of Moscow Oblast), Arkhitektura SSSR, no. 1 (1962): 30-32.

Zelichonok, M., and I. Miliavskii. "The Brigade Takes on a Contract: What Economic Accountability Yields on Moscow Construction Projects," Pravda, October 18, 1970.

Zhilishchno-bytovye voprosy: sbornik rukovodiashchikh materialov, (Housing and Everyday Living Questions: Collection of Guiding Materials). Moscow: Profizdat, 1964.

"Zhiloi dom" (Residential Building), Official Department, Ekonomicheskaia gazeta, no. 5 (January 1971): 16.

Zhuchok, Yu., and Ye. Zuikova. "House of the New Way of Life: Building with Privileges," Literaturnaia gazeta, no. 2 (January 8, 1969): 11 (CDSP XXI, no. 4: 15-17).

Zhukhovitsky, "Will the New Way of Life Housing Complex Remain?" Literaturnaia gazeta, no. 3 (January 14, 1969).

Zhuravlyev, A., and M. Fyodorov. "The Microdistrict and New Living Conditions," Nauki i zhizn', no. 9 (1960) (Soviet Review II, no. 4 [April 1961]: 37-40).

JOURNALS AND NEWSPAPERS

WESTERN SOURCES

Balinsky, Alexander S. "Non-Housing Objectives of Soviet Housing Policy," Problems of Communism X, no. 4, (July-August 1961): 17-23.

Barry, Donald D. "Cities and Towns," Problems of Communism XVIII, no. 3 (May-June 1969): 1-11.

Bates, A. Allan. "Low Cost Housing in the Soviet Union," in Industrialized Housing, pp. 1-21. Washington: Government Printing Office, 1969.

Berg, Voldemar. "The Soviet Urban Housing Problem," Bulletin, Institute for the Study of the USSR IV, no. 11 (November 1957): 38-42.

Block, Alexander. "Soviet Housing—The Historical Aspect; Problems
of Amount, Cost, and Quality in Urban Housing—I," Soviet Studies
I, no. 3 (January 1954): 246-277.

_____. "Soviet Housing—The Historical Aspect; Some Notes on
Problems of Policy—I," Soviet Studies III, no. 1 (July 1951):
1-15.

_____. "Soviet Housing—The Historical Aspect; Some Notes on
Problems of Policy—II," Soviet Studies III, no. 3 (January 1952):
229-257.

Butler, Scot. "The Soviet Capital Investment Program," in Economic
Performance and the Military Burden in the Soviet Union.
Studies prepared for the Joint Economic Committee, U.S. Con-
gress. Washington: Government Printing Office, 1970.

Cattell, David T. Leningrad: A Case Study of Soviet Urban Government.
New York: Praeger Publishers, 1968.

_____. "Local Government and the Sovnarkhoz in the USSR, 1957-
1962," Soviet Studies XV no. 4 (April 1964): 430-442.

Chossudovsky. "The Development of Housing in the USSR," U.N.
Housing and Town and Country Planning Bulletin, no. 5 (1951).

Churchward, L. G. "Soviet Local Government Today," Soviet Studies
XVII, no. 4 (April 1966): 431-452.

Frolic, B. Michael. Annotated Bibliography on Soviet Municipal
Planning and Administration. Oakland: Institute of Planning
Librarians, 1963.

_____. "The Soviet City," Town Planning Review (Department of
Civic Design, Liverpool School of Architecture, University of
Liverpool) XXXIV, no. 4 (January 1964): 285-306.

Geiger, Kent H. The Family in Soviet Russia. Cambridge: Harvard
University Press, 1968.

Hazard, John N. Communists and Their Law. Chicago: University
of Chicago Press, 1969.

_____. Soviet Housing Law. New Haven: Yale University Press,
1939.

Herman, Leon M. "Urbanization and New Housing Construction in the Soviet Union," The American Journal of Economics and Sociology XXX, no. 2 (April 1971): 203-219.

_____. "Urbanization and New Housing Construction in the USSR," in Industrialized Housing, pp. 22-40. Washington: Government Printing Office, 1969.

Hodgetts, Craig, and Lester Walker. "Redesigning New York—An Immodest Proposal," New York II, no. 8 (February 24, 1969): 33-43.

Industrialized Housing. Studies prepared for the Subcommittee on Urban Affairs of the Joint Economic Committee, U.S. Congress, April, 1969. Washington: Government Printing Office, 1969.

Kerblay, M. Basile. "La Ville: essai de confrontation des doctrines sovietiques et occidentales sur le phenomene urbain" (The City: An Essay of the Confrontation of Soviet and Western Doctrines on the Urban Phenomenon), in Annuaire de l' URSS 1967, pp. 727-739. Paris, 1968.

_____, ed. "Les grandes villes du monde: Moscou" (The Great Cities of the World: Moscow), Notes et études documentaires, no. 3493 (May 24, 1968), La documentation française.

Marx, Karl, and Frederick Engels. Karl Marx and Frederick Engels, Selected Works, Vol. I. Moscow: Foreign Languages Publishing House, 1962.

Morton, Henry W. "The Leningrad District of Moscow—an Inside Look," Soviet Studies XX, no. 2 (October 1968): 206-218.

Mote, Max E. "Leningrad Municipal Administration: Structure and Functions." Doctoral Thesis, University of Washington, 1966.

New Directions in the Soviet Economy. Studies prepared for the Subcommittee on Foreign Economic Policy of the Joint Economic Committee, U.S. Congress. Washington: Government Printing Office, 1966.

Osborn, Robert J., and Thomas A. Reiner. "Soviet City Planning: Current Issues and Future Perspectives," Journal of the American Institute of Planners XXVIII, no. 4 (November 1962): 239-250.

Parkins, Maurice F. City Planning in Soviet Russia. Chicago: University of Chicago Press, 1953.

Rusis, Armins. Home Rule in Moscow. Washington: Library of Congress European Law Division Law Library, 1963.

Sosnovy, Timothy. "Housing Conditions and Urban Development in the USSR," in New Directions in the Soviet Economy, 1966, pp. 533-553. Studies prepared for the Subcommittee on Foreign Economic Policy of the Joint Economic Committee, U.S. Congress, Washington: Government Printing Office, 1966.

_____. "Housing in a Workers' State," Problems of Communism V, no. 6 (November-December 1956): 31-39.

_____. The Housing Problem in the Soviet Union. New York: Research Program on the USSR, 1954.

_____. "The Soviet Housing Situation Today," Soviet Studies XI, no. 1 (July 1959): 1-21.

Triska, Jan F., ed. Soviet Communism: Programs and Rules. San Francisco: Chandler, 1962.

Troyat, Henri. Daily Life in Russia Under the Last Tsar. London: George Allen and Unwin, 1961.

Zile, Zigurds L. "Private Rights in a Collectivist Society: A Study of the Non-Socialist Effort in Soviet Urban Housing Construction." Thesis for Doctor of Juridical Science, Harvard Law School, 1967.

_____. "Problems and Programs of City Planning in the Soviet Union," Washington University Law Quarterly V (1963): 19-59.

JOURNALS AND NEWSPAPERS

Biulleten' verkhovnogo suda RSFSR (Bulletin of the Supreme Court of the RSFSR).

Biulleten' verkhovnogo suda SSSR (Bulletin of the Supreme Court of the USSR).

Bulletin, Institute for the Study of the USSR.

Current Abstracts of the Soviet Press (CASP).

Current Digest of the Soviet Press (CDSP).

Ekonomicheskaia gazeta (Economic Gazette). Gazette of the Central
    Committee of the CPSU.

Gorodskoe khoziaistvo Moskvy (The Municipal Economy of Moscow).
    Monthly of the Executive Committee of the Moscow City Soviet.

Izvestia. Official newspaper of the USSR government.

Journal of the American Institute of Planners.

Kazakhstanskaia pravda. Official newspaper of the Central Committee
    of the Kazakhstan Communist Party.

Kommunist. The official theoretical and political journal of the Central
    Committee of the CPSU.

Kommunist Tadzhikistana. Official newspaper of the Central Com-
    mittee of the Tadzhik Communist Party and of the Supreme
    Soviet of the Tadzhik Republic.

Krokodil. Satirical gazette published by Pravda.

Literaturnaia gazeta (Literary Gazette). Organ of the Board of the
    USSR Union of Writers.

The New York Times.

Novyi mir (New World). Literary and socio-political Journal, organ
    of the USSR Union of Writers.

Partiinaia zhizn' (Party Life). Journal of the Central Committee of
    the CPSU.

Planovoe khoziaistvo (Planned Economy). Journal of USSR Gosplan.

Pravda. Official newspaper of the Central Committee of the CPSU.

Pravda Ukrainy. Official newspaper of the Central Committee of the
    Ukrainian Communist Party and of the Supreme Soviet and
    Council of Ministers of the Ukrainian Republic.

Pravda vostoka. Official newspaper of the Central Committee of the Uzbek Communist Party and of the Supreme Soviet and Council of Ministers of the Uzbek Republic.

Problems of Communism.

Problems of Economics.

Recherches internationales à la lumière du Marxisme.

Sotsialisticheskaia zakonnost' (Socialist Legality). Organ of the Office of Procurator of the USSR.

Sovetskaia Belorussiia. Official newspaper of the Central Committee of the Belorussian Communist Party and of the Supreme Soviet and Council of Ministers of the Belorussian Republic.

Sovetskaia iustitsiia (Soviet Justice). Journal of the RSFSR Supreme Court.

Sovetskaia Kirgiziia. Official newspaper of the Central Committee of the Kirghiz Communist Party and of the Supreme Soviet and Council of Ministers of the Kirgiz Republic.

Sovetskaia Latviia. Official newspaper of the Central Committee of the Latvian Communist Party and Supreme Soviet of the Latvian Republic.

Sovetskaia Rossiia. Daily of the Central Committee of the Communist Party of the Soviet Union. Formerly, official newspaper of the Russian Bureau of the Central Committee of the CPSU.

Sovetskie profsoiuzy. (Soviet Trade Unions). Journal of the All-Union Central Council of Trade Unions.

Sovetskoe gosudarstvo i pravo (Soviet State and Law). Organ of the Institute of State and Law of the USSR Academy of Sciences.

Soviet Review.

Soviet Sociology.

Soviet Studies.

Survey of the Soviet Press.

Stroitel'naia gazeta (Construction Gazette). Organ of the State Committee on Construction and Central Committee of Trade Unions of the building and building materials workers.

Town Planning Review.

Trud (Labor). Official newspaper of the All-Union Central Council of Trade Unions.

Vechernaia Moskva (Moscow Evening News). Daily of the Moscow City Committee of the CPSU and of the Moscow Soviet.

Vedomosti verkhovnogo soveta RSFSR (The Gazette of the Supreme Soviet of the RSFSR).

Vedomosti verkhovnogo soveta SSSR (The Gazette of the Supreme Soviet of the USSR).

Vestnik statistiki (Bulletin of Statistics). Organ of the Central Statistical Administration under the USSR Council of Ministers.

Voprosy ekonomiki (Problems of Economics). Journal of the USSR Academy of Sciences, Institute of Economics.

Voprosy filosofii (Problems of Philosophy). Journal of the USSR Academy of Sciences' Institute of Philosophy.

Voprosy istorii (Problems of History). Journal of the USSR Academy of Sciences' History Division and of the Ministry of Higher and Secondary Specialized Education.

Zaria vostoka (Dawn of the East). Official newspaper of the Central Committee of the Georgian Communist Party and of the Supreme Soviet and Council of Ministers of the Georgian Republic.

ALFRED JOHN DiMAIO, Jr. is Assistant Professor of Government at John Jay College of Criminal Justice, The City University of New York. He received an M.A. degree in Soviet regional studies and a Ph.D. degree in political science at Harvard University. He was a Graduate Fellow at Harvard's Russian Research Center.

COMMUNITY DEVELOPMENT STRATEGIES
IN THE MODEL CITIES PROGRAM: Impact of
the Program on Eight Major Cities
George J. Washnis

GOVERNING SOVIET CITIES: Bureaucratic
Politics and Urban Development in the USSR
William Taubman

SPATIAL DESIGN AND PLANNING IN THE U.K.:
Its Relevance to Developing Countries
Edited by Robert J. Marshall

URBANIZATION AND THE DEVELOPING
COUNTRIES: Report on the Sixth Rehovot
Conference
Edited by Raanan Weitz